Hans H. Penner

Impasse and Resolution

A Critique
of the Study of Religion

PETER LANG
New York • Bern • Frankfurt am Main • Paris

Library of Congress Cataloging-in-Publication Data

Penner, Hans H.
    Impasse and resolution : a critique of the study of
religion / Hans H. Penner.
        p. cm. — (Toronto studies in religion ; vol. 8)
    Bibliography: p.
    1. Religion—Methodology.   2. Structuralism.
I. Title. II. Series.
BL41.P46   1989   200'.1—dc20   89-2573
ISBN 0-8204-0976-6   CIP
ISSN 8756-7385

CIP-Titelaufnahme der Deutschen Bibliothek

Penner, Hans H.:
Impasse and resolution : a critique of the study
of religion / Hans. H. Penner. — New York; Bern;
Frankfurt am Main; Paris: Lang, 1989.
    (Toronto Studies in Religion; Vol. 8)
    ISBN 0-8204-0976-6

NE: GT

© Peter Lang Publishing, Inc., New York 1989

Printed by Weihert-Druck GmbH, Darmstadt, West Germany

TO ANNA

*With gratitude and love for
thirty years of good life together.*

TABLE OF CONTENTS

PREFACE

This book assumes that you are familiar with the academic study of religion as this is practiced among historians of religion, phenomenologists of religion and anthropologists of religion. Meeting colleagues from these disciplines over the years confirmed my opinion that there is much that is wrong in the study of religion. This book attempts to describe what is wrong and how we might go about correcting the errors in order to contribute to the further developments in the human sciences. I think of the book as something like books on chess which analyze traps, pitfalls and blunders and how to avoid them. It also gives you the pleasure of knowing that such a text does not necessarily come from the hand of a grand master. In fact the book may be about the blunders and pitfalls made by grandmasters! In any case I have done what I think needs to be done and the result after many years of reading, reflecting and discussing is not always as diplomatic as it might be. One of the problems in writing a book such as this is to keep out of the pitfalls and the blunders you have discovered. I am certain there are traps that remain concealed in the approach I argue for in Part II of the book. But the only way I know of discovering where they are is through the critical process used in Part I. Criticism yields knowledge. The guiding principle throughout this book is that what is central to the study of religion is criticism and construction of theories of religion. It involves asking how is it that Tambiah and Spiro, for example, can write such different if not contradictory texts about Buddhism using almost identical kinds of data. And then ask, which one is right? Or, are they both wrong? I find it curious that the last pair of questions are seldom asked. Perhaps Part I will provide us with an answwer for why this is the case.

I am grateful to The Bucknell Review, for publishing a version of chapter two many years ago, (1970) and to The Journal of The

American Academy Of Religion, for accepting a version of chapter three for publication in 1986. I am deeply grateful to colleagues and friends for their patient help in reading and commenting upon several versions of the manuscript. I am especially grateful to Professors Willis Doney, Timothy Duggan (Dartmouth College) and Merrie Bergmann (formerly of Dartmouth College) for their comments on the chapter on the logic of functionalism. Professors Duggan and William Green (University of Rochester) were of tremendous help in their critique of chapter three. Professors Ronald Green and Robert Oden, colleagues in my own department at Dartmouth, together with Professor E. Thomas Lawson (Western Michigan) read through and commented on the penultimate version of the manuscript. Their comments confirmed that criticism and the growth of knowledge do indeed entail each other. I thank them once again. Last, but not least, I am grateful to Michael Gildersleeve, an honor's student in the department, for his careful reading and editing of the manuscript.

I have named in the dedication the one to whom all language of structural relations can be applied in an existential mode; I know because I am known, I value because I am of value, and love because I am loved.

INTRODUCTION

*"If our ordinary concepts suggest
a confused theory we should look
for a better theory, not give up
theorizing." David Davidson*

It is not a simple thing to travel from Hanover, New Hampshire to Chicago, especially late in the fall. I made the trip for one of those huge professional meetings. While standing in a long line for registration, I met a friend at the annual gathering of scholars interested in the study of religion. We had not met for several years. As usual, he wanted to know what I was doing, and I told him that I was working my way through a study of the rites of passage in Hinduism. "You mean to say," he responded, "that you have finally dropped methodology and have actually turned to the study of religion?" I tried to explain that this was a test case for a new theory I was working out, but we were interrupted by the appearance of colleagues we both knew.

Later, with map in hand, I found the room for the first set of papers I wanted to hear. I sat down beside a distinguished scholar of religion. He looked somewhat perplexed and soon told me that he had just heard that a department of Religion in a famous Eastern University was looking for someone competent in methodology. What bothered him was this -- he simply could not understand what it was they were looking for. I thought I might be able to explain, but the moderator of the session called the assembled to order for the first paper. This is the short story of my academic life and the following chapters of this book are my response to such encounters.

Notice that my colleague in the registration line seemed to know what methodology is all about. It is something scholars do when they are not engaged in the study of religion. It is something abstract, perhaps esoteric, and thus quite different from the empirical investigation and description of the history of religions.

This view of methodology is quite popular. It assumes, to use an analogy from Bacon, that we have two alternatives. The first is to become like scholastic spiders, spinning intricate theoretical webs out of our mental substances. The second alternative is to become like empiricist ants, collecting and classifying huge piles of data on religion. The subtle implication, of course, is that given the alternatives we ought to be empiricist ants. Fortunately, we have a third alternative, to become like bees, going to the history of religions for our natural data and working it into a new product called knowledge.

Many years ago, this critical approach to the study of religion was called "methodology." This was certainly the case during my days as a graduate student at the University of Chicago. There was something distinctive, almost unique, about this kind of research and intellectual debate among graduate students and professors interested in religion. Unfortunately, this is no longer true. I am not sure why this is the case. As this book will demonstrate, we have yet to begin working on some of the crucial problems and puzzles in the study of religion. The point I wish to make throughout the book is that the various solutions to the problems and puzzles are theoretical or methodological.

It is important to remember that this book encompasses the academic study of religion, which from my point of view includes more than what has become known as "religious studies." Although the disciplines of "the history of religion" and "phenomenology of religion" receive a great deal of attention, I shall also focus on the significant problem of rationality and religion in the recent debate in sociology and anthropology. Both of these disciplines are known for their use of functionalism as the major theory for explaining religion. A separate chapter is devoted to a critical examination of this theory. This is not an arbitrary decision. Most readers of this book will agree that departments of religion are deeply indebted to the research done in religion by anthropology and sociology. Since at the moment there is very little being done in linguistics or philosophy on the subject of religion I leave them aside. (This is ironic, since Saussure, the father of modern linguistics, did think that the science he called "semiotics" included religion. I have devoted a short chapter to his work as the foundation for structuralism.)

I cannot help but believe that the study of religion has much to contribute to the continued development of the cognitive sciences. Before this can happen we will have to break through some of the deadlocks we have created for ourselves. The first four chapters describe and analyze the impasse we have reached in the history, phenomenology and anthropology of religion. Chapters Five and Six make a case for structuralism as one way out of the impasse. Chapter Seven is a brief demonstration of how structuralism provides new theoretical advances for explaining religion.

I was tempted to revise the title of one of Ian Hacking's books and call this work, "Why Does Language Matter To The Study Of Religion."1 I am convinced that the last part of the twentieth century will be remembered for discovering the significance of language for explaining human nature, culture and religion. Structuralism would not exist without this discovery.

I believe, therefore, that the study of religion can avoid structuralism only at its peril. This is not a popular position to take, especially in the field of study known as the history and phenomenology of religion. This field has been quite defensive if not hostile to structuralism - - the anthropology of religion has both defenders and critics and, it is fair to say, has been much more receptive to the basic postulates of structuralism. The reasons for this hostility should become clear to you by the end of the book. Briefly stated, the primary source for the hostility is theological.

The origin of both the history and the phenomenology of religion as academic disciplines can be traced to theological faculties. One of the ironies in the history of these disciplines is that the idea of an autonomous "wissenschaft," free of all "reductionisms," was doomed from the very beginning, since the definition of the subject as the study of manifestations of The Sacred was essentially theological. The consequences of this beginning, as we shall see, were devastating to the growth and development of both the history and phenomenology of religion as academic disciplines.

This may sound like an unfair judgment concerning the openness of the history and phenomenology of religion to both criticism and change. Let me defend the assertion with a single piece of evidence which I believe proves my point. All scholars of religion are aware of an important fact that took place in 1987. It is the year of the appearance of a 15 volume Encyclopedia of Religion edited by Mircea Eliade. We have seen nothing like it since The Encyclopaedia Of Religion And Ethics, in 13 volumes, which was published beginning in 1908. In the new Encyclopedia, Lévi-Strauss's multi-volumed study on mythology is cited in the bibliography but not in the text of an article on "History and Myth." In the lead article on "Myth," Lévi-Strauss is mentioned in passing in the text but not cited in the bibliography.

How did this come about? No one at the end of this century can write about myth at any level without confronting Lévi-Strauss. The magnitude of this problem can be clearly seen if we imagine a new "Encyclopedia of Language" which treats Chomsky as insignificant to modern developments in linguistics. That, of course, is unthinkable! The consequence of such an omission makes the Encyclopedia incomplete and out of date before its publication.

Anyone familiar with the cultural sciences will agree, I believe, that significant problems have been resolved by scholars who have explicitly identified the theoretical importance of structuralism for their research. I have selected two examples in the study of religion as part of the last chapter. I now feel compelled to state the obvious-- this does not mean that we have reached the final theoretical answer; structuralism is not the absolute solution to our problems in the study of religion. No one has ever held such absurd notions the opposition notwithstanding. In fact, as we shall see, the problem of meaning in religion, is not solved by structuralism. Structuralism, however, may be the foundation upon which a well formed theory of meaning can be built. In any case, we are not alone at this junction. The question at the moment is, which semantic theory do we choose? None seem adequate for explaining the complex issues of meaning. There are very few scholars in the academic study of religion who are focusing their attention on this crucial problem. And yet, we all talk and write about "the meaning of religion" as if the theoretical issues are solved.

Are there any alternatives? Indeed there are. Functionalism remains the leading theory for explaining religion. Functionalism is a theory that explains cultural and social elements as satisfying certain needs. The needs can be defined as sociological, psychological or biological. It has been called the theory of the social sciences. It has become common sense to explain religion as satisfying some or all of these needs.

I think it is important to remember that functionalism was born from within the positivist-empiricist tradition. I believe it was Malinowski who defined its origins in the following way, "Since we cannot explain the object of religion perhaps we can explain its functions." I interpret this assertion to mean that it is indeed impossible to explain an object that does not exist! To put it in other terms, only those beliefs or assertions that are empirically verifiable are meaningful. Although functionalists agree that religion is based on needs, they do not agree on what the needs are. For some, the needs are social, for others they are psychological or individual. The debate, as usual, ended in compromise, the needs are psycho-social as well as biological.

Functionalists also disagree on the status of religious belief and myth. For some, religious belief is as rational as can be. Such beliefs are attempts to explain our experience of the world. They are, of course, mistaken or false, but to hold a mistaken belief or false theory does not entail that you are irrational. There are functionalists who take an opposite point of view. Religion is not rational in the sense that it entails truth conditions. Religious beliefs and rituals from this point of view are expressive of emotions and function to satisfy this need. They are purely symbolic and are not to be taken as cognitive. The basic problem with this approach to religion is that it must deny that religion is or entails language. I know of no language which is purely symbolic or expressive.

Chapter Three is a critical analysis of the debate between the "intellectualist" and "expressive/symbolist" approaches to religion. What is important to remember is that both sides are in agreement on a crucial issue -- truth conditions are given in the correspondence of a belief with reality, and correspondence can only be validated empirically. Functionalism in its many variations is "realist" and empirical in its epistemology. It would seem that these basic assumptions create a rather large abyss between functionalism and the approach to religion taken by historians and phenomenologists of religion. After all, The Sacred is certainly not something that can be empirically verified. The abyss between the two approaches is only illusory. Although the marriage between the two has been troublesome, it continues because of what I call "the robust fideism" which unites them. Since Chapters One and Two provide many examples of this from the history and phenomenology of religion, let me provide a classic example from anthropology. Martin Hollis closes his essay on "Reason and Ritual" with the following quote from Evans-Pritchard: "Though prayer and sacrifice are exterior actions, Nuer religion is ultimately an interior state. This state is externalized in rites which we can observe, but their meaning depends finally on an awareness of God and that men are dependent on him and must be resigned to his will. At this point the theologian takes over from the anthropologist." Hollis then closes with this curious remark, "The theologian seems already to have taken over from the anthropologist. But why not? Sacred anthropology is sceptical theology."2

Chapter Four demonstrates that the logic of functionalism is seriously flawed and that any attempt at revision only produces trivial conclusions. What we need is a disciple of Kuhn to explain why functionalism has persisted as the major "paradigm" in the study of social institutions for at least the last eight decades.

I am convinced that the arguments in Part I of this book are valid. If this is the case, then what we need is a way out of the impasse that both the phenomenology of religion and functionalism have created in the study of religion. It seems clear that both of these approaches lead to a dead end. I then argue that structuralism provides us with a way out. Thus, Part II of this book describes the basic principles of this theory together with three cases which demonstrate its power and success.

A great deal of nonsense has been written about structuralism, and not all of it has come from the pens of critics. Many of us are deeply indebted to the work of Claude Lévi-Strauss and his insight that at least some of our problems might be solved by taking linguistics seriously. Part II of this book attempts to follow that insight. If the basic principles of the theory are correct, and I think they are, then much, if not all, of what has been written about religion will need to be rewritten. This in itself should provide younger scholars interested in religion with the energy to carry on with the research. A structuralist approach to the study of religion also unites us with other cognitive disciplines in the human sciences. I am afraid that the quest for an autonomous "science of religion" has led to the irrelevance of a great deal that has been done in the study of religion.

My intention in writing this book is to provide you with an argument that will identify and analyze the various traps and pitfalls in the study of religion. Once we have identified them, I suggest that the use of structural theory is one way we can avoid repeating them. I have also written this book to demonstrate once again to some of my colleagues why I think reflection on theory and methodology is of prime importance to anyone interested in the study of religion. Before we begin, I think I owe you at least one important clarification -- what do I mean by the word "religion?" Defining the term "religion" is not, as some scholars think, a hopeless task. Given the ambiguities and various uses of the term, it is imperative that we clarify what we mean by the word. The problem with most definitions of religion is not because the task is hopeless or the fact that there does not seem to be any agreement on a particular definition. The problem with most definitions of religion is that they are weak or bad definitions. All we need to do is follow a few agreed upon rules for defining terms. The definition (definiens) for example should not be wider than the word we want to define (definiendum), nor should it be narrower than the definiendum. The definition should not include ambiguous, figurative or obscure language, and it should not be expressed in negative terms.3 Thus, "Religion is ultimate concern" or "Religion is worldview" or "Religion is the sacred" are good examples of bad definitions. The first and second examples are too wide, and the last is ambiguous involving another term which also needs clarification. Note that the "sacred" is often defined as "not the profane." This only compounds the problem.

Here is my definition of religion: Religion is a "verbal and nonverbal structure of interaction with superhuman being(s)." Let me just point out a few of the features of this definition which I think are positive and make it better than most definitions of religion that I have come across. First, it is not unique or new. It is a variation on the definition of religion given by Tylor many years ago and used by such contemporary scholars as Horton and Spiro. The definition includes the terms "verbal" and "nonverbal" because I want to include myth, ritual, art and belief in the definition. The term "structure" is the only technical term in the definition. By structure I mean a system of elements that are defined holistically. Thus, the elements of a system do not define the system. In fact, it is the relations that elements enter into that define or constitute the system. Part II of this book offers a full description of this theory of "structure." The last chapter will provide three case studies to illustrate the revolutionary consequences of applied structuralism.

The words "interaction with superhuman being(s)" sets religion apart from other systems that, although related, should not be confused with religion. Thus, for example, this definition will exclude Nazism, Marxism, Humanism and Capitalism. It also excludes vague notions such as "worldview" as helpful definitions of religion. Such vague, or ambiguous, definitions of religion usually hide a hidden agenda that contains theological premises. My definition does include all of the monotheistic, polytheistic, and "spirit" systems that I am aware of. Thus, the definition includes an immense amount of religious data for study and explanation. There will, of course, always be border line cases, but this is true of all definitions.

Myths and rituals are obviously very important in religions. As I have already noted, myth and ritual are embedded in the above definition, and we can easily define both terms for further clarification. A myth is a story that has a beginning, middle and end, is or was orally transmitted and consists of the actions of superhuman being(s). The term "ritual" can be defined as "verbal and nonverbal modes of behavior that consist of interactions with superhuman being(s)." These clarifications indicate once again that Nazism is not a myth or a ritual. This definition of the term "myth" obviously excludes novels and such notions as "the myth of our economy." The definition of "ritual" also excludes habits or routines.

The distinctive feature which runs through all of the above definitions is "superhuman being(s)." I am not completely happy with the term but I cannot think of anything better. By "superhuman being"

I mean someone who does things we cannot do; create the world, perform miracles, transform itself into different states or modes of being, and the like.

I have come across two criticisms of definitions of religion which include the terms "superhuman being(s)." The first, known since Durkheim, seems quite serious. Such definitions exclude Buddhism which is supposedly "atheistic." I do not deny that there is a sense in which Buddhism is atheistic. But, Durkheim was wrong when he thought that Buddhism must be excluded from definitions of religion that include the notion of "spiritual beings" or "superhuman being(s)." The Buddha was no ordinary human being. Durkheim forgot, or for some reason excluded, parts of Buddhism that tell us that the Buddha's birth was miraculous and that he struggled with Mara and other hosts of superhuman beings at the time of his enlightenment and again at the time of his death. Durkheim also forgot, or excluded, that after his enlightenment the Buddha ascended into heaven and converted his mother along with other deities. The Buddha, on meeting his father, rose into the air and shot fire and water out of his hands and feet. I believe that these are things that we ordinary human beings cannot do. Moreover, Buddhism has never denied the realm of deities and spirits. Durkheim was led astray by the modern quest for the historical Buddha and the pejorative notion that myth is illusory, false, or the opiate of the masses. Whatever the relation is between myth and history, the quest for the historical Buddha is simply irrelevant to the significance of the Buddha in Buddhism as a religion. The Buddha is a mythical figure. (I can find no reason why it should be any different for Jesus, or Moses. One of our problems is that we have tremendous difficulties with the term "mythical.")

The second difficulty that has been raised comes from the classroom. Students have pointed out rather quickly that mysticism seems to be excluded from this definition of religion. I could respond, and in a sense the response is true, that definitions always have border lines which are unclear, that no definition is perfect, and that perhaps the students could come up with either a better definition or a good substitute for "superhuman being(s)." This response, however, would gloss over a crucial point concerning what is wrong with the contemporary study of religion. Mysticism seems to be excluded from my definition because we think of mysticism as a system or experience, that is unique. Some scholars think that mysticism is the origin and essence of religion. Others think that there is no such thing as mysticism, only Jewish mysticism, Buddhist mysticism, and so on. I have argued elsewhere that both positions are wrong and that the history of the study of mysticism contains striking similarities to the study and demise of "Totemism."4 The relevant point of that argument is that most studies of "mysticism" distort what I call its "semantic field." Mysticism is not a thing in itself but an element in a system. And once we define mysticism by means of its relation to other elements in the system we shall discover that its significance is not as mysterious or nonsensical as it sometimes seems.

I have borrowed the notion of "semantic field" from Saussure. Chapter Five is a brief description of his theory of linguistics. He has taught us that it is grossly misleading to consider terms in isolation from the system, taking the terms one by one thinking that by aggregation we can construct a system. On the contrary, we must start from the interdependent whole and through analysis discover the elements as defined by the relations. It is the relations which define the elements. This basic principle, the essence of holism, is demonstrated in the last chapter. In that chapter I argue that Hindu and Buddhist "mysticism" as the "Wisdom of the East" have significance only in their relation to caste; the yogi and the monk are literally in opposition to caste. Thus, Hinduism as a religious system is constituted by a basic pair of oppositions -- caste-householder/ascetic-renouncer. My definition of religion, therefore, does not omit mysticism but encompasses it as an element in the structure. Once the definition is applied to Hinduism or Buddhism or Christianity as structures, we will, following Saussure and Lévi-Strauss, obtain the elements. Mysticism is one element in the structure, and why it appears in some structures and not others is just one of the problems we may now begin to answer. From the theoretical standpoint of Part II of this book, it is clear that the answer will not be an historical one. I am now getting ahead of myself.

In reading the last few paragraphs again I am at a loss to explain why one of my critics thought that my definition is theological and thus exposed to "the same devastating criticism" that I mount in the first two chapters. Nothing can be farther from the truth. My definition does not translate into "no god(s), no religion." The Buddha is not a god, but he is "superhuman." The Nats and Phii in Theravada Buddhism are not gods, but they are "superhuman." It is precisely the accounts of such beings and their relations to human beings that remains one of the major unresolved puzzles in the study of religion. The history of the study of religion clearly indicates that "the history of superhuman beings" is not the private domain of theology. And when we tie the definition of religion to myth and ritual we have marked out a clear domain that we can recognize as religion.

My critic was also somewhat surprised that the definition of religion I offer is not used throughout the book, especially in the last chapter. He thought my definition of religion excludes the case I make for Hinduism in the last chapter which is founded on the opposition renouncer/householder. I simply assumed too much. I am grateful for the comment and wish to correct the misunderstanding. My definition simply clarifies the term "religion." It is neither true nor false, it is not a theoretical term; it does not explain religion. It tells you how I will go about marking out what counts as religion. In testing this definition over several years, I have found that although I have not been able to improve on "superhuman beings," students are quite capable of using the definition to identify the data we want to explain. And this is a crucial test of the definition.

The last chapter assumes my definition of religion. Caste, as we now know, is constituted by the opposition pure/impure. Now, pure/impure is a ritual relation, and the study of these rituals clearly marks them as having to do with superhuman and human beings. No Hindu rite of passage that I am aware of excludes "mantras." The mantra can be indentified as the "language" of the superhuman beings that are significant in Hinduism. Brahmins, the ritual specialists, are in direct genealogical relationship to the mythical ancestors. The second case in the last chapter describes Buddhism as a system constituted by the opposition monk/laity. I assume that you will remember that a monk is "the son of Buddha." That the monk's chanting of the sutra is a chanting of "the words of the Buddha." and, that the Buddha is a superhuman being. Finally, it is important to keep in mind that a definition of religion does not constitute the structure of a religion.

One final word before you begin reading the text. I have been told that it does not take a careful study of structuralism to come up with the cases I describe in the last chapter. As one colleague put it, "You could have presented the argument without any reference to Lévi-Strauss and structuralism." All it takes is "insight." Both assertions are true. Of course, I could have written the last chapter without reference to structuralism. Of course, it takes "insight" to see things from a new perspective. My argument, however, rests on the assumption that "insight" presupposes theory. Moreover, in response I ask why it is the case that it is a fact that explanations of religion such as those found in the publications of Dumont and Tambiah did not exist before 1958? Why did Edmund Leach, to name one important anthropologist, abandoned his functionalist approach to religion after reading Lévi-Strauss? Finally, I wish to make explicit to younger scholars of religion, especially in departments of religious studies, just where some of these ideas originated. I am constantly astonished at the theoretical illiteracy of many graduate students of religion that I have met especially in the United States and Britain. Nevertheless, I am deeply satisfied to discover that they are eager to learn about the theoretical sources I find indispensible for my own reflection on the problems we face in the study of religion. The lesson to be learned is this: know your intellectual ancestors! To dismiss them, to ignore them, can be fatal.

NOTES

1. I recommend Ian Hacking, *Why Does Language Matter to Philosophy?* (Cambridge: Cambridge UP, 1975) to anyone interested in the study of religion.

2. Martin Hollis, "Reason and Ritual," *Rationality*, ed. Bryan R. Wilson (New York: Blackwell, 1970) 239. The quote from Evans-Pritchard is taken from *Nuer Religion* (Oxford: Oxford UP, 1956) 322.

3. See Hans H. Penner and Edward A. Yonan, "Is a Science of Religion Possible?" *The Journal of Religion* 52 (1972): 107-33, for more details and sources.

4. See Hans H. Penner, "The Mystical Illusion," *Mysticism and Religious Traditions*, ed. Steven T. Katz (Oxford: Oxford UP, 1983). The argument took Lévi-Strauss's analysis of "Totemism" as its model. See Claude Lévi-Strauss, *Totemism* (Boston: Beacon, 1963).

PART I IMPASSE

CHAPTER ONE

UNDERSTANDING RELIGION AS THE SACRED

The term "understanding" is often used to mark a methodological distinction between two domains of knowledge -- the natural sciences and the human sciences. As Dilthey put it, "we explain nature, but we understand man." Many scholars of religion have taken this distinction into the study of religion.1 Thus, the proper study of religion entails a unique or specific "understanding" of religion which identifies the study as within the domain of the human sciences. Moreover, the proper understanding of religion, from this point of view makes, a distinction between adequate and inadequate interpretations of religion from within the human sciences. To "understand" religion in this sense, therefore, entails the notion that religion is sui generis, that the sui generis object of religion is The Sacred.2 Because religion is sui generis, the study of religion requires its own special method and an autonomous discipline for a proper understanding or interpretation of the Sacred. To understand religion, therefore, is to study religion without reducing it to something else. To understand religion as religion, as a manifestation of The Sacred, is to view human beings as essentially homo religiosus. From these sets of assertions, it is obvious that the academic discipline for the autonomous study of religion requires a special methodology. Such assertions become the basis for an argument for the establishment of separate departments of religion in academic communities.

I shall attempt to demonstrate in this chapter and chapter two that this approach to the study of religion has ended in failure. The intention of historians and phenomenologists of religion who have taken this approach to the study of religion is an honorable one -- the establishment of a "science of religion." The irony, if not contradiction, inherent in this

When we trace the history of this "autonomous discipline" with its special methodology, we are led into surprising discoveries. Here are two examples from a number that are well known. The first can be found in Waardenburg's anthology on classical approaches to religion. The context for the anthology can be found in what Waardenburg has to say about the new phenomenology of religion in an essay on meaning in religion, "At this point we may broach the question to which we shall return later: what might we understand, in the approach by 'religion'? In our opinion, from a descriptive point of view, a particular religion might be considered to be a certain, often complicated system of meanings or significances ... to what might be called the transcendent sources of these meanings, or better the 'intended object' of their intention(s)."3 The phrase "the transcendent sources of these meanings" is well known to historians and phenomenologists of religion who base their approach to the study of religion on the notion that religion is sui generis, that the object of religion is The Sacred. All this is familiar to anyone who has read the publications of historians and phenomenologists of religion.

We are confronted with an immediate problem when an attempt is made to create a list of scholars who represent the discipline. For example, in preparing his massive anthology on classical approaches to religion, Waardenburg presents this rule as a guideline, "In the first place, all methodology which concerns literary, historical, sociological, anthropological, and psychological research as such has been left out. Our choice has been made only from those methodological texts which have to do with religious subjects."4 The anthology then goes on to include among the founders of the study of religion as an autonomous discipline Max Müller, as well as Freud, a psychologist; Durkheim, a sociologist; and Malinowski, an anthropologist. Neither Müller, Freud, Durkheim nor Malinowski would have anything to do with an understanding of religion which involved "transcendent sources of meaning." None of them thought of religion as sui generis. In fact, all of their methods have been cited at one time or another as good examples of "reductionism" and, therefore, inadequate as proper approaches to an understanding of religion!

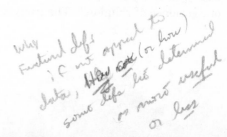

My second example, taken from a famous statement by Eliade, should make this crystal clear. A religious phenomenon, writes Eliade, "will only be recognized as such if it is grasped at its own level, that is to say, if it is studied as something religious. To try to grasp the essence of such a phenomenon by means of physiology, psychology, sociology, economics, linguistics, art, or any other study is false; it misses the one unique and irreducible element in it --the element of the sacred.... I do not mean to deny the usefulness of approaching the religious phenomenon from various different angles; but it must be looked at first of all in itself, in that which belongs to it alone and can be explained in no other terms."5 One is left wondering about what usefulness psychology, anthropology and sociology might have at all for explaining religion if such explanations are false. We are, of course, never told.

Several years later, Eliade was invited to write an essay on a survey of the history of religions over the past fifty years. One would expect, after reading the above assertion, that the essay would cover scholars of religion beginning with Rudolf Otto The essay, in fact, begins with Durkheim and Freud, and includes Mauss, Gernet, Malinowski, Evans-Pritchard, and Parsons to name a few. Since none of these scholars are historians or phenomenologists of religion, why include them? Because, says Eliade, "their theories were to play a considerable role in the cultural life of the following decades." Freud and Jung especially, "have contributed to the Zeitgeist of the last generations, and their interpretations of religion still enjoy a certain prestige among nonspecialists."6 Later in the essay, we find that the works of Freud and Durkheim are something more than a variable in a specific Zeitgeist. After having included the various disciplines in the human sciences under the rubric of "branches of Religionswissenschaft", we find this explanation for including them: "Indeed there is no such thing as a 'pure' religious fact. Such a fact is always also a historical, sociological, cultural, and psychological fact, to name only the most important contexts.... The confusion starts when only one aspect of religious life is accepted as primary and meaningful, and the other aspects or functions are regarded as secondary or even illusory." This is helpful. But then we read, "Such a reductionist method was applied by Durkheim and other sociologists of religion. An even more drastic reductionism was brought forward by Freud in his Totem und Tabu."7

I would agree with Eliade that it doesn't make much sense to talk about "pure" fact. Perhaps it would make more sense to talk about psychological, sociological and anthropological meanings of a religious "fact". If so, it is because such meanings are theoretical. However, even this tolerable interpretation will not help us out of the confusion. The problem with Eliade's position, as well as similar approaches to the study of religion, is that they cannot have it both ways. Either religion is sui generis and entails a special hermeneutics for interpretation or it is not. If it is, then those who attempt to explain religion sociologically, or psychologically, may grasp a secondary feature of religion, but not its "essential" meaning.

The hierarchy of the branches of religionswissenschaft from this point of view is clear. Durkheim and Freud did not just take one aspect of religion and lift it into a primary level. They were wrong in thinking that the secondary aspects of religion, the sociological and psychological, are essential to understanding the true essence of religion. What remains unexplainable is why historians and phenomenologists of religion continue to insist that sociology, anthropology and psychology remain "useful" for understanding religion.

It is not unusual to find scholars in the human sciences talking about consciousness, society or language as sui generis. Religion is often placed in this framework as a phenomenon that is unique, in a class by itself. A special method of understanding, or hermeneutics, is therefore necessary for an accurate assessment of religion. Indeed, methods of explanation such as those used in the natural sciences are clearly not appropriate. As we have seen, any attempt to explain religion as other than a sui generis phenomena, as The Sacred, is a mistake and a sign that religion is misunderstood. Moreover, it is usually argued that such explanations are "reductions" of religion.

I do not wish to be misunderstood. I find nothing wrong, in principle, with the claim that a certain subject matter is sui generis. That is to say, the subject demands certain theoretical principles and terms for explanation that are not available from theoretical sources external to the subject to be explained. This was precisely Durkheim's argument for the establishment of sociology, since neither psychology nor philosophical anthropology contained adequate theoretical principles for explaining social facts. As we shall see in Part II of this book, Saussure argued a similar case for language. And if we assume, as I do, that there is growth as well as continuity in our theoretical knowledge, then we must expect that at certain times new theories will encompass older theories as more adequate for explaining the data we are interested in The sui generis nature of a particular subject matter is then never absolute but dependent upon the adequacy of our theory. Or, the sui generis nature of a subject matter is relative to the adequacy of the theoretical object which explains the subject. It is, therefore, the revision and construction of theory which produces the continuity and growth of knowledge.

As far as I know, no one in the history or phenomenology of religion has presented an argument for the sui generis nature of religion from a theoretical perspective. In fact, Waardenburg and Eliade's descriptions of the "autonomous" discipline for the study of religion fail precisely because they are incomplete; both must appeal to, or include, external methods for a complete understanding of religion. The basic problem, as we shall soon see, is that the history and phenomenology of religion are not concerned with developing the theoretical object for the study of religion.

It may well be that a complete explanation of this situation must reach back to the romantic philosophers. I am thinking of Moritz, Schelling, the Schlegels, Schleiermacher and Creuzer. What I have in mind can be summed up in the following quote on mythology from Schelling: "Since the representations and the expressions [of mythology] are neither governed nor created by consciousness, it is the case that mythology is born directly as such, and in no other sense than the one it . expresses.... Because of the necessity with which its form is likewise born, [its meaning] is entirely literal, that is to say, everything in mythology must be understood just as it expresses itself, and not as if something else was being thought or said. Mythology is not allegorical, it is tautegorical. The gods, for mythology, are beings that really exist, they are not something else, nor do they signify something else, they signify only what they are."8 Although Schelling does not use the terms "sui generis," he is clearly asserting that the significance of myth cannot be reduced to meanings external to myth itself.

It would seem that the "romantic spirit" is with us more than we are willing to admit. It might help explain the continued interest in Max Müller. Although Eliade begins his review of the history of religions with Durkheim, he is fully aware of the fact that the study of religion as we know it today has its roots in "orientalism." He puts it this way in a remarkable essay on the present status of the study of religion, "The history of religions constituted itself an autonomous discipline shortly after the beginnings of Orientalism, in some respects relying on the researches of the Orientalists, and it has profited enormously from the progress of anthropology. In other words, the two principle documentary sources for the history of religions have been, and still are, the cultures of Asia and the peoples whom one calls (for lack of a more adequate term) 'primitive'."9 This genuine insight into the origins of what is now known as the history and phenomenology of religion completely overlooks a crucial corpus of material that has had tremendous influence on modern thought about religion. It is hard to explain, and I must confess I did not notice it myself on first reading Eliade's essay, why such texts as Creuzer's Symbolik und Mythologie der alten Völker, Moritz's Götterlehre, F. Schlegel's Über die Sprache und Weisheit der Inder, and Schelling's Philosophie der Mythology are overlooked. Although we might want to assert that these works are evidence of a "creative hermeneutics" running wild, there should be no doubt that they are also a source for our understanding of religious symbols as having "intransitive significance" and the notion that myth and religion are sui generis.10

If Schlegel and Schelling have been forgotten as important sources for the autonomous study of religion, there is one text that remains basic for most contemporary discussion of the study of religion. This text is The Idea of The Holy. The following quotation from Rudolph Otto can be taken as the motto for most of what is written by historians and phenomenologists of religion:

If there be any single domain of human experience that presents us with something unmistakably specific and unique, peculiar to itself, assuredly it is that of the religious life.... I shall speak, then, of a unique 'numinous' category of value and of a definitely 'numinous' state of mind, which is always found wherever the category is applied. This mental state is perfectly sui generis and irreducible to any other; and therefore, like every absolutely primary and elementary data, while it admits of being discussed, it cannot be strictly defined.11

Although Schlegel and Schelling are not mentioned by Otto, it is significant to recall that his use of Fichte, Goethe, Kant, Schiller, and Schleiermacher more than make up for this omission. One cannot overestimate the impact of this quotation from Otto on the study of religion. It became the motto for most scholars in what Eliade has called the autonomous study of religion.

Those who have read The Idea Of The Holy will recall that soon after Otto wrote the above passage about "numinous" states of the mind he added the famous (infamous?) assertion that, "whoever knows no such moments of experience is requested to read no farther." When I read the book I did not ponder this odd statement. I did not think, how strange that only those who have this numinous state of mind will know what Otto is talking about. I kept reading it because I did not want my peers to think I was mentally defective! It was, therefore, somewhat of a shock to read only recently that a scholar of religion believes that this assertion by Otto is "a challenge... as compelling today as when Otto wrote it, [it] will be with us for a long time."12

Understanding religion has come to mean, do not reduce religion to another level that is not religion. Grasping the essence of religion means having some intuitive understanding of the essence of religion, or the transcendent, or the ultimate reality to which religion refers. Methodologies that do not employ this approach to the study of religion are not just reductionistic; they are false. I will examine these assertions in the following chapter. For the moment I want to focus on the notion of "reductionism."

As far as I know, the terms, "reduction" and "reductionistic" are never adequately defined or explained by historians and phenomenologists who use them. Although the use of the terms is widespread in the literature on religion, reductionism is used against anyone who does not begin with the notion that religion is a manifestation of The Sacred. At best we usually find a sentence or two about the usefulness of these theories for purposes other than the study of religion. The term "reduction," then, is often used as a negative judgment on research in religion with which we disagree. It can also be used in order to ignore what others have written about religion.

As we have noticed, many scholars of religion use the term "reduction" as indicating the use of a theory which explains religion away. Reduction can also mean a methodology which diminishes the value of religion. When we turn to the history and philosophy of science, however, we find that the term "reduction" means something quite different.13

Reduction in most sciences is the explanation of a theory in one area of research by a theory which is used in another area. Ernest Nagel has defined reduction as "the explanation of a theory or a set of experimental laws established in one area of inquiry by a theory usually though not invariably formulated for some other domain."14 Thus, when a reduction is formulated in such a way that chemistry "becomes" physics, what we really mean is that theories or laws formulated in physics are now capable of explaining the theories of chemistry. Chemistry still exists. However, we now have greater explanatory power because of the reducing theories in physics. This point must be stressed simply because it is the core of our misunderstanding of reduction.

According to many scholars of religion, reduction explains religion away, or at least diminishes the value of the data. According to philosophers of science, what is being reduced is not data, but theories. It is quite conceivable that the data of one discipline or domain of study can be explained more adequately and more extensively by a theory from another domain or area of research. This has happened time and time again in the physical sciences, and it marks the advance or progress of those sciences.15 But, once again, this must not be taken in an absolute sense. There may well be domains within biology, for example, that, at least for the present, cannot be explained by theories external to the discipline itself.

This is clearly not the case, however, with the approach to religion under investigation in this chapter. As we have seen, religion cannot be reduced because according to this approach the essence of religion, its transcendent truth or nature, cannot be comprehended by any theory. What we must clearly see here is that The Sacred, the transcendent source of religion, the essence of religion, is not a theoretical object. The sacred is "ultimate reality." It is, as Eliade consistently expressed it, "the REAL." Thus, understanding the various manifestations of religion as manifestations of the Sacred is not a theoretical operation, or at least it is not presented as such.

If this approach is correct, then the reduction of religion is impossible. If we follow the above argument, it would seem that psychological or sociological explanations of religion are not really "false" or "reductionistic" but totally incommensurable with understanding religion, since religion, as The Sacred, cannot be explained. Whatever social scientists think they are explaining, it cannot be religion because the essence of religion, the numinous, is an ultimate, transcendent reality, a thing-in-itself. To argue this way, however, is to place the understanding of religion beyond theoretical bounds and to locate the study of religion beyond science. It should be clear that if we push these claims to their final conclusion there is no way we can determine whether they are either true or false.

I believe that such claims are either mistaken or they are dogmas to be taken on faith. Reductionism, as the term is used by scholars in religion , usually indicates that the nature or essence of religion has not been understood. Ernest Nagel maintains that this is misleading. According to Nagel,

> it suggests that the question of whether science is reducible to another is to be settled by inspecting the 'properties' or alleged nature of things rather than by investigating the logical consequences of certain explicitly formulated theories (that is, systems of statements).... The conception ignores the crucial point that the 'natures' of things, are not accessible to

direct inspection and that we cannot read off by simply inspection what it is they do or do not imply. Such 'natures' must be stated as a theory and are not the objects of observation.16

It should now be obvious that Nagel's idea of theory and the approach taken by most historians and phenomenologists of religion are two entirely different things. Nagel is saying that such terms as "essence," "nature" and "the sacred" are theoretical terms which are not empirical objects of observation. Moreover, the intuition of essences is at best a personal operation not open to confirmation by others. But, as Nagel has said, "it is clearly a slipshod formulation, and at best an elliptic one, which talks about 'deduction' of properties from one another, as if in the reduction of one science to another one were engaged in the black magic of extricating one set of phenomena from others incommensurably different from the first."17

If historians and phenomenologists of religion wish to claim that the study of religion is one science among others and if the discipline also declares that its claims are open to confirmation, that is, that its claims have truth value, then it would seem that such terms as "The Sacred" must be formulated within some theory of religion. Thus, to assert that religion is The Sacred would be equivalent to stating some theory about religion. I know of no published work in this discipline which has set The Sacred in a theoretical context.

To deny the process of reduction is to deny the possibility of development. Reduction is not concerned with falsifying a theory. Reduction takes place when, given two theories, we find that one of the theories is a more comprehensive theory for explaining the data. That is, the reducing theory is able to explain more than the reduced theory can, while including the data of the reduced theory. Reduction often solves problems which are not solved in the reduced theory. It should be clear that intertheoretic reduction is primarily concerned with theories, not "data" or "realities."

If historians and phenomenologists want to argue that their subject matter and methodology are not open to criticism from other sciences because of the sui generis nature of religion, it would then become quite difficult to understand in what sense the study of religion is ✓ a science, a knowledge. Furthermore, it would become impossible to judge whether any progress or growth in knowledge is being made. How would others who are interested in the study of religion be able to determine whether the assertions made are true or false? What would provide us with the proper framework for discovering new problems?

If the study of religion is exempted from intertheoretical reduction because the proper object of religion is The Sacred, then historians and phenomenologists of religion cannot accuse other disciplines interested in the subject of being reductionistic. The study of religion as a science sui generis is simply incommensurable with other sciences. Such a "science" has nothing in common with any other discipline by which it can be either reduced or criticized; no methodology can possibly evaluate it or contradict it. To argue for such a view consistently would put an end to the study of religion as a viable academic discipline. Anyone familiar with the publications of historians and phenomenologists of religion knows quite well that no one has ever held such a position. All these studies have been parasitic, using developments in sociology, psychology, anthropology and philosophy. The label "reductionistic" is attached only after the borrowing of terms, definitions, and models from these academic domains occurs. Since I will be borrowing terms and ideas from structuralism in later chapters of this book, I do not want to be misunderstood. I see nothing wrong with borrowing from other disciplines when this might be helpful in the development of our own. What is wrong, what I find contradictory, is the persistent claim that an autonomous study of religion exists that does not reduce religion to ✓ another plane of reference and then borrows some of its most important concepts from those very disciplines it finds guilty of reductionism -- you cannot have it both ways!

Scholars of religion interested in the problem of reduction often miss this important point. For example, Wayne Proudfoot correctly identifies Eliade as among those who have spoken against reductionism. He quotes the same pages from Eliade as I have and concludes that, "Eliade employs the term sacred to characterize the object of religious experience."18 He then asserts that, "The notorious obscurity of that term need not concern us here.... The point is that when Eliade refers to

Object = experienced (handwritten marginal note)

Otto (handwritten marginal note)

the irreducibility of the sacred, he is claiming that it is the intentional object of the religious experience which must not be reduced. To do so is to lose the experience, or to attend to something else altogether."19 This is unfortunate because it is precisely The Sacred as the object of religious experience that is central to the debate concerning reductionism. What Proudfoot and others continue to overlook is that the anti-reductionist in the study of religion is not offering us an obscure term. The Sacred as the object of religion is about as clear as can be. It is the "wholly other," and, as we shall soon see, this notion is loaded with theological meaning.

It is somewhat bewildering to read, therefore, that I was unable to fully clarify the discussion of this problem, in an essay I co-authored about a decade ago, because I lacked appreciation "of why the attack on reductionism has such an appeal."20 There is much that is intellectually stimulating in Proudfoot's essay on "explanation." Although many of us would agree with his distinction between two kinds of reduction I do not think they shed new light on the problem or its appeal for the study of religion. Proudfoot calls the first type "descriptive reduction." It involves "failure to identify an emotion, practice, or experience under the description by which the subject identifies it."21 An example would be to describe "I believe in God" as "I believe in society." Clearly the sense of the two assertions is not synonymous. Proudfoot calls the second type of reduction "explanatory." This involves "offering an explanation of an experience in terms that are not those of the subject and that might not meet with his approval."22 An example might be, the belief that "Christ is the hope of the world," can be explained by the hypothesis that "the origin and cause of religious belief is society." Proudfoot thinks that "This is perfectly justifiable and is, in fact, normal procedure. The explanandum is set in a new context, whether that be one of covering laws and initial conditions, narrative structure, or some other explanatory model.... The explanation stands or falls according to how well it can account for all the available evidence."23 I agree. It is important to notice that given this argument explanatory reduction need not meet with the believers approval. In fact, "it may be that the correct explanation requires no reference to religious realities."24 This is precisely the thesis of the essay I co-

Comparative philosophy of religion ; comp. systematics

authored over a decade ago! The burden of that essay was to convince the reader that the issue of reduction is primarily theoretical!25

Proudfoot's analysis of reductionism reinforces that conviction. If I understand him correctly, he thinks that Eliade and others are wrong for attacking "explanatory reduction" (I agree) but right in their battle against "descriptive reduction" which consists of a mistaken description of the subject's experience. The problem with this interpretation is that none of the anti-reductionists, as far as I can see, have followed their own advice. Surely, Eliade's description of religious experience as expressing The Sacred, to take just one example, would cause great difficulties for many believers as descriptions of their experiences, beliefs and practices. The reason for this difficulty will become clear in a moment.

The attack on "reductionists" produces a serious dilemma. On the one hand, scholars want to study religion empirically with criteria that are objective and public, open to the kind of criticism which provides for growth in our knowledge of religion. On the other hand, the claim that religion refers to The Sacred prevents serious theoretical discussion of religion from taking place. In fact, it blocks any attempt at genuine methodological discussion. How can we make sense out of this situation? How can we explain the contradiction inherent in an academic discipline which produces both a quest for scientific status and the refusal to become one? The answer, I believe, is to be found in the third tradition which gave the history and phenomenology of religion its birth, the tradition Eliade somehow overlooked when he traced his intellectual ancestors back to "orientalism" and anthropology. This tradition sheds a great deal of light on the historian and phenomenologist's "object" of religion.

It may be the case that the influence of theology on the history and phenomenology of religion is so obvious that it need not be mentioned. If this is incorrect, which I believe is the case, then it becomes all the more urgent to make clear why this tradition has been repressed. Why, for example, are scholars of religion continually perplexed about the influence of a small book called The Idea Of The Holy? When they do mention Otto, usually in a footnote, they must confront the fact, and its significance, that Otto was a professor of theology at Göttingen and

Marburg. The sign of what is wrong is that theologians like Otto are forgotten when historians of religion try to remember the intellectual ancestors of their discipline. It is almost as if they were in a state of amnesia when the problems inherent in what is known as religionswissenschaft are encountered. Perhaps "repression" is a better term, for how else can one explain the lack of concern most historians and phenomenologists have about the significance of the theological past for the problems inherent in their own discipline?

At least some theologians who later became phenomenologists or historians of religion were quite certain about what they were doing. For an example, here is a statement from a well known and often quoted phenomenologist of religion who never forgot that he was also a theologian, "Le premier point d'intersection -et le principal ...est la découverte de ce qui est «autre», cette découverte que nous appelons l'éveil à la conscience ou l'émergence de l'homme. Cet «autre» s'appelle dans la religion «Ce qui est tout autre» (das ganz Andere), Dieu."26 Do contemporary scholars of the history and phenomenology of religion agree with this statement, or is it an embarrassment to them? If they are unwilling to affirm what van der Leeuw asserts, then what do they mean by homo religiosus, "transcendent sources," The Sacred, and "the wholly other"? Surely, the significance of The Sacred as used by historians and phenomenologists is not synonymous with the "reductionistic" concepts of Freud's unconscious, Malinowski's primary and secondary needs, Marxian superstructures, or Durkheim's collective conscience. If this were so, it would be impossible to understand the well-worn assertions about the autonomy of the study of religion, that homo religiosus cannot be reduced, that religion is an autonomous reality, and therefore, sui generis. The ghosts of Otto, van der Leeuw, Wach and other theologians will not be put to rest by generous quotes from Freud, Malinowski, and Durkheim or, for that matter, from Douglas, V. Turner and Geertz.

There is nothing "notoriously obscure" in the above quotation from van der Leeuw. And there is a good deal of empirical evidence to confirm this. Many scholars of religion have refused to leave their theological ancestors alone; they do not wish them to rest in peace, eventually to be forgotten. It is the metaphysical relations with these ancestors that chains them to the past. Let us for example, recall the volume The History of Religions: Essays On The Problem Of Understanding. Published in 1967, this collection of essays begins with a piece by Wach in which he states that "An exemplary model for training oneself to grasp the significant from the fullness of the materials of Religionswissenschaft is still Rudolf Otto's Das Heilige. This study, besides being important for the phenomenology of religion, also has great methodological significance."27 The book closes with an essay by Paul Tillich on "The Significance of the History of Religions for the Systematic Theologian" in which Tillich refers to Otto, his colleague, as "an historian of religion!"

Two more examples suffice to show that this situation is not something peculiar to what was once known as "the Chicago school." The first example is taken a contemporary theologian interested in the meaning of symbols. Here is what Paul Ricoeur thinks the discipline is all about. His statement is in the context of discovering a hermeneutics as the "restoration of meaning." This hermeneutics is in opposition to what he has called "the school of suspicion" (Marx, Freud, et al.). The opposition to the "school of suspicion" Ricoeur calls "postcritical faith." He finds this "postcritical faith," the faith that has undergone criticism, in the phenomenology of religion. The significance of his "discovery" deserves to be quoted at length.

Let us look for [the postcritical faith] in the series of philosophical decisions that secretly animate a phenomenology of religion and lie hidden even within its apparent neutrality. It is a rational faith, for it interprets; but it is a faith because it seeks through interpretation, a second naivete....

We will take our examples from the phenomenology of religion in the wide sense, embracing here the work of Leenhardt, Van der Leeuw, and Eliade.... The first imprint of this faith in a revelation through the word is to be seen in the care and concern for the OBJECT, a characteristic of all phenomenological analysis. That concern, as we know, presents itself as a 'neutral' wish to describe and not to reduce.... To generalize from this, we shall say that the theme of phenomenology of religion is the SOMETHING intended in ritual actions, in mythical speech, in belief or mystical feeling...Let us call this intended object the 'sacred', without determining its nature, whether it be the TREMENDUM NUMINOSUM, according to Rudolf Otto; 'the powerful,' according to Van der Leeuw; or 'fundamental time,' according to Eliade. In this general sense, and with a view of underlining the concern for the intentional object, we may say that every phenomenology of religion is a phenomenology of the sacred.28

Indeed it is! What is striking in these passages is the theologian's discovery of a secret which phenomenologists and historians of religion have tried to conceal or deny, "the series of philosophic decisions that secretly animate a phenomenology of religion and lie hidden even within its <u>apparent</u> neutrality". Is Ricoeur wrong? Has he misunderstood what is going on? Well, some may respond, gathering their apparent phenomenological robes around them, that may be true of Otto and van der Leeuw, but who reads them now? We have gone beyond them in our neutrality and objectivity regarding the study of religion. For further clarification let us move to the Netherlands for a second example.

Phenomenologists and historians of religion at Groningen formed a study group consisting of "mostly younger scholars" to reflect on some of the fundamental problems and methods in the science of religion. We are told that the group shared "dissatisfaction with phenomenology of religion in the old style." After stressing this dissatisfaction with the "old style" anyone who reads the collected papers will be startled, as I was, by the title of the very first essay, "Theology, Philosophy and Science of Religion"! Here is what Hubbeling has to say about a "science of religion," "It also includes a study of religion as such. This study ought to be done in as neutral a way as possible, in that the student gives an objective and impartial description and explanation of the religious phenomena. Neither does he give a moral or other evaluation of these phenomena, nor does he inquire into the truth of them. He does not show his own religious or atheistic preferences and by no means does he try to defend them within the scope of his discipline, the science of religion."29

Van Baaren, after generous quotes from Spiro, Turner, and Malinowski, agrees. "It can never," he asserts, "be the aim of science of religion to reduce religion to something else." He goes on to clarify this by saying that "Systematic science of religion is no historical discipline as history of religions is; it is a systematic one. It is distinguished from other systematic disciplines taught in the faculty of theology by its lack of normative character. It only studies religions as they are empirically and disclaims any statements concerning the value and truth of the phenomena studied. This does not imply that the student of this discipline is not allowed to entertain conceptions as a person, it only means that he acknowledges that those convictions are irrelevant for his scientific work and that he must rule them out as much as possible in his research.... As the truth of religion cannot be scientifically demonstrated, science of religion refrains from any judgment in this matter." He closes his essay with the following astounding assertion, "A term derived from our own culture is in case of need preferable to a term derived from a foreign culture. In the second case we operate with two unknown quantities, in the first case only one. In this way we can use the term revelation [!] as a terminus technicus of science of religion."30

Since no one from within the discipline of the history and phenomenology of religion is raising the question, let us ask Ricoeur's once again. What series of philosophical/theological decisions secretly animate this "science" and lie hidden even within its apparent neutrality? Who has decided, and on what grounds, that truth claims in religion cannot be "scientifically demonstrated"? Does this mean that there are two domains of truth, one in science and one in religion? If we follow this path it will surely lead us to total incoherence. Why have generations of historians, phenomenologists, and neo-phenomenologists of religion been taught to suppress their personal convictions as irrelevant in the pursuit of truth and objective knowledge?

Why have they decided, and on what grounds, that the object of religion (The Sacred) is inexpressible as such and that any other interpretation of the object of religion is a reduction and therefore,

indirectly

inadmissible? What do they really mean when they assert that the object of religion is "The Sacred"? And when they make such assertions are they making statements that are true or false? What is the epistemological or cognitive status of such statements as, religion expresses, manifests, or refers to The Sacred. Finally, who or what discipline determines the truth behind the empirical descriptions given by the phenomenologist of religion? None of these questions are raised by the younger scholars discussing <u>methodological</u> problems in the history and phenomenology of religion at Groningen, or, at any other University where the history and phenomenology of religion is the central concern.

It is, I believe, the suppression, not the repression, of these questions that allows them to contradict themselves by generous quotations from scholars and disciplines that are clearly reductionistic by their own principles. It is also the suppression of these questions that allows them to attack alternative methodologies as "methodological imperialism." It should be obvious that the "imperialism" is actually disguised in the robe of "neutrality." The irony in all of this is that a traditional logical positivist could agree with most of the assertions being made by contemporary historians and phenomenologists of religion. The irony is located in the claim that logical positivism is the enemy of the phenomenology of religion.

Let us confront this situation bluntly and in all honesty. Theology is very much a part of what has become known as the history and phenomenology of religion. But rather than agreeing with Ricoeur, I think we should take a stand that is in opposition to the claim that we either are, or should join, the "post-critical faithful." On the contrary, we should become suspicious of "neutrality" and develop the courage to expose the theological secrets behind the disguise of The Sacred as the object of religion; that SOMETHING which many scholars find so difficult to define.31

Once the apparent disguise of "neutrality" is seen for what it really is, an illusion, scholars will then be forced to take a stand. Will we take a stand among those who claim that the object of religion is the inexpressible, an ultimate mystery, the wholly other, that involves us in an endless hermeneutics incapable of being either confirmed or disconfirmed? If so, then let us clearly identify ourselves with what has been called the "post-critical faith." But then let those of us who choose this option also assume the responsibility for this faith rather then letting the theologian decipher the hidden meanings. Let us, in brief, expose to the public what we really mean when we write about homo religiosus and assert that religion "means" The Sacred. Let us fully explain the hidden agenda that provides the reasons for being anti-Marx, anti-Freud, anti-Durkheim and anti-reductionistic.

Of course, the historian and phenomenologist do say more about religion. But, the "more" that is said is placed under severe constraints due to the rule which stipulates that we remain "neutral" or "normless" in our study of religion. If we really did live up to the rule, the object of our study would never be defined. This, in turn, would be devastating for an academic discipline simply because no framework whatsoever would exist for identifying what is and what is not religion. Nothing of the kind ever happens. Why not? The constraint is an illusion. It is an illusion because there is one assumption or principle that is not neutral in the history and phenomenology of religion. It is the principle that religions are manifestations of The Sacred, the representation of a "transcendent source," "ultimate reality", or "the Real." It is only when we attempt to specify what this "reality" is that opens us to the accusation that we have now crossed over into theology from a discipline that is normless and neutral, i.e. not a theological enterprise.

We can now make sense of the claim that the historian and phenomenologist of religion are not concerned with whether the world's religions are true. Genuine neutrality in understanding religion involves sympathy or empathy regarding a reality that is transcendent, The Sacred Reality. It is not empathy for any specific religion, but empathy for what religions express, empathy for The Sacred. And since this reality cannot be described empirically, the best we can do is describe what religions have said about this reality without taking any position on the truth claims these expressions of The Sacred entail. Those who take this position do not seem to notice that this understanding of genuine neutrality, of objectivity and "systematics," presupposes a norm, The Sacred. That religion is The Sacred is not an empirical discovery or an historical "fact."

One of the best examples of what I have been describing can be found in the work of van der Leeuw. The essence of religion, he writes, is "not a phenomenon at all, and it is neither attainable nor understandable; what we obtain from it phenomenologically, therefore, is merely its reflection in experience."32 The same position is expressed from a slightly different perspective by Kristensen when he says that, "We gain a different conception of the 'holy' when we take the reality of the believer's faith as our starting point.... This reality proves to be self-subsistent and absolute; it is beyond all our rational criticism. The only difficulty for us is to form an accurate conception of this reality and to understand it from within."33

Notice that the difficulty is not understanding a certain religion, but the "reality" to which religions refer. Just how an historian of religion knows that this reality is "self-subsistent," "absolute," and/or "beyond all rational criticism" is never explained. Let us recall van Baaren's solution. It is "revelation" that is the "terminus technicus" for the study of religion, but, whose?   Perhaps at this point the phenomenologist of religion remembers the famous words Otto wrote at the beginning of his book.

The examples given above, and many more could be cited, illustrate the dilemma of an essentialist non-reductive understanding of religion. The exact criteria for forming an accurate conception of the reality of the "holy," or The Sacred, cannot be given by historians and phenomenologists of religion. This is not to say that such criteria are in themselves impossible to construct, but when they are constructed they will be theological.

If my interpretation of this academic discipline for the study of religion is accurate, it would seem that Durkheim is not the only one for whom it can be said that petitio principii is a scholarly vice. As we have seen, a description of how various religions express The Sacred clearly presupposes some understanding of the nature of The Sacred, not as a theoretical postulate, but as a reality sui generis. According to the defenders of this "science," the sui generis nature of religion, The Sacred as such, cannot be described by any methodological procedure. It is this circular argument that helps explain why it is the case that methodological analysis is often considered to be of little value. But the problem becomes much more severe when we recall that we have no criteria for deciding which interpretation of religion is more adequate than another as an understanding of The Sacred. In the end it would seem that not only all religions but all interpretations of religion are of equal value. This path surely leads to incoherence. We can view the development of the phenomenology of religion as an attempt to close the entrance to this path. In the next chapter we shall see this attempt failed.

NOTES

1. Two very good surveys of this type of academic study of religion have been written. See Ursula King, "Historical and Phenomenological Approaches," *Contemporary Approaches to the Study of Religion, Vol. I: The Humanities,* ed. Frank Whaling (The Hague: Mouton, 1983) and E. Sharp, *Comparative Religion: A History,* 2nd ed. (La Salle, Ill.: Open Court, 1986).

2. I shall use capitols for "The Sacred" when I intend this term to denote an ontological, metaphysical or "ultimate reality," as this term is used by many historians and phenomenologists of religion.

3. J. D. J. Waardenburg, "Research on Meaning in Religion," *Religion, Culture and Methodology,* eds. Th. P. van Baaren and H. J. W. Drijvers (The Hague: Mouton, 1973) 126-128.

4. J. D. J. Waardenburg, *Classical Approaches to the Study of Religion* (The Hague: Mouton, 1973) 6.

5. Mircea Eliade, *Patterns in Comparative Religion*, trans. Rosemary Sheed (New York: World, 1958) xi.

6. Mircea Eliade, "The History of Religions in Retrospect: 1912 and After," *The Quest* (Chicago: U of Chicago P, 1969) 13.

7. Eliade, "The History of Religions," 19.

8. *Schellings Werke*, Sechster Band (Müchen: Beck, 1928) 197-198. The original text is as follows: "Weil das Bewusstsein weder die Vorstellung selbst, noch deren Ausdruck wält order erfindet, so entsteht die Mythologie gleich als solche, und in keinen andern Sinn, als in dem sie sich ausspricht... zufolge der Notwendigkeit, mit welcher auch die Form entsteht, ist sie durchaus eigentlich, d. h. es ist alles in ihr so zu verstehen wie sie es ausspricht, nicht als ob etwas anderes gedacht, etwas anderes gesagt wäre. Die Mythologie ist nicht allegorisch, sie ist tautegorisch. Die Götter sind ihr wirklich existirende Wesen, die nicht etwas anderes sind, etwas anderes bedeuten, sondern nur das bedeuten, was sie sind."

9. Mircea Eliade, "Crisis and Renewal," *The Quest* 57. There is, of course, a third source which Eliade overlooks, or dismisses much too easily; the third source is theology.

10. "Intransitive significance" is taken from Tzvetan Todorov's excellent book which includes an analysis of Romantic thought on modern theories of meaning. See Tzvetan Todorov, *Theories of the Symbol* (Ithaca: Cornell UP, 1982) Chapter 6, "The Romantic Crisis."

There are two excellent studies of the rise of "Orientalism" in the West which should become a resource for scholars interested in this important development. The first is, Raymond Schwab, *The Oriental Renaissance*, trans. Gene Patterson-Black and Victor Reinking (New York: Columbia UP, 1984). The second volume is, Edward W. Said, *Orientalism* (New York: Pantheon, 1978).

11. Rudolph Otto, *The Idea of the Holy* (Oxford: Oxford UP, 1957) 4, 7.

12. Willard Oxtoby, "The Idea of the Holy," *Encyclopedia of Religion*, ed. Mircea Eliade, vol. 6 (New York: Macmillan, 1987) 437. The reference from Otto, *The Idea of the Holy* will be found on page 8.

13. Edward Yonan and I addressed this issue over a decade ago in "Is a Science of Religion Possible?" *Journal of Religion* 52 (1972). I have every reason to believe that the issue is as important now as it was then.

14. Ernest Nagel, *The Structure of Science* (New York: Harcourt, 1961) 338. I am fully aware of the ongoing debate concerning "reductionism" in the sciences. I would agree with many philosophers of science that the logical positivist account of reductionism is afflicted with unresolvable problems. Nevertheless, I do think that Nagel is on the right side of the issues which are theoretical in nature. For the pros and cons concerning the issues, see Fredrick Suppe, *The Structure of Scientific Theories* (Urbana: U of Illinois P, 1977) and Peter Achinstein, *Concepts of Science* (Baltimore: Johns Hopkins UP, 1968). It seems clear that Kuhn and Feyerabend are not an option; see the discussion in the above volume edited by Suppe and Kuhn's second thoughts on his notion of "paradigm" in the same volume. The relativistic consequences of positions such as Kuhn's for the study of religion will be discussed in Chapter Five. For a trenchant criticism of Feyerabend, see Hilary Putnam, "How Not to Talk About Meaning," *Mind, Language and Reality: Philosophical Papers*, vol. 2 (Cambridge: Cambridge UP, 1975). Putnam also thinks that, "The Nagel view [of reduction] does not appear to me to be so seriously false" (Putnam 118).

15. For some good examples and another review of the issues see Tryg A. Ager, Jerrold L. Aronson, and Robert Weingard, "Are Bridge Laws Really Necessary?" *Nous* VIII (1974): 119-134.

16. Ernest Nagel, *The Structure of Science* 364.

17. Ernest Nagel, "The Meaning of Reduction in the Natural Sciences," *Science and Civilization*, ed. Robert C. Stauffer (Madison: U of Wisconsin P, 1949) 131.

18. Wayne Proudfoot, *Religious Experience* (Berkeley: U of California P, 1985) 192.

19. Proudfoot 192. Proudfoot is certainly correct even though I cannot recall Eliade ever describing The Sacred as the "intentional object."

20. Proudfoot 190.

21. Proudfoot 196.

22. Proudfoot 197.

23. Proudfoot 197.

24. Proudfoot 201. See Terry F. Godlove, "Interpretation, Reductionism, and Belief in God," *Journal Of Religion* 69 (1989): 184-198, for a very interesting argument for the strong claim that the "explanatory" type of reduction may prove the believer to be right. Godlove uses Davidson's truth-conditional semantics as the basis for this argument, using Durkheim as his example.

25. See Penner and Yonan 107-33. The difficulty we had that Proudfoot alludes to is not "why the appeal of anti-reductionism," but rather the problem of specifying the meaning of "covering laws" and "initial conditions." This difficulty reflects the serious problems inherent in the nomological-deductive model for scientific explanations. Some of these difficulties will be discussed in Chapter Three. I wish to insist once again, however, that the problem of "reduction" is basically theoretical. I see no disagreement between Proudfoot and myself on this point.

26. G. van der Leeuw, *L'Homme Primitif et la Religion* (Paris: Presses U de France, 1940) 120.

27. Joachim Wach, "Introduction: The Meaning and Task of the History of Religions (Religionswissenschaft)," *The History of Religions: Essays on the Problem of Understanding*, ed. Joseph M. Kitagawa (Chicago: U of Chicago P, 1967) 18. There is an earlier version of the theological foundations of the history of religions which should not be forgotten; Mircea Eliade and Joseph M. Kitagawa, eds., *The History of Religions: Essays in Methodology* (Chicago: U of Chicago P, 1959). The point of the book is expressed in "The Preface" in the following way: "In spite of the favorable contemporary circumstances, it will not be easy for the

history of religions to establish itself as one of the leading scholarly activities in the modern university. In fact, the great danger is that it will be completely absorbed by certain other fields. The history of religions deals with materials handled also by philosophy of religion, psychology, sociology, anthropology, history and theology. Its problem is to demonstrate that it is not merely ancillary to these other studies but is a discipline in its own right, drawing on, yet making unique additions to, these areas of knowledge" (ix). This is indeed a good summary of how we perceive ourselves. The fact that there is not one methodological essay in the volume is no longer surprising. What is surprising, after reading this quotation in the preface, are the essays by Wilfred Cantwell Smith, Jean Daniélou, and Friedrich Heiler. Given the Christian theological nature of these essays in a book on methodology in the history of religions, it becomes obvious that the discipline as described in the preface was aborted before it had the chance for life on its own in the modern university. In reading these essays there is a sense in which our next example from Ricoeur is wrong; nothing is hidden here. The odd fact is that some historians of religions are unaware of this fact. The question then arises, what is the future of this illusion; how long will it last?

28. Paul Ricoeur, *Freud and Philosophy: An Essay on Interpretation* (New Haven: Yale UP, 1970) 28-29. Ricoeur repeats this description in "The Hermeneutics of Symbols: II," *The Conflict of Interpretations: Essays in Hermeneutics* (Evanston, Ill.: Northwestern UP, 1974) 318.

29. H. G. Hubbeling, "Theology, Philosophy and Science of Religion and their Logical and Empirical Presuppositions," *Religion, Culture and Methodology*, ed. Th. P. van Baaren and H. J. W. Drijvers (The Hague: Mouton, 1973) 9-10.

30. Th. P. van Baaren, "Science of Religion as a Systematic Discipline: Some Introductory Remarks," *Religion, Culture and Methodology* 37, 47-48, 54.

31. It would appear that these issues are finally coming to the surface. See Donald Wiebe's essay, "The failure of nerve in the academic study of religion," and the acerbic theological response by the editor in, *Studies in Religion / Sciences Religieuses* 13 (1984). In my own response to the editorial outburst (see *Studies in*

Religion / Sciences Religieuses 15 (1986): 165-175), I tried to point out that Wiebe's only error was in assuming that the history of religions had become free of theological assumptions concerning religion.

32. G. van der Leeuw, *Religion in Essence and Manifestation* (London: Allen, 1938) 680.

33. W. Brede Kristensen, *The Meaning of Religion* (The Hague: Nijhoff, 1960) 23.

CHAPTER TWO

THE PHENOMENOLOGY OF RELIGION

In this chapter we will extend the analysis presented in the first chapter by focusing on phenomenology as a method for the study of religion. We will, therefore, be able to penetrate more deeply into some of the methodological problems presented to us in the history and phenomenology of religion. This will be done in three parts. The first part will briefly outline what the phenomenology of religion is all about. This approach to religion is often located in the phenomenological movement which began with Husserl. Part two, therefore, will describe Husserl's phenomenological project. Part three will critically apply Husserl's phenomenology to well-known assertions by phenomenologists of religion.

I am fully aware of the fact that not one well-known anthology or history of the phenomenological movement includes an essay on the phenomenology of religion. The two volume study of the movement by Herbert Spiegelberg refers to G. van der Leeuw's use of philosophical phenomenology as an afterthought to the possibility of a phenomenology of religion.1 Despite this conclusion, scholars of religion have persisted in identifying not only van der Leeuw but also Otto and Eliade as influenced by the phenomenological movement, especially by Husserl. Thus, Willard Oxtoby writes in the recently published Encyclopedia of Religion that "One of the principal options in the study of religion in the mid-twentieth century has been termed the 'phenomenology' of religion.... Understood strictly, the phenomenology of religion is supposed to be a precise application to religion of insights from the European philosophical movement known as phenomenology, launched by Edmund Husserl."2

Douglas Allen is more direct. He places Otto, van der Leeuw and Eliade, "the three most influential" scholars of religion, directly in the phenomenological movement and states that they "have used a phenomenological method and have been influenced, at least partially, by phenomenological philosophy." The first bibliographical reference to this article is the two volume work by Herbert Spiegelberg. Allen repeats this assertion in another article he wrote on Husserl, "Husserl's influence can be seen in the phenomenological works of Max Scheler, Gerardus van der Leeuw, Paul Ricoeur and many others."3 The task in this chapter is to demonstrate that the influence of Husserl on what has become known as "phenomenology of religion" is at best a folk tale and that the history and phenomenology of religion as we know it today could reasonably be described as Christian theology carried on by other means. In order to carry out this demonstration we will proceed with a description of phenomenology of religion and then give a brief synopsis of Husserl's work on phenomenology.

I. The Phenomenology of Religion

The term "phenomenology" is used in many ways. It is often used in the title of a book to indicate that the work is a "pure" description of a particular subject. What the phenomenologist does is simply describe the phenomena as it appeared in an experiment, field work, or historical research. Of course, it is not quite so simple. We must learn to become suspicious of any work that is presented as a pure description unencumbered by theory. Descriptions are always theory laden. However, I see no compelling reasons that would argue against the use of phenomenology to indicate that what we are doing is primarily descriptive (always within the framework of some theory) rather than theoretical research.

The phenomenology of religion is different. It has flourished primarily in theological faculties and divinity schools. We are repeatedly told by its practitioners that the phenomenology of religion is a distinct methodology for the understanding of religion that should not be confused with history, sociology, anthropology or theology. When we inquire about the distinctive characteristics of this methodology, we are given the reply that it involves taking The Sacred, the "essence" of religion, seriously.

Anyone familiar with the phenomenology of religion will recall that most practitioners of this method make the following claims: 1. Religion is a sui generis reality, and, therefore, the study of religion requires its own unique methodology. But, the essence of religion never manifests itself in a naked and unaccommodated form. 2. Because of the unique nature of religion all "reductions" must be avoided. 3. The ultimate aim of a phenomenology of religion is the formulation of the essence of religion. 4. Phenomenology of religion is free from value judgments; it is an objective account of religion. It can teach us to recognize what is genuine and what is spurious in religion. 5. By using Husserl's notion of the "epoche," phenomenologists of religion are able to suspend the question of the truth of religion. 6. Guided by the principle of "epoche" the phenomenologist of religion does not use the term "revelation" but substitutes the concept of "hierophany" in its place.4

The father of the phenomenology of religion put it this way: 1. The phenomenology of religion "is the systematic discussion of what appears (rede über das Sich-zeigende). Religion however, is an ultimate experience, a revelation which in its very essence is, and remains concealed." 2. The phenomenology of religion is not, "history of religions," "psychology of religion," or "philosophy" of "theology" since the latter two "claim to search for truth, which phenomenology, in this respect, exercises the intellectual suspense of the epoche."5 At this point, van der Leeuw refers to Husserl's use of the term epoche as implying that "no judgement is expressed concerning the objective world, which is thus placed 'between brackets,' as it were. All phenomena, therefore, are considered solely as they are presented to the mind, without any further aspects such as their real existence, or their value being taken into account." 3. The observer thus adopts "the attitude of complete intellectual suspense or of abstention from judgement, regarding these controversial topics."6

More recently we are informed that "one of the principal options in the study of religion in the mid-twentieth century has been termed the 'phenomenology' of religion." This option is then described as "a precise application to religion of the insights from the European philosophical movement known as phenomenology, launched by Edmund Husserl."7

II. Husserl and Phenomenology.

Clarification of the meaning of phenomenology requires knowledge of the phenomenological movement itself. The available studies of this movement are as enormous as they are complex, and the debate on the issues has at times become emotional. The point of departure, nevertheless, has always remained the thought of Edmund Husserl, and my attempt to clarify the meaning of phenomenology will, therefore, be based on his work.8 This approach follows the practice of leading phenomenologists in philosophy and the human sciences.

Within the limits of this initial analysis, two points must be emphasized from the beginning. First, phenomenology is neither a neutral method nor a pure description of phenomena. It is a transcendental philosophy. Second, the denial of this assertion, as we shall see, is a rejection of the aims of phenomenology itself.

The notion that phenomenology is only a method for pure description is based on an influential interpretation of Husserl set forth in an article by Eugene Fink in 1933.9 Ironically, Husserl endorsed this article! One of Fink's main assertions concerning Husserl's work and the meaning of phenomenology is that Husserl moved from a method of "eidetic analysis" to an idealistic philosophy. This interpretation of Husserl splits the development of his thought into two parts. The first involves an eidetic or essential analysis of the mundane world, or the real world, of everyday phenomena. The second moves to an idealistic analysis of subjectivity, of the pure ego. The first generation of phenomenologists which Husserl fathered accepted this interpretation as involving two "reductions" or stages in Husserl's phenomenology.

This interpretation of Husserl's phenomenology as "early" and "later" led to the repudiation of the "later Husserl" as a return to metaphysical-idealism. Phenomenologists on the Kantian side accepted the eidetic, mundane reduction as good phenomenology but concluded that the transcendental reduction was a return to ontologism. It was, therefore, not just unnecessary but impossible for the construction of a genuine phenomenological method. Philosophers influenced by the Marxist tradition repudiated Husserl as the last of the bourgeois idealists. And the British analytic tradition viewed his later thought as intuitional mysticism.10

Why Husserl sanctioned Fink's article remains a mystery.11 Given the evidence of his own publications Husserl did not think of phenomenology as two methods of reduction, the eidetic and the transcendental, the second of which could be eliminated. The judgement that the transcendental reduction commits him to an idealistic metaphysics must be reconciled with his own denial of this judgement as a misunderstanding of his thought.12 An adequate account of phenomenology will someday have to come to terms with the fact that Husserl made a distinction between "idealistic epistemology" and "idealistic metaphysics."13

The generation of scholars who split Husserl's work into a phenomenology (i.e. an intuitive description of the mundane world) and an idealistic metaphysics (i.e. taking the pure ego as an absolute entity or being) produced a phenomenology that has been suspect of mystical vision, traditional introspectionism or intuitionism.14

The central problem Husserl attempted to solve was epistemological or cognitional. In the preface to the _Logische Untersuchungen_, Husserl states that he continuously saw himself pushed to higher levels of reflection "concerning the relation between the subjectivity of cognition and the objectivity of the content of cognition."15 Or, as he says in the introduction to the first investigation, the question that is always raised is, "how to understand that the 'in itself' of objectivity comes to 'presentation,' grasped by cognition; in the end becoming again subjective."16 This problem is highlighted again in the _Cartesian Meditations_, where the problem is exhibited in reflection. Reflection on self always manifests the self as a subject for the world, but at the same time as an object to be grasped as a part of the world. In _Krisis_ the problem is raised in his discussion of the relation between the lived-world and subjectivity. In _Ideen_ II the problem is raised in relation to the natural and human sciences.17

This problem, or paradox, is not the result of phenomenology; on the contrary, the various phenomenological reflections specify the problem and seek to overcome it. The solution to the riddle is one more attempt to overcome the dualism of subject and object which has vexed our philosophical tradition and scientific disciplines. Husserl saw this problem as the root of philosophical and theoretical skepticism.

Skepticism, according to Husserl, is the result of the attempt to found subjectivity on the basis of the world. That is to say, it results from an attempt to solve the problem through an emphasis on the subject as a part of the world. As a component of the world, subjectivity is conditioned through its relation with other components of the world, and thus the acceptance of the world can only be relatively binding. We know there is objective truth and, on reflection, we also know it is always valid for us, or for me. Since my concrete subjectivity, however, is a component of the world, grasped only as an object in the world, my cognition remains a particular fact only relatively binding. It cannot be raised to the level of universal and necessary validity. Husserl often called this "empiricist" or "common sense" view of existence "the natural orientation" toward the world.

Husserl also used the term "psychologism" as the foundation for the skeptical consequences which result from the attempt to found the validity of cognition in the "natural orientation." He never failed to point out that skepticism (also, subjectivism or relativism) involved contradiction. In the L. U. this is revealed logically by showing that skepticism must in the end commit itself to saying that "It is true that there is no truth" or "what is true for someone is false for another" or "the same content of judgement can be both true and false."18 In Krisis, the contradiction is manifested as an annulment of relativism itself. Psychologism must take as valid, as universal, its cognition of the world and its component relations, which in turn cancels out the self and its relative cognition as ONLY a part of the world.19

According to Husserl, therefore, any philosophy or scientific method which grounds itself in the "natural orientation," the uncritical mundane world of "common sense" experiences, inevitably ends in skepticism.20 And the effect of this skepticism, according to Husserl, is dogmatism.

III. The Solution: Reduction and Intentionality

As I have noted, Husserl's primary concern was skepticism. His main project was to establish a basis for the acceptance of the world in both the natural and human sciences by founding them on a transcendental, "pretheoretical" experience. This basis, which he also called "transcendental subjectivity," the stream or process of experience, is the starting point for Husserl's attempt to overcome the cognitive dualism which is the result of remaining in the mundane or empirically given "natural orientation." Phenomenology in this sense is universal in its critical demands and in its attempt to penetrate and solve the problems of skepticism and relativism. According to Husserl, this is what makes phenomenology more than a science among sciences; it is, therefore, first philosophy.

In stressing that phenomenology is not just a method of description I have suggested that what it entails is a definite orientation which Husserl calls "transcendental" in contrast to what we could call a transcendent or "natural" orientation. Phenomenology in this sense continues to have a consistent meaning throughout Husserl's writing and is best described by an examination of reduction and intentionality.

Reduction has two meanings. It means a restriction of interest in that it signifies a turn or a return to something. This is its most general meaning, and in this sense every science implies reduction, a limitation of interest. In other words all scientific interest, engages in the use of that well-known Husserlian term "epoche." An analysis of the reductions used in both the natural and human sciences would reveal therefore, two aspects; on one side a negative aspect which brackets or suspends something, on the other side a positive aspect which is a turn or "orientation" toward the residue resulting from the bracketing.

It is important to notice that from Husserl's point of view this general sense of reduction has nothing to do with the phenomenological transcendental reduction. All such reductions are performed from within what he calls the natural or mundane orientation. The phenomenological reduction which is of central concern in the writings of Husserl is a bracketing of the natural orientation itself. It is a turn to pure subjectivity as the foundation of all cognition and certainty.21

Since many phenomenologists of religion have made use of Husserl's notion of "epoche" and "bracketing," it is important that we understand what Husserl means by these terms in the context of the natural orientation. Once we have understood them, it will become very clear that the use of these terms in the phenomenology of religion is at best metaphorical and lacks any methodological substance whatsoever.

Husserl is clear on what he means by the thesis of the natural orientation. In the natural orientation, according to Husserl, "I know of a world that is infinitely extended in space and infinitely become and becoming in time, I know it means above all that I find it there as immediately intuited, as existing, I experience it. Through seeing, hearing, tasting, etc., in the various modes of sense perception, bodily things are simply there for me in particular spatial division; 'at hand' in verbal or pictured senses, whether I am particularly attentive to them or not."22 The general thesis of the world can be summed up as an orientation in which I continually find at hand a spatial-temporal actuality opposite myself to which I belong as do all other people equally related to it;23 the world as actuality is always there.24

It is this thesis which must be "bracketed," "put out of action," or "suspended." But what can possibly remain as a basis for a science if the entire world, including human beings, is suspended or placed in brackets? Or, better yet, what can be posited as being when the total world, the totality of reality, remains bracketed? Husserl answers that what is exhibited is what he designates as the "pure subjective process of experience" and its "pure ego."25

This position on the meaning of the term phenomenology is made explicit when Husserl states, "without having grasped the specific transcendental orientation, without actually appropriating the basis of pure phenomenology [i.e., the pure ego, etc.] we may indeed use the word phenomenology but we do not have the subject itself."26

The transcendental reduction has often been interpreted as a flight from the real world, a mystical adventure which results in a loss of the world itself. Husserl has often been accused of denying the world of common experience. He was well aware of the possibility of this misunderstanding. In spite of his emphatic denial that transcendental-phenomenological reduction is a negation of the world, the criticism persists. Yet, his own understanding of reduction permits him to state, "If I do it [set the natural thesis out of action] then I do not negate this world."27

In other words, Husserl is arguing that just as the reductions in the natural and human sciences do not negate that aspect of the world placed in brackets in order to focus on the residue, so phenomenology does not negate the natural orientation which it brackets. Reductions within the natural orientation are abstractions in that they suspend a part of the world from within the natural orientation itself. Or, in other words, the reduction is employed on a part of the world, on the mathematical, biological, psychological or sociological world. The phenomenological reduction, however, is total, concrete and employed from a different orientation.

The reduction to transcendental subjectivity, according to Husserl, provides us with a valid basis for grounding the world of facts. The key to the entrance into this mode of reflection is the notion of "intentionality." This is the second term which requires a brief explanation.

Intentionality is certainly a key concept in Husserl's thought. There is no doubt that he stressed the meaning of this term as "consciousness of something."28 The term itself, however, requires an extensive critical analysis in most interpretations of Husserl's phenomenology. Husserl considered intentionality to be the main theme of his phenomenology; it "characterizes consciousness in an exact sense and justifies the designation of the stream of consciousness as a stream of consciousness and at the same time as a unity of consciousness."29 Intentionality is the other side, or the bipolar term, of transcendental reduction. In itself, without the reduction, it has only psychological significance.30

As is usually the case, primary theoretical terms in a scholar's system are often the most problematic. Husserl was not unaware of this. "Consciousness of something", he wrote, "is something self-evident, yet at the same time highly misunderstood" and more explicitly, "The problematical title which encompasses all phenomenology is called intentionality."31

From the specific character of intentionality as consciousness of something, described within the structural correlation of "noesis" and "noema" in Ideen I, the term continues to develop in its complexity. By the time we reach his last writings, as found in Krisis, Husserl describes it in much more sophisticated terms. Here we find three words which designate the concept of intentionality. The three words are ego-cogito-cogitato, and an analysis of their interrelation is the focus of attention.

Intentionality, analyzed completely, would involve an analysis of its threefold complexity as "directed toward something [the ego pole], appearance of something [the subjective pole] and something [the object pole]."32

Husserl makes it clear in his early publications that consciousness as an "intentional act" is one experience or fact. We must never think of intention as bifurcated. That is, analysis of intentional experience is not to be described as presenting two things; an object experienced and, beside it or along with it, an intentional experience, which somehow directs itself to the object. "There are," says Husserl, "no two facts in the sense of a part and a surrounding totality, but only one fact is present, the intentional experience... [and] If this experience is present so is eo ipso, the object 'intentionally presenting.'"33 Husserl, of course, includes objects which do not exist, that are not "real," such as in fantasy and the like. Some of the most fascinating pages in Husserl's writing are those where he is concerned with the intentionality of fantasy, dreams and fiction.

In Ideen I, the two terms which characterize intentionality are noesis and noema. Noesis can be designated as the psychical side of intentionality. It is the experiencing, or "sense-giving," in the act itself.34 Noesis is not to be understood as sensation. It is made explicitly clear in the analysis that I do indeed experience sensations, but I do not perceive them. When I perceive a tree, for example, I do not perceive the sensations, or the HYLE, as Husserl calls it. Sensations are non-intentional. Noesis as "consciousness of something" is not a designation of "psychic complexes," or "streams" of sensations. Noesis as the subject of experiencing the specific act is thoroughly conscious.35

Noema is the "sense" of the object as well as "how" it is given. Noema is not the object itself; it is an ideal sense, or, as Husserl calls it, an "irreal" signification.36 The noesis or noetic aspect of the intentional correlation is a multiplicity of acts. The noematic side is "irreal" because it remains identical as sense. It is the sense of the object as "how" it is given as such. Every judgement, for example, is a judgement about something. Every perception includes that which is perceived and "how" it is perceived, judged or felt. The existence or non-existence of the object does not effect the analysis of intentionality itself. Whether the object exists or not, is real or "irreal," every intentional process of experience has its intentional object, which means its "objectivating sense."37 The essential rule which must be remembered is that there is "no noetic moment without its specific noematic moment which belongs to it."38 Or, to put it in other words, "no sense without 'something' and no 'something' without the sense, when we say, 'consciousness of something'."39

All the above statements describe what Husserl means by transcendental phenomenology. The generous quotations from Husserl should confirm that, at least for Husserl, phenomenology is not just a method for description, nor is it a neutral method for gaining objectivity. It is neither an idealistic nor a realistic metaphysics but is an attempt to go beyond these traditional philosophical positions and the impasse of the long debate between them. I must add at this point that the argument that Husserl's phenomenology is naive in its proclamation that it is "presuppositionless" is at best misguided. The term appears in the context of the "natural orientation" which, as we have seen, Husserl defines as the uncritical empiricist assumption that there is an objective world in which subjectivity remains anonymous if not non-existent.

Husserl asserts in Ideen I that a phenomenology of natural science, nature and culture should be possible since transcendence as bracketed is not negated. All transcendence, that is to say, all reality including the world, is a correlate of consciousness. We should, then, be able to work out a phenomenology of these realities, he thinks, not just from the side of consciousness but also from their modes, the "how" of their giveness.40 This kind of analysis would follow the bipolar structures of reduction and intentionality as an analysis of noetic-noematic correlations. Seebohm believes this correlation is a new way of stating that "a world without ego, but also, an ego without world, is unthinkable."41

Husserl was well aware of his own assumptions and subjected them to the same critical reflections as others. At the end of his career he was also aware of how his thought was being misunderstood, misused, if not abused, by the interpretations of his students, such as Scheler, Heidegger and others.42 The major misunderstanding, or abuse, was the revision of the notion of "the lived-world" (lebenswelt) in his system of thought. This revision seriously undermined Husserl's critique of the natural attitude and its consequences. Richard Rorty calls this revisionism the "miseries" of the phenomenological movement. After quoting from Ryle's review that phenomenology was heading for bankruptcy and disaster ending either in "self-ruinous Subjectivism or in windy Mysticism." Rorty adds, "Ryle's prescient point was that the coming of 'existential phenomenology' meant the end of phenomenology as a 'rigorous science."43 Thus, phenomenologists of religion who think that we can recover our losses by turning to the existentialist phenomenologists had better think long and hard.

The rest is history, which for the most part is a metaphorical use of Husserl's phenomenology -- a lesson on why revisions are seldom interesting.

IV. A Phenomenological Critique of Phenomenology of Religion.

I believe that it is worthwhile reflecting for a moment on the relevance of this analysis for the study of religion. To do this we must, of course, take Husserl's point of departure as an important problem. We must share, in other words, his concern to establish knowledge on a rational basis. We must also share his concern, if not his analysis, for the genesis of skepticism and dogmatism. If we do, it becomes clear that the study of religion is also threatened by them.

One of the main aims in the study of religion is objectivity. The search for a proper grounding for objectivity has often led to explanations of the meaning of religion as primarily sociological, psychological, or both. For Husserl, the basic issue involved here is not whether we find the right theory and its premises in either the human or natural sciences. Husserl explicitly defended the importance of both. His problem was to find a valid basis for the <u>claims</u> they make. For Husserl, it made no difference, relative to skepticism (which is finally irrationalism), whether we attempt to found our method on the "objective" or the "subjective"; the consequences are the same. If, for example, we take our departure from the natural sciences, seeking validity in the physical world, we gain an "objective" world. We gain it, however, until we return to the subject for whom the world is an object. Or, we may turn to the "positive sciences" (psychological in the widest sense) and lose any sense of objective validity whatsoever, since subjectivism swallows the world in its own solipsism. As Husserl describes the situation in a different context, "purely factual sciences produce purely factual men."44 We should add that "purely subjective sciences produce no men at all." Of course, Husserl would deny that there ever is such a thing as a consistent "pure science" in either of these cases.

Durkheim's sociology of religion is a classic example of the attempt to ground cognition as well as religion in social reality. His attempt to sociologize Kant's transcendental subject, however, only accentuates the problem. The question is not whether religion is social or has a social function. The crucial question for Husserl is what are the critical grounds for accepting the "collective conscience" as the a priori of all religious and social life? It is this question that phenomenologists of religion fail to ask in their haste to brand sociology of religion "reductionistic."

In the same form, Husserlian phenomenology would ask Freud, what is the critical basis for accepting the unconscious? Husserl's own theory of motivation led him to conclude that "what I do not 'know,' what in my experience, my presentation, thinking, or doing does not stand counter to it as presented, perceived, remembered, or thought, etc., does not 'determine' me psychically [geistig]. And what is not inherent in my experiences [erlebnissen], whether it is unthought or contained as implicit intention, does not motivate me, not even in an unconscious manner."45 Such assertions do not strike us as unusual. We have become familiar with talk about "pre-theoretical," or "pre-reflective," knowledge, of "competence" in a language which is "innate." This is especially the case in those cognitive sciences interested in social and psychological topics. For the most part, there is little interest in these developments by phenomenologists of religion. This is most unfortunate.

There is another approach in the search for objectivity in the study of religion. It can be called the metaphysical-theological basis for solving some of our problems. The use of the terms metaphysical and theological is intentional. They not only take us back to what has been described in the first chapter, but their use fits in nicely with Husserl's own description of them. It is clear that they are closely related, if not synonymous, in Husserl's thought.46   Husserl means something limited when he speaks of metaphysics or theology.   They are systems of thought which assume that there are "things-in-themselves" or a "thing-in-itself" which we cannot know.47   The Logische Untersuchungen is an explicit denial of this kind of metaphysical skepticism.

Whether a phenomenology of religion is a possibility or not, Husserl's critique at this point becomes relevant to a predominant theme we have discussed in the first chapter; the view that religion is in some sense a manifestation of The Sacred. As we have seen, the exact sense of this notion is ambiguous, if not mysterious. If we take the widely quoted work of Rudolf Otto as our example, it becomes clear that The Sacred as such can never be known. As we saw, van der Leeuw, Kristensen and Eliade, to name the most well-known scholars in the discipline make similar assertions about The Sacred.

Now, whether we accept Husserl's phenomenology or not, his analysis of the constitution of skepticism applies to the core of the history and phenomenology of religion. This problem is often hidden by statements which insist on objectivity. Thus, we may read that the task is not explanation but understanding or that religious expressions wherever and whenever they occur are of equal value or validity, that the history and phenomenology of religion make no judgement about the validity of religious expressions. Yet, The Sacred as a thing-in-itself is THE judgement on which all other statements are made.

Once again, the problem here seems clear.   The solution to the problem, however, is anything but clear.   The issue is simply as follows: if The Sacred is indeed the religious reality, the religious a priori, the reality wholly other, das ganz andere and if this "reality" in principle cannot be known,   then the history and phenomenology of religion is in contradiction with itself; it cannot assert that it is objectively describing the manifestation of religion as The Sacred in history while at the same time denying that The Sacred as such can be known.   Following Husserl, this assertion not only drives us into skepticism concerning the knowledge of the object of religion, but it leads inevitably to dogmatism.

This judgement is certainly harsh and difficult to accept.   Yet, there are scholars of religion who do not see anything wrong with the assertion that their discipline is a series of contradictions which lead to incoherence. Whatever the reasons for such acquiescence to incoherence, it would seem that if a phenomenology of religion is to be developed, The Sacred as the object, a 'wholly other' reality, must be rejected. Conversely, if the history and phenomenology of religion is to be grounded on The Sacred as in principle wholly other, then a phenomenology of religion becomes an impossibility. A phenomenology of religion as pure description only prolongs the problem; it does not overcome it. The pseudo-neutrality of such a position can be immediately unmasked by the question, "pure description of what?" or "what is the object of your pure description?"

We are repeatedly told that the phenomenology of religion is a distinct methodology that should not be confused with history, sociology, anthropology or theology. When we inquire about the distinctive characteristics of this methodology, we are given the reply that it involves taking The Sacred, the "essence" of religion, seriously. I believe that it is an indisputable fact that no methodology of religion can hope to succeed which asserts that it is necessary that we take a certain reality seriously while denying at the same time the availability of that reality for rational, critical inspection. A science of religion based on a mystery remains a mysterious science! It may well be the case that there are individuals who do not know the meaning of their religion. It would be odd, however, for a science of religion to proceed with descriptions and explanations of data whose reference, by definition, can never be known. This places us in the peculiar position of admitting that the subject we wish to describe has in the end escaped our method for describing it.

Why, then, do scholars construct a method which self-destructs the moment it actually begins to explain or understand a particular subject matter? The answer, of course, is that no one in the phenomenology of religion has pursued such a bizarre course of study. It is the result of taking phenomenologists of religion literally. Once we become accustomed to the language phenomenologists of religion have learned to use, it becomes obvious that they do not always mean what they say.

Once we have learned this lesson, we will be in a better position to interpret the assertions of phenomenologists of religion. It is not the case that The Sacred cannot be known. It is not the case, as Ricoeur thinks it is, that phenomenologists have "secretly" decided to remain neutral regarding the truth of religion. What is the case is that phenomenologists have explicitly refused to answer these questions in some situations rather than others. As we have seen in Chapter One, van der Leeuw knows very well what The Sacred is; it is "the wholly other," it is God. And van der Leeuw also knows that it is the theologian who knows who God is! It is the theologian who seeks the truth about God. Let us recall that the truth embodied in religion cannot be "scientifically demonstrated" because the essence of religion is "revelation." In brief, the phenomenology of religion and theology are two sides of the same coin! The only problem, of course, is that the phenomenology of religion, as the applied side of this "science," cannot call upon theology to confirm its applications in any straightforward manner simply because the object of theology, God, Faith, or Revelation, is not theoretical.

It is significant, therefore, that at the end of the symposium on methodology in the study of religion, Drijvers and Leertouwer conclude that the problems presented at the symposium demonstrate once again "how strongly phenomenology [of religion] is bound up with the crisis of the Christian religion [and theology] in Western culture."48   The paper responsible for this judgement was written by Professor Waardenburg, who as we have seen, knows the phenomenological movement in the study of religion very well. He argues that one of the problems in what he calls "classical" phenomenology of religion is its insistence on grasping the meaning of religion by typologies, patterns and classifications of religion. His argument is certainly persuasive when we remember that typologies and taxonomies do not explain anything, including the meaning of religion. Waardenburg wants to shift the emphasis in the phenomenology of religion, he wants a "new style" of phenomenology which interprets the "intentionality" of religious expressions.49   This is indeed a refreshing proposition. Waardenburg suggests that we reformulate the phenomenological problem; instead of "back to the facts" we should concentrate on "back to basic intentions."50   Once again, it would seem that phenomenologists of religion have returned to Husserl,

focus on interpretation of intentionality

who, as we have seen, made "intentionality" central to his phenomenological system.

Unfortunately, the "new style" of phenomenology of religion is a variation on the classical approach. All the classical problems are embedded in the reformulation; the threat of theology, defense against "reductions", suspension of the recognized problem of truth in religious expressions, and recognition of "transcendence" as the special, sui generis nature of religion. After specifying that the new phenomenology of religion would concentrate on reconstructing religious meaning, on formulating the intention of what is meant in religious texts and expressions, Waardenburg concludes that phenomenological analysis of this kind will remain "scholarly guesswork." Now why, we must ask, does a new style of phenomenology of religion end up as a guessing game? Because "it is the trans-empirical, 'transcendent' reference of such facts which makes them what we call, at least from a phenomenological point of view, 'religious'."51

Note again how the new phenomenology of religion has borrowed a crucial term from Husserl's phenomenology. But we must not be led astray. Waardenburg's use of "intention," "meaning" and "signification" have no relation whatsoever to the phenomenological movement which begins with Husserl. This is unfortunate because we are left without any theoretical framework by which we might understand the procedure for putting "intentional analysis" into practice. Perhaps a new slogan might be suggested to scholars interested in developing a phenomenology of religion. Instead of "back to intentionality" it should be "back to Husserl."

This would not involve accepting every word of Husserl. If, for example, a phenomenologist of religion were interested in working out the implications of the meaning of religious expressions as "intentional acts," it just might be helpful to discover both what Husserl meant by "intentionality" and how he used this theoretical term. The phenomenologist of religion might well reject Husserl's sense of the term, showing us why it is inadequate for an analysis of meaning in religion. We would then fully understand why and where the phenomenologist differs from Husserl's phenomenology. Since this has not been done, we are left with technical terms which lack theoretical substance, studies in methodology without analysis, and assertions which are contradictory and meaningless.

We must, then, make our own attempt at linking a phenomenology of religion to the work of Husserl. This linkage does not produce a "new style" of phenomenology of religion but a radical departure from everything which is known as phenomenology of religion. First, as we have seen, the category, or reality, of The Sacred will either be radically revised or rejected. This will take place as a result of a denial of things-in-themselves which remain unknown. In the second place, it will not hold metaphysical or theological assertions in suspension, as if it could remain neutral to them. Instead, in defining the meaning of a phenomenology of religion it might well provide us with critical limitations or restrictions which are necessary to prevent either metaphysics or theology from becoming substitutes for a phenomenological description of religion.

Third, such a linkage might overcome what can be called the "paradox of final agnosticism" which can be found at the center of all phenomenologies of religion as we know them. This paradox is our counterpart to the problem of ethnocentrism in the human sciences. It might also be called the "nirvana paradox" in which we describe a religion, cult, or myth and then admit that we do not know its meaning because it refers to The Sacred. Few of the phenomenologists I have read hold to this paradox for long. It inevitably leads to a destructive skepticism. It is usually overcome in one of two ways: either move to the social sciences, thereby increasing the threat of relativism and "reductionism" or move to subjectivism. The first choice swallows up the term "religion," the second choice vaporizes the term "history," in the phenomenologist's task of understanding and describing the history of religions.

A fourth feature which this linkage might focus on is a new analysis of myth and ritual as religious phenomena. Here Husserl's reflections on "expression," "signification," "object" and "symbol" might prove helpful. Most historians and phenomenologists of religion are no longer influenced by the notion that myths are statements about the origin of the world in some proto-scientific sense. It is not altogether clear, however, just what significance they do have as religious expressions. If I have analyzed the "paradox of final agnosticism" correctly, the referent of myths as sacred remains unknown. A phenomenology of religion which went back to Husserl might be able to show that myths are expressions of, a) particular psychical experiences functioning as giving sense to expressions; b) that these expressions have a sense; and c) that they have a reference to an object. It might show furthermore, that the signification of myths a)indicates how the object is meant, b) implies reference to an object and c) indicates an object by virtue of its own signification. And it would show, I think, that this signification is not sensation but has a reference to an ideal object. This would follow from Husserl's own assertion that sensations are experienced but never perceived.

The question of whether myths have any cognitive value might be determined phenomenologically on the basis of whether myths as expressions have any possible sense at all. Phenomenologically speaking, this is a contradiction since an expression has signification, or it is not an expression. This kind of analysis would precede any consideration of the relation of myths to "reality" -- in a social or psychological sense -- i.e. as "real." It would suspend this question as a question from within the natural orientation.

The analysis of myths and rituals in the social sciences usually assumes that the meaning of myths and rituals is to be determined by their reference to social reality. (We shall take a close look at this assumption in the next two chapters.) Instead of accusing such analyses of being "reductionistic," a phenomenology of religion might provide a critique of the social science approach to myth and ritual by showing that myths and rituals as expressions of religion have a significance that cannot simply be reduced to sociological or psychological theories of meaning. The phenomenologist of religion, of course, would have to determine what this significance is and then show how it is given by intentional analysis, and how this analysis is more adequate than sociological and psychological explanations of myth and ritual. This is indeed a big order to fill. Let us remember, however, that the same kind of orders have been filled in other successful human sciences. I am thinking especially of structuralism, linguistics and other cognate disciplines.

I have intentionally hedged my description of possibilities for a phenomenology of religion that is explicitly linked to the actual work of Husserl. My description of such a phenomenology of religion is provisional simply because of the difficulty in constructing such an approach to the study of religion. The difficulty is not to be found in the complex nature of Husserl's thought, although this would be enough to halt the timid. The difficulty is due to the critique that "post-structural" scholars have directed at phenomenology in general and Husserl in particular. This critique has dealt a devastating blow to Husserl's notion of a transcendental reduction and the apodictic value of his notion of the transcendental ego. Foucault, for example, describes his own project as a correction of "the search for origins, for formal a prioris, for founding acts... its aim is to free history from the grip of phenomenology."52   It will simply not do for the phenomenologist of religion once again to call this movement a Parisian fashion which is reductionistic in its thought, and nihilistic in its outcome. A new phenomenology of religion will have to struggle with this contemporary intellectual movement. And if it disagrees with it, then it will have to articulate why it disagrees and show where someone like Foucault has gone wrong. This is precisely what the construction of theories is all about.

In the meantime, I would suggest the following set of methodological rules for constructing a phenomenology of religion.   1. The truth of our description of religious meaning does not entail that the intentional object exists, since it is not necessarily the case that meaning entails reference.   2. The suspension of truth regarding religious expressions and statements is a serious mistake, for it may well be the case that the meaning of religious expressions entails truth conditions. 3. Empathy for or experiencing another religion is theoretically irrelevant to an analysis of the meaning of religion. 4. The meaning of religion does not entail whether The Sacred exists or not. 5. The meaning of religion does not entail an inference that we have the ability to intuit the existence of The Sacred. 6. A phenomenological analysis of the meaning of religion entails a theoretical reduction of religious expressions as intentional acts.

The development of a phenomenology of religion from within the above framework would mean an end to the phenomenology of religion as it is practiced today. If the Husserlian tradition does not provide the proper theoretical framework for phenomenologists of religion, then they should stop referring to Husserl and describe what they think the theory is that leads to objectivity in our understanding of religion. One thing is certain. It is time phenomenologists of religion drop the disguise of "neutrality." Rather than taking a stand on the autonomy of religion and the sui generis nature of the sacred they need to produce an argument that can withstand critical examination.

NOTES.

1. Herbert Spiegelberg, *The Phenomenological Movement: A Historical Introduction*, 2 vols. (The Hague: Nijhoff, 1960).

2. Willard Oxtoby, "The Idea of the Holy," *Encyclopedia of Religion*, ed. Mircea Eliade, vol. 6 (New York: Macmillan, 1987) 436.

3. Douglas Allen, "The Phenomenology of Religion," *Encyclopedia of Religion*, vol. 11, 273ff., and "Edmund Husserl," vol. 6, 539. See also J. D. J. Waardenburg's article on van der Leeuw, vol. 8, for a similar assessment.

4. All of these assertions can be found in the publication of a well-known phenomenologist of religion. See C. J. Bleeker, *The Rainbow: A Collection of Studies in the Science of Religion* (Leiden: Brill, 1975). The fact that he has put them all together in a single publication allows us to keep this note short.

5. G. van der Leeuw, *Religion in Essence and Manifestation* (London: Allen, 1938) 683-85.

6. van der Leeuw 646, note 1. This note is not in the original German edition and is obviously an afterthought. There are no notes on the use of *epoche* in Chapter

109, "The Phenomenology of Religion."   At one place van der Leeuw defines *epoche* as "restraint" (zurückhaltung). See *Phänomenologie Der Religion* (Tübingen: Mohr Verlag, 1933) 640. The English edition of the book translates *epoche* as "intellectual suspense." Thus, at one point, we get the nonsense sentence "exercises the intellectual suspense of the *epoche.*" van der Leeuw 687. The only explicit reference to Husserl is made on page 675 (Eng. ed.) where van der Leeuw asserts that "Phenomenology is concerned only with 'phenomena' that is with 'appearance'; for it, there is nothing whatsoever 'behind' the phenomena." This is clearly not Husserl's view of the subject.

7. Willard Oxtoby, "Holy, The Idea of," *Encyclopedia of Religion*, vol. 6, 436.

8. Abbreviations used for notes on Husserl are as follows: L.U.I; L.U.II; L.U.III = *Logische Untersuchungen*, 5th ed. (Tübingen: Mohr Verlag, 1968).   Ideen I = *Ideen zu einer reinen Phänomenologie und phänomenologischen Philosophie*, vol. I (Den Haag: Nijhoff, 1950).   Ideen II = *Ideen zu einer reinen Phänomenologie und phänomenologischen Philosophie*, vol. II (Den Haag: Nijhoff, 1952). C.M. = *Cartesian Meditations*, trans. Dorian Cairns (The Hague: Nijhoff, 1960).   Krisis = *Die Krisis der europäischen Wissenschaften und die transzendentale Phänomenologie* (Den Haag: Nijhoff, 1954).

9. Eugene Fink, "Die Phänomenologische Philosophie Edmund Husserl in der Gegenwärtigen Kritik," *Kantstudien* 38 (1933): 319-383.

10. For examples see T. Adorno, *Zur Metakritik der Erkenntnistheorie: Studien über Husserl und die Phänomenologischen Antinomien* (Stuttgart: Kolhammer, 1956);   Herbert Marcuse, "Zum Begriff des Wesens," *Zeitschrift für Socialforschung* 5 (1936); and G. Ryle, "Phenomenology," *Aristotelian Society Supplement* 11 (1932): 68ff.

11. For two possible answers to the riddle see T. M. Seebohm, *Die Bedingungen der Möglichkeit der Transzendentalephilosophie* (Bonn: Bouvier, 1962) 48ff. and Ernst Wolfgang Orth, *Bedeutung, Sinn, Gegenstand: Studien zur Sprach Philosophie Edmund Husserls und Richard Höningswald* (Bonn: Bouvier, 1967) 245ff.   For an excellent introduction to Husserl's thought and the problems of

interpretation, see Wolfgang H. Müller, *Die Philosophie Edmund Husserls* (Bonn, 1956).

12. See Ideen I 134; L. U. II 20, 80; and L. U. I 113.

13. L. U. II 108.

14. Ryle's critique is certainly correct on this particular development within the phenomenological movement. See note #10 above for reference.

15. L. U. I vii.

16. L. U. II 8; also Krisis 182-190.

17. For an excellent analysis of this crucial problem in Husserl see Seebohm 43-47.

18. L. U. I 112, 114-115, 117; also Ideen I 44ff., 189.

19. Krisis 182ff., 265, 501ff.

20. The term "orientation" is my translation for "*einstellung*" which is usually translated as "attitude" and tends to convey psychological overtones contrary to Husserl's usage of the term.

21. See Seebohm 76-77 for an excellent summary of the meaning of reduction.

22. Ideen I 57.

23. Ideen I 59

24. Ideen I 63; also Ideen II 1-4, 174, 179ff.; and Krisis 308-309, 326-328.

25. Ideen I 70.

26. Ideen I 216.

27. Ideen I 67; also 174, "The bracketed is not wiped off the phenomenological slate."

28. L. U. II 130; Ideen I 207, 216.

29. See Ideen I 203ff.; also Ideen II 336.

30. Ideen I 216.

31. Ideen I 217, 357.

32. Krisis 174. Orth, *Bedeutung*, has attempted a schema of these interrelated terms in Chapter Five, p. 248.   If I understand Orth correctly, he does not understand the central theme of intentionality in Husserl's work as applicable to a so-called "mundane phenomenology."   I agree.   How Husserl's notion of intentionality becomes reduced to a "mundane phenomenology" is important but quite beyond the purpose of this chapter.

33. L. U. II 372.

34. Ideen I 210-211.

35. Ideen I 213.   Cf. Aron Gurwitsch on Husserl's doctrine of intentionality in *Studies in Phenomenology and Psychology* (Evanston, Ill.: Northwestern UP, 1966) 124ff.

36. Ideen I 245. Those familiar with Husserl's thought will know that his concept of "noema" as well as "intentionality" are difficult to interpret.   The difficulty is illustrated by the different interpretations of these terms in the secondary literature on Husserl. For examples see Dagfinn Føllesdal, "Husserl's Notion of Noema," *The Journal of Philosophy* 66 (1969): 680-87; Richard H. Holmes, "An Explication of Husserl's Theory of the Noema," *Research in Phenomenology* 5 (1975): 143-53; Robert C. Solomon, "Husserl's Concept of the Noema," *Husserl: Expositions and Appraisals*, eds. Fredrick A. Elliston and Peter McCormick (Notre Dame: U of Notre Dame P, 1977) 168-81; Robert Sokolowski, "Intentional Analysis and the Noema," *Dialectica* 38 (1984): 113-129; and Lenore Langsdorf, "The Noema as Intentional Entity: A Critique of Føllesdal," *The Review of Metaphysics* 37 (1984): 757ff.

37. Ideen I 223.

38. Ideen I 232.

39. Ideen I 321, 322.

40. Ideen I 175; Ideen II and Krisis are attempts to work this out relative to the natural and human sciences.

41. Seebohm 154.

42. For an example of his awareness see Krisis 439-440.

43. Richard Rorty, *Philosophy and the Mirror of Nature* (Princeton: Princeton UP, 1980) 167-68, note 5.

44. Krisis 4; see 60ff. and 70ff. for the dualism of objective and subjective worlds.

45. Ideen II 231.

46. Examples of this close relationship can be found in the scattered instances where Husserl speaks of God, existence, etc. See Ideen I 121-122, 138-140; Ideen II 85; and Krisis 67, 95.

47. L. U. I 113-114, 110-125, and Husserl's assertion that "Everything that is, is 'in itself' capable of being known...," L. U. II 90.

48. Th P. van Baaren and H. J. W. Drijvers, eds., *Religion, Culture and Methodology* (The Hague: Mouton, 1973) 168.

49. J. D. J. Waardenburg, "Research on Meaning in Religion," *Religion, Culture and Methodology* 117.

50. Waardenburg, "Research on Meaning..." 112.

51. Waardenburg, "Research on Meaning..." 122; also 113, 114, 117 and 121.

52. Michel Foucault, *The Archaeology of Knowledge* (New York: Pantheon, 1972) 203. In addition to his published work, I have found Hubert L. Dreyfus and Paul Rabinow, *Michel Foucault: Beyond Structuralism and Hermeneutics*, 2nd ed. (Chicago: U of Chicago P, 1983), to be an excellent reading of Foucault in both its appreciation for his brilliant insights and its criticism of the development of his thought.

CHAPTER THREE

RATIONALITY, RELIGION AND SCIENCE

All scholars of religion, with the possible exception of historians and phenomenologists, have at one time or another struggled with the question about the relation between modern science and religious beliefs. For the historian or phenomenologist of religion this question is a good example of "reductionism," or a confusion between the "sacred and the "profane." Such questions are simply "bracketed" or suspended. As a result the historian and phenomenologist of religion have become mostly irrelevant to the progress being made in the human sciences. This is most unfortunate. The argument from "neutrality" has effectively cut off debate about the truth of religious beliefs or religious assertions as cognitive or non-cognitive, rational or irrational and the relation between science and religion.

In this chapter, I want to focus on the debate about the relation between science and religion. I have chosen this issue for three reasons. First, it is an old debate. Second, it is an important debate and a good example of how a powerful theory, logical positivism, can become the accepted theory for positions which are radically different in the answers they give us. Third, the history of the debate may indicate we are using a defective theory and thus asking the wrong questions. Finally, it is about time that scholars devoted to the study of religion, as historians and phenomenologists, join the debate because of their competence. The issues in this debate will not go away because we refuse to recognize the relevance of the questions for an adequate explanation of religion.

If, then, you are tempted to ask, "What has this to do with me?" my answer is it has everything to do with you. If you take the position that religion, the sacred, and science, the profane, are two different modes of thought, you are on the side of Lévi-Bruhl and Eliade. If, on the other hand, you make no distinctions between religion and science as modes of thought, then you find yourself with scholars such as Durkheim and Horton. Take either side and you will discover serious problems. It is this impasse that is opened up for discussion in this chapter.

Ever since Tylor, scholars of religion have debated the similarities and differences between religion and science, or "traditional" thought and modern "Western" thought. The classical positions in the dispute are those of Tylor and Lévi-Bruhl, which Evans-Pritchard labeled respectively the "intellectualist" and "sociological" schools.1 Despite the charges of ethnocentrism leveled against them, neither "school" disappeared. Rather, scholars such as Evans-Pritchard, Radcliffe-Brown and Malinowski transformed them into new explanations of religious beliefs and practices. The uneasy truce between these two dominant positions was broken by Robin Horton's article on "African Traditional Thought And Western Science."2 Horton's important and controversial work raises issues that ought to be central to the study of religion: the relation between religion and science, the cognitive significance of religious thought, the problem of comparative studies, and the adequacy of relativism as an approach to understanding religion.

The debate over Horton's theories has taken place largely in Britain among anthropologists, sociologists, and philosophers. Sadly and inexplicably, it has been neglected by American students of religion who, aside from those who prescind from the question about the truth of religion, should have much to contribute to the discussion.

I. Two Alternatives to Horton.

Before turning to a description and critical analysis of Horton's project, it will be useful to describe two competing views of religion, myth and ritual that clearly oppose Horton's position. Attention to them should highlight what Horton opposes and why his project is important to the comparative study of religion. The first can be called the "symbolic approach," and the second the "relativist alternative."

A. The Symbolic Approach.

The symbolic approach holds that religious beliefs, myths and rituals are not to be taken literally. Here is .i.Leach's statement about the matter:

Tylor, Frazer and the latter day new-Tylorians assume that statements of dogma start out as mistaken attempts to explain cause and effect in the world of nature. Dogma then persists because these mistaken ideas satisfy psychological desires. As a vulgar positivist I repudiate such speculation about causes which are inaccessible to observation and verification. It may seem surprising that men persist in expressing formal beliefs which are palpably untrue, but you won't get anywhere by applying canons of rationality to principles of faith.3

The task, therefore, is to "decode" the symbols in order to discover their "hidden" meaning. But, there seems to be no agreement about just what the "hidden" meaning is.

Since John Beattie is a participant in the debate with Horton, let us turn to his account. Beattie asks, "What, if any, is the essential difference between 'ritual' procedures and so-called 'practical' or 'scientific' ones?"4 His answer, which has been repeatedly emphasized before, is that there is a crucial difference between the two. Ritual procedures are essentially expressive of desires. Myth, ritual and magic, the central institutions of religion, dramatize the universe. Beattie concludes that myth, "whatever its form, is not science and is nothing like it; it operates not by 'trial and error, guided by observation', but by symbolism and drama," thus, "myth dramatizes the universe, science analyzes it." 5

If we equate "modern society" with "Western scientific society" and "knowledge" with "scientific knowledge," then this variation on the symbolic approach yields the conclusion that any attempt to relate traditional religious beliefs to modern beliefs (science) is simply misdirected. Traditional beliefs and rituals are essentially expressive. This theory makes it senseless to ask whether religious beliefs or rituals are true or false because by definition they are not statements, utterances, assertions, or actions that entail true or false propositions about the world. Traditional religious beliefs are not to be taken as hypothetico-deductive, or inductive statements and ritual does not qualify as rational behavior (i.e., a means-end action). For most symbolists it is a serious epistemological error to take religious beliefs in form or function to be explanatory statements. As Beattie puts it, "The sensible student of myth, magic and religion will, I think, be well advised to recognize that their tenets are not scientific propositions, based upon experience and on a belief in the uniformity of nature, and they cannot be understood as if they were." 6

The symbolist approach attempts to avoid the ethnocentric trap of asserting that traditional societies are stupid or childish. In his debate with Spiro, Leach rebukes him in the following way: "In anthropological writing, ignorance is a term of abuse. To say that a native is ignorant amounts to saying that he is childish, stupid, superstitious. Ignorance is the opposite of logical rationality."7 The symbolist approach holds that all societies have both expressive (symbolic) and instrumental (rational) modes of thinking. That sounds sensible enough. To make their point, however, symbolists must persuade us that traditional religion is basically and essentially expressive or symbolic and that religious beliefs and rituals are not goal-oriented.

Beattie and others are well aware that their informants do not validate this approach to traditional religion, myth, and ritual. On the contrary, informants report that the performance of a sacrifice is the means to an end. It aims to change, persuade, or coerce a god, spirit or ancestor to do what the petitioner requests. Beattie and other symbolists do not dispute that such beliefs are actually held, but they assert that when the natives "think deeply" about it "they will conclude that the efficacy of ritual lies in its very expressiveness."8

No one who endorses this position would deny for example, that South Asian Buddhists believe that giving gifts to the sangha is a means for gaining good merit in this life and the next. But the symbolist must deny that the ritual is instrumental. This, it seems to me, amounts to the denial that South Asian Buddhists know what they are doing. But, if they "think deeply" about it, they might discover that what they believed to be rational action was in reality expressive or symbolic action.

Emphasis on the efficacy (function) of expressive action often overshadows the important point that the symbolic approach does indeed agree with Tylor; the beliefs are mistaken if they are taken as hypothetico-deductive theories or instrumental means for obtaining a goal. The difference is that the symbolic approach claims that we can make sense out of the ritual action despite, or without considering, the mistaken belief!9

This tradition has remained reasonably consistent from Durkheim to the present. From a symbolist point of view, traditional kinship, political and economic systems can be explained by reference to the empirical infrastructures and their objective relations. The problem is the gods, goddesses, and spirits. The belief about superhuman beings cannot be explained by reference to the objective nature of these beings because they do not exist. Therefore, the belief must refer to something else in nature or culture, or they may not refer at all as expressions which are ends-in-themselves. As David Schneider puts it, "Without blaming it all on Durkheim, the fact remains that since his time, anthropologists have held pretty consistently to this premise. Where institutions are related to real, existential facts, it is presumed that they must somehow be 'based on' or 'related to' them, but where no such facts can be shown to exist, then the institution tends to be treated as primarily symbolic and expressive."10

One of the strengths of the symbolic approach is its criticism of ethnocentric explanations of religious beliefs and practices. But, the assumption that we can not take such beliefs and practices literally leads to a search for their meanings, which are necessarily hidden. Thus, religion should be understood as a symbolic or indirect, expression of metaphysical concerns, political relations, morality, classification categories, or The Sacred itself. But this raises the question of why only some societies express such concerns and relations symbolically. Furthermore, if these meanings are hidden, unknown to the believers themselves, then in what sense can we say that the believers are fully rational? As Sperber points out, when Filate asked him to go out and kill a dragon he was not asking Sperber to decipher a cryptic message!11

Moreover, the symbolic alternative to intellectualism seems trapped in a paradox. Most adherents to this approach distinguish between the practical life (instrumental action, science, technology) and the symbolic and/or expressive life (religious beliefs, practices, etc.). But whence does this distinction derive? Certainly not from the "primitive" societies that have been studied, for they have made no such distinctions. As Taylor points out, "It is a feature of our civilization that we have developed a practice of scientific research and technological application from which the symbolic and expressive dimensions have been to a great extent purged."12

The symbolist solution to the problem of ethnocentrism is at best illusory. Bluntly, the distinction between practical knowledge and symbolic expression is no less ethnocentric than the criticism leveled against Horton. The question that this approach does not answer is why traditional societies fail to discover or recognize the "hidden symbolic meanings" in their own religious beliefs and practices.

B. The Relativist Alternative.

If the intellectualist and symbolic approaches to religion have been unable to fully solve the problem of understanding other cultures without the intrusion of ethnocentrism, then the relativist approach appears to be an attractive alternative.   It seems able to solve all the problems by asserting that cognition, rationality, and perception are culturally determined.   What counts as rational, or of cognitive significance, is determined by a "Weltanschauung," "Lebenswelt," or "form of life." As Winch states it, "Reality is not what gives language sense. What is real and what is unreal shows itself in the sense that language has."13 Thus, we cannot conclude that traditional beliefs are "not in accord with reality" or mistaken because what is or is not in accord with reality is dependent on the sense that language has. Moreover, the search for "hidden meanings" is unnecessary. Sperber describes this alternative as follows: "To be of relevance, relativism must maintain that not only opinions, interests, and skills, but also fundamental concepts, meanings and possibly postulates used in human cognition are culturally determined... Propositions that can be entertained, expressed, asserted are, according to relativists, language and culture specific."14

F. Suppe provides a useful summary of the relativist position from within the philosophy of science. He uses the term "Weltanschauung" to identify the position. He describes this as follows:

(1) Observation is theory-laden: The Weltanschauung position determines or influences how one views, describes, or interprets the world; hence adherents to different theories will observe different things when they view the same phenomena. (2) Meanings are theory-dependent: The descriptive terms (both observational and theoretical) used by science undergo a shift of meaning when incorporated into, or used in conjunction with, a theory; thus the principles of a theory help determine the meaning of such terms occurring in them, and so the meanings of such terms will vary from theory to theory; hence changes in theory result in changes in meaning. (3) Facts are theory-laden: What counts as a fact is determined by the "Weltanschauung" associated with a theory; as such there is no neutral set of facts for assessing the relative adequacy of two competing theories; rather, the adequacy of a theory must be assessed according to standards set by its associated "Weltanschauung."15

For Peter Achinstein, the relativist position rejects the fundamental positivist assumption "that there are, and indeed must be, terms in a theory (the nontheoretical terms) whose meaning can be given independently of the theory and can remain constant from theory to theory," viz., that observational statements are invariable. 16

For various reasons, escape from ethnocentrism among them, many scholars in the human sciences have embraced the relativist approach. This is unfortunate because, as we shall soon see, this alternative entails unacceptable consequences.17

For our purposes let us concentrate on Suppe's second thesis. If "meanings are theory-laden," then no theory could contradict any other theory because the terms in one theory have different meanings than the terms in another theory; the theories express incommensurable concepts. If we substitute "lebenswelt" or "form of life" for the term "theory," we have Winch's position.18   Winch claims that Evans-Pritchard cannot assert that Zande beliefs are "not in accord with reality." If the Azande assert p and Evans-Pritchard asserts not-p, they are not really disagreeing since the terms in the Azande assertions are p-laden and mean one thing, while Evans-Pritchard's not-p terms are not-p-laden and thus mean something different. As Achinstein points out, "Not-p, then, is not the negative of p.   In short, negation is impossible."19

If this analysis is valid, then the extension of the second thesis becomes even more problematic. For ceteris paribus, it would then imply not only that Evans-Pritchard's disagreements with the Azande are an illusion but also that disagreements between religions, and even within religions, are also illusions. Thus, Shankara (an advaitan Hindu) must have been mistaken when he claimed that Buddhist doctrines were not in accord with reality, and Nagarjuna (a Buddhist) must have been equally mistaken when he claimed that the Sarvastivadins (a Buddhist school) contradicted themselves!

Moreover, if disagreement between two theories (or forms of life) is impossible, then agreement between two theories is also impossible for the same reasons. But if there can be neither agreement nor disagreement between, let us say, two theories of traditional religious thought (Horton and Winch, or Horton and Beattie), what sense can it make to say that they are about the same thing? Furthermore, what sense can it make to say, ceteris paribus, that two different religious traditions are rival theories or "forms of life," about the same thing, e.g. salvation, suffering, death, or the nature of man? Clearly, the logical consequences of this alternative make cross-cultural comparison impossible.

If thesis two is true, then "a person could not learn a theory by having it explained to him using any words whose meanings he understands before he learns the theory."20 We must remember that one of the principles of the relativist approach is that there are no theory-neutral or paradigm-neutral terms. By extension, it would seem that in order to learn about Buddhism we would have to become Buddhists. But how? Certainly not by reading a translation of a Pali text in English, for a further consequence of thesis two is that translations are also impossible. What happens when we do field work, come home, and publish the results remains utterly mysterious.

Finally, how could we validate, confirm, or falsify the relativist point of view? Winch, Horton, and Beattie seem to disagree with each other. But how is this possible? To put it another way, how could we validate the proposition that meanings, beliefs, etc. are culturally determined, since that proposition itself must arise out of a particular "form of life" or "lebenswelt." To answer these questions, relativists must somehow rise above the position they are taking. In so doing they contradict themselves.

Such counter-arguments may well put an end to the relativism approach to religion. But, do we not have evidence that can take us beyond argument, evidence that can settle the debate? The "Sapir-Whorf" hypothesis often serves as a defense for relativism. Whorf was convinced that,

The categories and types that we isolate from the world of phenomena we do not find there because they stare every observer in the face; on the contrary the world is presented in a kaleidoscopic flux of impressions which has to be organized in our minds -- and that means largely by the linguistic system in our minds. We cut nature up, organize it into concepts, and ascribe significances as we do, largely because we are partners to an agreement to organize it in this way -- an agreement that holds throughout our speech community and is codified in the pattern of our language.21

One of Whorf's more famous lexical examples is the use of the term "snow" in Western and Eskimo cultures. "We have the same word for falling snow, snow on the ground, snow packed hard like ice, slushy snow, wind-driven snow -- whatever the situation may be. To an Eskimo, this all-inclusive word would be almost unthinkable; he would say that falling snow, slushy snow, and so on, are sensuously and operationally different, different things to contend with; he uses different words for them and for other kinds.22

Roger Brown, summarized the Whorfian hypothesis this way:

1. Structural differences between language systems will, in general, be paralleled by non-linguistic cognitive differences, of an unspecified sort, in the native speakers of the two languages.

2. The structure of anyone's native language strongly influences or fully determines the world-view he will acquire as he learns the language.23

Brown and Lenneberg chose the semantic domain of color as a means of testing the hypothesis. Brown concludes his research with a surprising admission: "The fascinating irony of this research is that it began with a spirit of strong relativism and linguistic determinism and has now come to a position of cultural universalism and linguistic insignificance.24   It was indeed a major discovery in the human sciences. Most people assume that the perception of color is the obvious example of cultural and linguistic relativism. We slice up the world of color according to our categories of color, and these categories are relative to a specific language; "true blue" is in the eye of the beholder. What Brown and Lenneberg discovered, and others have confirmed, is that there is a logic in the perception of color which is universal across cultures and that there seems to be an evolution in the development of basic color categories as represented in Figure 1.

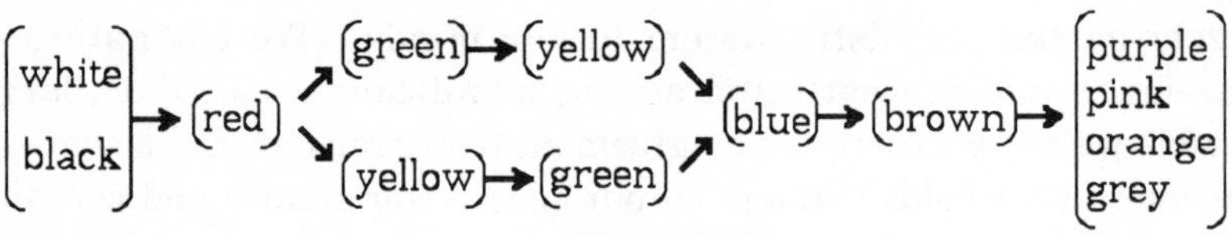

Figure 1

Roger Brown provides us with the following interpretation:

It would appear that languages have added color terms in a fixed universal order. A dichotomous system, like that of the Dani, using only *white* and *black*. is the most primitive, with *red* being the next addition and then either *yellow* or *green*, followed by whichever of the two has not evolved, then *blue* and *brown*, and finally a set of 4 that cannot be ordered among themselves. This partially ordered sequence is offered by Berlin and Kay as a universal sequence of linguistic evolution. From the extreme relativism of Whorf and the anthropologists of his day, we have come to an extreme cultural universality and presumptive nativism.25

Kay and McDaniel have confirmed Brown's judgment. They conclude that "the semantics of color display substantial linguistic universals; and that these semantic universals, which explain a considerable range of both synchronic and diachronic fact, are based upon pan-human neurophysiological processes in the perception of color. We interpret these findings as placing strict limits on the applicability of the Sapir-Whorf hypothesis and related hypotheses of extreme linguistic/cultural relativity.26 The red/yellow/green sequence of our traffic lights may not be so arbitrary after all!

Kay and Kempton agree with Brown's (or Lenneberg's) statement of the two theses of the Whorfian hypothesis. They argue, however, that Whorf's followers tacitly add and employ a third: "The semantic systems of different languages vary without constraint."27 This third thesis, whose accuracy would strengthen the second, has drawn the attention of most scholars concerned with the applicability of the Sapir-Whorf hypothesis in the semantic domain of color.

Kay and Kempton contend that the third thesis is discredited: "There appear to be strong constraints on possible inter-linguistic variation in the encoding of color" After describing new experiments they conclude that, "The case seems to be, first, that languages differ semantically but not without constraint, and second, that linguistic differences may induce nonlinguistic cognitive differences but not so absolutely under appropriate contextual conditions."28

Thus, the evidence does not support a strong version of cultural or cognitive relativism, and it is precisely the strong version that is of interest for a theory of religion, culture and language.

The work of Kay and Kempton appears to end strong versions of cultural relativism, and participants in the ongoing debate between Horton and his critics should be able to use the conclusions of this research as a powerful weapon against those who side with Winch. Unfortunately, this cannot be done. As Kay and Kempton point out, all of the experiments have focused only on the semantic domain of color, and "There are other areas of human thought and belief -- religion is an obvious example -- in which constraints like those imposed by peripheral neural mechanisms on possible color classifications seem a priori unlikely to operate. Some domains therefore offer greater potential scope for application of notions like [thesis] II and III."29 In other words, the door leading into cultural or cognitive relativism is not shut. Indeed, the debate in linguistics seems to indicate that the door is wide open!30 Marshall Sahlins, in an article that deserves far more attention, does not quarrel with the basic findings. He does point out, however, that the significance of the basic color terms, their meaning, is certainly not "reference to Munsell color chips!"31 But, then, what is the relation between the discovery of basic color terms across cultures and the social significance colors? Sahlins' reflection on this issue indicates that the semantics of color terms is anything but settled.

These disagreements, and the questions which cut across several disciplines in the human sciences, are of major importance, and it is unfortunate that students of religion have contributed very little to this debate. The paucity of interest in theoretical and methodological issues, and the present ethos of the study of religion, make it hard to be sanguine about our willingness or ability to take up this challenge.

There is no indication that Horton and his critics are aware of the implications of this corpus of material either. The focus of the debate seems to be the issue of ethnocentrism. Horton thinks that Winch is "wildly off course" in his interpretation of African religious thought. The task, then, is to discover what led him astray. Horton provides an interesting answer:

> In short, up till this late date in Western history [about four hundred years ago] there was little or no sense of contrast between religious discourse and scientific discourse, religious

activity and scientific activity. It was later, when post-Newtonian paradigms in the physical sciences began to dispense with the theistic component, and when the achievements of these sciences became increasingly difficult to challenge, that religious leaders began to grope for definitions of their calling which emphasized its distinctiveness from the sciences. It was then that the theologians began to emphasize that the ends of religion were quite different from the ends of science and to deny that they were in any sort of competition with scientists. The sort of definition propounded by Wittgenstein, Phillips, and Winch is simply the culmination of this trend.32

Thus, "whereas he [Winch] repeatedly insists on a reverential readiness to learn from other peoples, his interpretation of mystical beliefs involves the projection on to these peoples of his own anti-scientific fantasies."33

However compelling Horton's description of the fideistic solution to the conflict between science and religion, and however accurately it describes scholarly tendencies in the study of religion, it does not resolve the problem of cultural or linguistic relativism. Therefore, it does not help establish rational grounds for comparative, cross-cultural studies.34

II. Horton's Position: The Continuity Thesis.

Horton has tried to develop an approach to traditional religion that contrasts with the sociological, symbolic and/or expressive explanations of religion. His 1967 article, the most complete expression of his position, claims that social anthropologists have not perceived the theoretical character of traditional religion either because they are not familiar with Western theoretical thought or "because they have been blinded by a difference of idiom."35 Horton does not equate scientific thinking with traditional thinking, but suggests that his explanations of their important differences can help account for the emergence of science in Western culture.

Part I of the article lists eight propositions Horton deems fundamental to the "nature and functions of theoretical thinking" and shows how they are "highly relevant" to traditional religion. In fact, what is often called bizarre, non-rational or incomprehensible in traditional religious thought becomes rational and comprehensible when viewed in terms of the propositions of theoretical thinking.

The eight propositions are these:

1. "The quest for explanatory theory is basically the quest for unity underlying apparent diversity; for simplicity underlying apparent complexity; for order underlying apparent disorder; for regularity underlying apparent anomaly."36   Since this proposition is the foundation of the others, it is best to quote Horton's exposition of it at some length.

> Typically, this quest involves the elaboration of a scheme of entities or forces operating 'behind' or 'within' the the world of common-sense observations. These entities must be of a limited number of kinds and their behavior must be governed by a limited number of general principles. Such a theoretical scheme is linked to the world of everyday experience by statements identifying happenings within it with happenings in the everyday world. In the language of Philosophy of Science, such identification statements are known as Correspondence Rules. Explanations of observed happenings are generated from statements about the behavior of entities in the theoretical scheme, plus Correspondence-Rule statements.37

Horton is aware of the problems posed by "Correspondence Rules." He asks, "In what sense can we really say that an increase of pressure in a gas 'is' an increase in the velocity of a myriad tiny particles moving in an otherwise empty space? How can we say that a thing is once itself and something quite different?"38 Noting the variety of solutions from Locke to modern positivism, he concludes: "Perhaps the most up-to-date line is that there are good reasons for conceding the reality both of common-sense things and of theoretical entities. Taking this line implies the admission that the 'is' of Correspondence-Rule statements is neither the 'is' of identity nor the 'is' of class-membership. Rather, it stands for a unity-in-duality characteristic of the relation between the world of common sense and the world of theory." 39

Horton suggests that this proposition can explain traditional religious thought. In traditional societies, ancestors, water spirits, and gods have the intellectual function of unobservable theoretical entities. "Like atoms, molecules, and waves, then, the gods serve to introduce unity into diversity, simplicity into complexity, order into disorder, regularity into anomaly."40 Lévi-Bruhl's pre-logical and mystical puzzles are solved!

2. "Theory places things in a causal context wider than that provided by common sense."41 The exposition of this proposition stresses the function of theory as a means of transcending the limitations of common sense in explaining why things happen. Horton illustrates this proposition with the case of the African diviner, who, when faced with a disease, "does not just refer to a spiritual agency. He uses ideas about the agency to link disease to causes in the world of visible, tangible events."42

3. "Common sense and theory have complementary roles in everyday life."43 Horton asserts that "traditional African relations between common sense and theory are essentially the same as they are in Europe... there are certain circumstances that can only be coped with in terms of a wider causal vision than common sense provides. And in these circumstances there is a jump to theoretical thinking."44

4. Level of theory varies with context."45 A "low-level" theory will work very well for limited tasks. If the task is placed in a wider context, then a theory of a "higher-level" will be selected for an adequate explanation of the task to be done. However, as Horton notes, "As the area covered by lower-level theory is part of the area covered by the higher-level scheme, so too the entities postulated by the lower-level theory are seen as special manifestations of those postulated at the

higher level. Hence, they pose all the old problems of things which are once themselves and at the same time manifestations of other quite different things."46 This postulate is then applied to the puzzling mystery of the relation of many spirits and one god in African thought.

5. "All theory breaks up the unitary objects of common sense into aspects, then places the resulting elements in a wider causal context. That is, it first abstracts and analyzes, then re-integrates."47 Horton illustrates this proposition with another perplexing aspect of West African thought, the "theory" of the individual and society and the belief in "multiple souls."

6. "In evolving a theoretical scheme, the human mind seems constrained to draw inspiration from analogy between puzzling observations to be explained and certain already familiar phenomena."48 This proposition, Horton suggests, is amply demonstrated in both modern Western and traditional African thought. "Whether we look amongst atoms, electrons, and waves, or amongst gods, spirits, and entelechies, we find that theoretical notions nearly always have their roots in relatively homely everyday experiences, in analogies with the familiar."49 The difference between the two is that modern Western explanations are expressed in an "impersonal idiom" while African traditional thought uses a "personal idiom."

7. "Where theory is founded on analogy between puzzling observations and familiar phenomena, it is generally only a limited aspect of such phenomena that is incorporated into the resulting model."50 Horton applies this proposition in the following way:

> The definition of a god may omit any referenceto his physical appearance, his diet, his modeof lodging... and so on. Asking questions aboutsuch attributes is as inappropriate as askingquestions about the color of a molecule or the temperature of an electron. It is the resultof the same process of abstraction as the one wesee at work in Western theoretical models: theprocess whereby features of the

prototype phenomena which have explanatory relevance areincorporated into a theoretical schema, whilefeatures which lack such relevance are omitted.51

8. "A theoretical mode, once built, is developed in ways which sometimes obscure the analogy on which it was founded."52 This proposition suggests that the "theoretical models of traditional African thought are the products of developmental processes comparable to those affecting the models of science."53

Horton concludes Part I by stating that "For the progressive acquisition of knowledge, man needs both the right kind of theories and the right attitude to them. But it is only the latter which we call science."54 The stress in Part I is on the continuities between these modes of thinking. Horton denies any substantive or essential difference between Western scientific thought and African traditional thought.

Part II delimits the differences between traditional and scientific modes of thought. The essential distinction "is that in traditional cultures there is no developed awareness of alternatives to the established body of theoretical tenets; whereas in scientifically oriented cultures such an awareness is highly developed. It is this difference we refer to when we say that traditional cultures are 'closed' and scientifically oriented cultures are 'open'."55

For Horton, this basic difference between scientific and traditional thought has the following decisive consequence: "Where the established tenets have an absolute and exclusive validity for those who hold them, any challenge to them is a threat of chaos, of the cosmic abyss, and therefore evokes intense anxiety."56 The remainder of Part II is an intricate and detailed description of these two theses.

Horton's stress on the continuity between religious and scientific thought as theoretical modes of explaining how the world is contradicts the symbolic approaches to religion as sketched in part I of this essay. From Horton's point of view, we must take religious beliefs and practices literally rather than symbolically. They are "intellectual" attempts at explaining some of the puzzles of our common sense experience and instrumental means for attaining the aims in life which we desire. Religious beliefs and practices, therefore, are not to be interpreted as symbolic expressions, dramatizations of experience, or symbolic codes for the communication of "hidden" meaning in traditional societies. At the same time, Horton also attempted to show that modes of theoretical thinking are universal across cultures and not relative to different "forms of life."

The symbolic/relativist approach to religion, which could rightly be called the "received tradition" for theoretical thought in the human sciences, responded quickly to this challenge from a "neo-Tylorian." I shall let Horton describe the essence of the response in his own sharp reply:

> If we are wrong-headed enough to treat them as explanations, we have to admit that traditional beliefs are mistaken. And the only possible interpretation of such mistakes is that they are the product of childish ignorance. Neo-Tylorians... [thus] subscribe to the stereotype of the 'ignorant savage' and are illiberal racists... Anthropologists who take this line [that beliefs are quite other than explanatory] are therefore not committed to the 'ignorant savage' stereotype. They are good liberals... There is a short and sharp answer to this whole line of thought. It is that, by all normal criteria of assessment, many of the religious beliefs of pre-literate cultures <u>are</u> primarily explanatory in intent; that by the criteria of the sciences, many of them <u>are</u> mistaken; and that to wiggle out of admitting this by the pretense that such beliefs are somehow not really what they obviously are is simply to distort facts under the influence of extraneous values." [But what, he then asks] is so very dreadful about holding theories which later turn out to be mistaken? Explanations of such mistakes do not necessarily cast any slur whatsoever on the mental capacity or maturity of the peoples concerned.57 The hero of today will be the mistaken man of tomorrow.58

This stress on the "intellectualist" approach to traditional and scientific thought could be interpreted as a rejection of the Durkheimian school of thought regarding religion, religious symbols, the distinction between the sacred and the profane, and Durkheim's own rejection of Tylor. Horton clearly rejects this point of view in an analysis that firmly locates Durkheim on the "continuity/evolution" side of explanations of religious beliefs rather than on the "contrast/inversion" side of the debate. He uses these terms to indicate two basic points of view regarding scientific thought and religious thought. The first views scientific modern thought as a continuous, evolving process starting with religion. The second views scientific thought as in contrast with, different from and opposite religious expressions.

As an example of the continuity/evolution view, Horton cites a passage in Durkheim's Elementary Forms that he thinks contains "a treasury of profound reflections on the nature of theory and of its relation to common sense... [Durkheim wrote] 'Thus between the logic of religious thought and the logic of scientific thought there is no abyss. The two are made up of the same elements, though unequally and differently developed.'"59 Horton's reading of Durkheim should be taken seriously.60

Horton has reviewed the criticism of his position in an essay entitled "Tradition and Modernity Revisited."61 He agrees that such notions as "open" and "closed" societies are "ready for the scrap heap." In addition, he admits that the threat of anxiety to established or traditionally held theoretical frameworks "must go." Finally, the notion that there is a contrast between the presence or absence of an awareness of theoretical alternatives in various societies must be revised.62 He is convinced, however, that "the basic comparative exercise itself stands vindicated. The continuity thesis is virtually undamaged.63 Since Horton thinks that his "continuity" thesis still holds, despite the criticism and revisions, I think the best strategy is to bypass the political charges and counter charges of ethnocentrism and return to a close analysis of Horton's initial argument.

III. A Critical Review Of Horton's First Proposition.

I focus on Horton's first proposition: "The quest for explanatory theory is basically the quest for unity underlying diversity; for simplicity underlying complexity...." This proposition is of prime importance for Horton's larger thesis and has been overlooked by most of his critics. It is the basis for the coherence among the remaining seven propositions. If the first proposition fails, then the remaining seven are in serious trouble or lose much of their relevance for the problem Horton wants to solve.

It is important to remember that in his exposition of the first proposition Horton asserts that the quest for explanatory theory "typically involves the elaboration of a scheme of entities or forces operating 'behind' or 'within' the world of common-sense [later revised to 'primary theory'] observations.... Such a theoretical scheme is linked to the world of everyday experience by statements identifying happenings within it with happenings in the everyday world. In the Philosophy of Science, such identification statements are known as Correspondence-Rule statements...."64

This exposition appears to suggest that the typical elaboration of theoretical thinking involves theoretical statements or terms and non-theoretical statements or terms, together with correspondence-rule statements that interpret (Horton says, "links") the theoretical terms. Whether we wish to call the non-theoretical statements "common-sense observations" or "primary theory" is irrelevant to my argument. This elaboration familiar from the writings of Carnap, Nagel, Hempel and Braithwaite is known as the logical positivist construction of theory, or the nomological-deductive or hypothetico-deductive model for the elaboration of scientific theories.

According to this account, scientific theory, the foundation of modern knowledge, is based upon a distinction between theoretical terms ("entities" or "forces") and observational terms ("common-sense," observed happenings). Correspondence rules (operational definitions, rules of interpretation) define and guarantee the cognitive significance of theoretical terms as well as specify the procedure for applying the theory to what is observed.65

The power of this elaboration of the structure of a theory is its supposed ability to mark off scientific knowledge from traditional thought. For over fifty years, the logical positivist elaboration of scientific theory has excluded "mystical notions," "metaphysical entities," or theological discourse from scientific thought. Unobservable "entities" or "forces" beyond empirical verification (or falsification) were simply nonsense, unintelligible. We can now see more clearly why Horton's use of this elaboration of a scientific theory in his explanation of traditional thought is provocative in more ways than one.

This model of scientific theory has become axiomatic for the symbolic/expressive approach to traditional thought. Horton remains puzzled about this. Why, he asks, do social anthropologists persist in asserting that, when it comes to traditional religious thought, "things are not what they seem."66 Horton's answers, convincing as they are, simply miss the fundamental presupposition in all symbolic/expressive accounts of traditional religious thought; language or thought that involves unobservable entities, which are not empirically verifiable, is not scientifically meaningful. The problem, then, is how to account for this language or thought. Answer, it is expressive, dramatic, or a symbolic code. In brief, Beattie, for example, accepts Horton's "typical elaboration" of a scientific theory straight; metaphysical entities, mystical notions and the like, are simply unintelligible if they are taken literally or at their face value. Horton, however, clearly regards gods and spirits as similar to theoretical terms and the unobservable entities they denote. To this Beattie replies, "But, both the entities themselves and the procedures by which the idea of them is reached are so very different in the two cases that it is not easy to see what new light the comparison between them can throw on either."67 Thus, for Beattie, the nomological-deductive elaboration of scientific theory is as best incommensurable with religious thought.

Let us return to the logical positivist construction of theory contained in Horton's first proposition. The empiricist assumption that unobservable entities are unintelligible means that gods and water spirits must be ruled out of the domain of modern scientific knowledge. The question that must then be answered is, what about theoretical terms in a theory? Are they also unintelligible? Are "electron" and "kinetic energy" like "god" and "water spirit"? If the answer is yes, then the foundation of modern scientific knowledge, according to the logical positivist elaboration of scientific theory, is shattered simply because every metaphysical or mystical notion is re-admitted into what counts as scientific, "objective" knowledge. To use a phrase from Feyerabend, "anything goes." There would simply be no rigorous way to distinguish between modern scientific knowledge and ethics, drama, or traditional thought. It is also important to remember that theoretical terms are often postulated on the grounds that they complete the theory's logical coherence, and it is only later that such terms receive empirical status as well. A "quark" is a good example.68

Logical positivist elaborations of theory can be viewed as a mighty attempt to avoid the collapse of distinctions between scientific knowledge and religious thought. How is this collapse avoided? Peter Achinstein provides us with an answer: "Now the realm of unobservables is suspect; indeed for Positivists, who demand empiricism and eschew speculative metaphysics, such a realm is unintelligible. So instead of assigning a semantical rule to a theoretical term, which would make it refer to something unobservable, the proposal is to refrain from assigning any such rule."69

But, without semantical rules, how can theoretical terms be used in a theory? Achinstein replies that "connections are made between the theoretical and the non-theoretical terms to provide a 'partial' and 'indirect' interpretation for them. Statements expressing these connections are classified as correspondence rules (or postulates)."70

There are three important points in Achinstein's description of the logical positivist's model of a scientific theory. First, and this is crucial, we must distinguish between non-theoretical and theoretical terms in a theory. Exactly how we go about making this distinction is never clearly established. Second, since, according to this model, terms which refer to unobservables are meaningless, we must refrain from assigning any semantical rules to theoretical terms. If we do assign semantical rules to theoretical terms, we will designate them as referring to unobservables, which as we have noticed, is unintelligible or meaningless. Semantical rules, according to this model, operate, are applied, provide an interpretation or definition only in the domain of observational terms and descriptions. Third, the connection or link between non-theoretical and theoretical terms is a correspondence-rule statement which provides a 'partial' and 'indirect' interpretation of theoretical terms.

Correspondence-rule statements are mixed statements, they include at least one theoretical term and one non-theoretical term. They provide a 'partial' and 'indirect' interpretation of theoretical terms by reference to observable terms or observable descriptions.71 Anyone familiar with the history of logical positivism will note that there was little if any disagreement about the first two points. There was a great deal of disagreement about the precise nature of "correspondence-rule statements." And this became the "Achilles' heel" of logical positivism.

As we have already noted, Horton is aware of the problems posed by "correspondence rules." Let us return to his elaboration of the first proposition. Horton asserts that "a theoretical scheme is linked to the world of everyday experience by statements identifying happenings within it with happenings in the everyday world... such identification statements are known as Correspondence Rules."72 This is unfortunate since it seems to assert that "correspondence rules" are rules of "identity." If this were true, it would transform "correspondence rules" into "complete," rather than "partial" and "indirect," interpretations of theoretical terms. But, as we have seen this is precisely what the logical positivist model must avoid, for it would then be ascribing complete semantical meaning to theoretical terms. Horton attempts to avoid this problem by asserting that "Perhaps the most up-to-date line is that there are good reasons for conceding the reality of both common-sense things and of theoretical entities. Taking this line implies the admission that the 'is' of Correspondence-Rule statements is neither the 'is' of identity nor the 'is' of class-membership. Rather, it stands for a unity-in-duality characteristic of the relation between the world of common sense and the world of theory."73 I know of no possible interpretation of correspondence rules as designating a "unity-in-duality."

Horton does not provide the reasons for "conceding the reality of both common sense things and of theoretical entities." He does tell us what he means by "the unity-in-duality" problem in another essay. It has to do with Eddington's famous problem of the Two Tables; "the hard, solid table of common-sense thought and action, and the largely empty space, peopled by minuscule planetary systems, of theoretical thought and action. The key questions of the debate have been (a) which of the Two Tables is the real one? and (b) is there any sense at all in which both are real?"74 I think Horton is confused here. I shall not be able to resolve it here. But, briefly, to take an example from Putnam, it must surely be the case that "X has temperature so-and-so does not have the same meaning (is not analytically equivalent to) X has mean molecular kinetic energy blah-blah, even when 'blah-blah' is the value of the mean molecular kinetic energy that corresponds to the value 'so-and-so' of the temperature, yet the property of having the temperature so-and-so simply is, as a matter of contingent fact, the property of having the mean molecular kinetic energy blah-blah."75 As Putnam points out, the issue here is one of explanation, and "explanation is itself an epistemic notion."76

I suggest that, despite Horton's disclaimer, "unity-in-duality" is an assertion of identity.77 If this interpretation is right, then Horton's notion of a correspondence rule which "links" theoretical terms with non-theoretical terms becomes unintelligible. If Horton is thinking of contemporary philosophers of science who take correspondence rules as identity statements or perhaps a "bridge" between the "reality" of theoretical entities and the world of common sense, then I am not sure to whom he refers. Correspondence rules are not semantic rules of identity which define a "unity-in-duality"; they are "mixed" sentences that include both theoretical terms or sentences and non-theoretical terms or sentences.

Horton argues that contemporary scholarship shows "that each category of beings has its appointed function in relation to the world of observable happenings," that for the "religious expert charged with the diagnosis of spiritual agencies at work behind observed events, a basic modicum of regularity in their behavior is the major premise on which his work depends." But, then Horton goes on to say, "Like atoms, molecules, and waves, then, the gods serve to introduce unity into diversity, simplicity into complexity and order into disorder, regularity into anomaly."78 Perhaps so, but I am not persuaded by this argument.

First of all, what are the correspondence rules that bridge, "link," or logically relate, "spiritual agencies" with "observed happenings?" We are never told. Not a single example in Horton's ethnographic evidence is used to instantiate or construct, a correspondence rule. In fact, we are not given a description of what the theory is from which we can make the deduction that "gods serve to introduce unity into diversity, simplicity into complexity...." As we shall see in a moment, this is not a failure on Horton's part but a defect in the theory he is using. Once we agree to a model of scientific theory which defines observational statements as invariant and theoretical statements as variant, then the construction of correspondence rules which will bridge the two sets of statements becomes impossible.

Proposition one informs us that Horton is thinking of a particular kind of theoretical model that will illustrate the continuity between Western science and traditional thought. The model separates theoretical terms from non-theoretical terms and "links" them by correspondence rules. Let us interpret "links" as providing significance, meaning, to the theoretical terms. Let us also remember that Horton takes "gods," "water spirits," and the like, as theoretical terms and that he has not described or defined the correspondence rules which provide significance to the theoretical terms. He need not provide us with correspondence rules if he assumes that the theoretical terms are necessarily significant.

Horton appears to be saying something like "a term M (spirits), which occurs in a theory T (Kalabiri cosmology) is significant (meaningful) if and only if there is within the theory a correspondence rule for M." Thus, the Kalabiri cosmology (theory) contains a theoretical term S, and furthermore, the theory (T) logically implies O = T, where O is an observation statement. O = T is a correspondence rule for S, since it contains both S and observation statements, hence, S is significant. As Achinstein points out, "This is unacceptable, for it implies that any theory is significant, whether or not correspondence rules have been explicitly stated for that term...no matter what theoretical terms are employed in a theory, and no matter what the axioms or theorems of the theory might be, every theoretical term necessarily is significant."[79] It should be obvious that the consequence of such a rule makes theory construction completely trivial.

The problem is not, do the gods "serve to introduce unity into diversity..." and so on, but, rather, is there any significance at all to "the gods." An expert on religion may indeed presuppose "a basic modicum" of regularity in the behavior of the gods, but this assumes that "the gods" is a significant, intelligible, theoretical term! This is precisely the claim to which Beattie and others object, and Horton has not given us a theoretical basis for an argument which would prove Beattie and others wrong. As we have seen, the notion that correspondence rules "stand for a unity-in-duality" only compounds the problem.

To confirm the suspicion that Horton assumes the necessary significance of all theoretical terms, let us briefly turn to his second proposition (in so doing I shall demonstrate that the first proposition is of prime importance for understanding the others). It aims to show how traditional thought as theory "places things in a causal context wider than that provided by common-sense [or, as later revised, "primary theory]."80

After describing instances of the diagnosis of disease in Africa, Horton states, "The point in all this is that the traditional diviner faced with disease does not just refer to a spiritual agency. He uses ideas about this agency to link disease to causes in the world of visible, tangible events."81 This is ambiguous. What links "a spiritual agency" to the "world of visible, tangible events"? We are not told. But, let us return to my suggestion that Horton is following a principle which makes all theoretical terms significant. If this is correct, then he need not provide us with "the link" because "spiritual agency" is necessarily significant.

Alternatively, Horton might mean that the correspondence rule (the link) that provides significance to theoretical terms is the conjunction of theoretical and non-theoretical terms or statements.

Horton seems to be saying this in the following passage: The situation here is not very different from that in which a puzzled American layman, seeing a large mushroom cloud on the horizon, consults a friend who happens to be a physicist. On the one hand, the physicist may refer him to theoretical entities. 'Why this cloud?' 'Well, a massive fusion of hydrogen nuclei has just taken place.' Pushed further, however, the physicist is likely to refer to the assemblage and dropping of a bomb containing certain special substances. Substitute 'disease' for 'mushroom cloud,' 'spirit anger' for 'massive fusion of hydrogen nuclei,' and 'breach of kinship morality' for 'assemblage and dropping of a bomb' and we are again with the diviner.82

Are we? Putting aside the puzzles constituted by this odd analogy as a description of a physicist's theoretical explanation of "nuclear fusion," and "bombs containing special substances," let us assume we are. If so, the significance of "spirit anger" is its <u>conjunction</u> with "break of kinship morality." Let us assume that the above analogy can be turned into a good example of theoretical thinking along the lines Horton suggests in his first two propositions. (This would take a good bit of turning.) I must confess that I find the example very puzzling. For one thing, I am not certain about what the African diviner thinks about spirits. Let us assume for the moment that the diviner thinks like a scientist. He would then commit himself to the truth about the world, but he would not commit himself to the truth about any particular hypothesis about the nature of that natural world. Perhaps he would grant the truth of the following: "The spirit's anger is each appearance, and is all, but is not any one appearance as such" (T_1). That is to say, the diviner takes this statement as a true scientific axiom. Let us also assume that he would grant the truth of such observational statements as "the sky is blue," "this man is sick," and problematically "breach of kinship morality" (O_1). If the diviner grants the truth of T_1 and O_1, then he will also admit to the truth of their conjunction $T_1 \cdot O_1$.

Would such a correspondence rule provide significance for T_1? The fact that the diviner can relate T_1 and O_1 as $T_1 \cdot O_1$ sheds no light whatsoever on the significance, the meaning, of T_1. Yet the rule that theoretical terms are <u>necessarily</u> significant states that the following sentences provide meaning for the theoretical terms they refer to:

"The spirit's anger is each appearance, and is all, but it is not any one appearance as such, and the sky is blue."

"The spirit's anger is... and this man is sick."

"The spirit's anger is... and there is a breach in kinship morality."

Let us remember that the same rule would apply to the physicist as well! This argument is clearly unacceptable because it sheds no light whatsoever on the nature of "spirit's anger." The point is, it does not make a difference with regard to the <u>significance</u> of "spirit" just how much about the <u>visible</u> world of hatreds and misdeeds is added to the account.83

If the typical scientific elaboration of the first proposition is construed as a distinction between theoretical terms, observational terms and correspondence rules that somehow confer <u>significance</u> upon the theoretical terms, then Horton's account of traditional thought as similar to Western scientific thought has failed. Horton must first demonstrate the correspondence rules in African thought (theory). I doubt that he can. Be that as it may, since he has not stated this explicitly, it would seem from his examples and propositions that he is assuming a principle which specifies that theoretical terms are necessarily significant. Either way, the account simply fails because "anything goes"; theory construction becomes a trivial exercise. The fundamental problem, of course, is Horton's use of the logical positivist, nomological-deductive model as the typical elaboration of his first proposition. Philosophers of science have criticized this elaboration of scientific theory together with the notion of correspondence rules with devastating consequences.84 If we assume the logical positivist description of scientific theory, we inevitably have to conclude that gods, ancestors, and spirits are unintelligible, unless, of course, we assert that such terms are necessarily significant. If we assume that correspondence rules are necessary for the elaboration of scientific theory, then I do not know how the latter can be argued without making theory construction a trivial exercise.

Beattie also assumes the logical positivist model of scientific theory. And as we have seen, his answer to the question of the relation between science and religion is radically different from Horton's. But he seems unaware that the continued revision of correspondence rules has placed the logical positivist model of scientific theory in grave jeopardy. It would be ironic, after the long struggle to exclude traditional thought from scientific thought, to finally have to admit that scientific thought is similar to traditional religious thought; that when we think deeply about it, <u>both</u> are expressive, like art and drama! Something has clearly gone wrong.

NOTES.

1. See E. E. Evans-Pritchard, "The Intellectualist (English) Interpretation of Magic," *Bulletin of the Faculty of Arts*, vol. I, part 2 (Cairo: U of Egypt, 1933) 1-27 and "Lévi-Bruhl's Theory of Primitive Mentality," *Bulletin of the Faculty of Arts*, vol. II, part 1 (Cairo: U of Egypt, 1934) 1-36.

2. *Africa* XXXVII (1967): 50-71; 155-187. An abridged version of this article appeared in *Rationality*, ed. Bryan R. Wilson (New York: Blackwell, 1970). All references are from the original publication.

3. Edmund Leach, *Genesis as Myth and Other Essays* (London: Cape, 1969) 99.

4. John Beattie, "Ritual and Social Change," *Man* 1 (1966): 60.

5. Beattie 65.

6. Beattie 72.

7. Leach 92. This interpretation of the intellectualist approach is, of course, Leach's, not Horton's or Spiro's. They have vigorously denied these charges.

8. Beattie 69-70.

9. For further criticism of the symbolic approach, see John Skorupski, *Symbol and Theory* (Cambridge: Cambridge UP, 1976); I. C. Jarvie and Joseph Agassi, "The Problem of the Rationality of Magic," *Rationality*; the acerbic replies of J. D. Y. Peel, "Understanding Alien Belief-Systems," *British Journal of Sociology* 20 (1969): 55-74; and John Beattie, "On Understanding Ritual," *Rationality*.

10. David Schneider, "Notes Toward a Theory of Culture," *Meaning in Anthropology*, eds. Keith Basso and Henry A. Selby (Albuquerque: U of New Mexico P, 1976) 207.

11. Dan Sperber,"Apparently Irrational Beliefs," *Rationality and Relativism*, eds. Martin Hollis and Steven Lukes (Cambridge: MIT P, 1982) 149-150. See also Skorupski 40-41.

12. Charles Taylor, "Rationality," *Rationality and Relativism* 94.

13. Peter Winch, "Understanding a Primitive Society," *Rationality* 82.

14. Sperber 155.

15. Frederick Suppe, *The Structure of Scientific Theories* (Urbana: U of Illinois P, 1977) 191-92.

16. Peter Achinstein, *Concepts of Science* (Baltimore: Johns Hopkins UP, 1968) 93. Also see Hans H. Penner and Edward Yonan, "Is a Science of Religion Possible?" *The Journal of Religion* 52 (1972): 107-133. I did not at that time take Feyerabend, Kuhn, et al. seriously enough to perceive that the logical positivist notion of "theoretical reduction" was in great jeopardy. This does not mean that science is in jeopardy but that logical positivism as an adequate philosophy of science is afflicted with unresolvable problems.

17. See Suppe for a complete roster on the side of the philosophy of science. Also see I. C. Jarvie, *Concepts and Society* (London: Routledge, 1972) for a bibliography in anthropology and Ernest Gellner, *Cause and Meaning in the Social Sciences* (London: Routledge, 1973).

18. Since Kuhn (1977) has decided to drop the term "paradigm" because of its ambiguity, it is not clear that he remains in this position. See Thomas Kuhn, "Second Thoughts on Paradigms" and the discussion in Suppe 459-517. Moreover, I do not recall that Kuhn has ever agreed in print or in a public forum to the use of the term "paradigm" in domains other than the physical sciences.

19. Achinstein 93. I have taken the first three consequences of "meaning-dependence" from Achinstein 92-98.

20. Achinstein 97.

21. Benjamin Lee Whorf, *Language, Thought and Reality* (Cambridge: MIT P, 1956) 212-213.

22. Whorf 216.

23. Roger Brown, "Reference: In memorial tribute to Eric Lenneberg," *Cognition* 4 (1976): 125.

24. Brown 152. Brown's essay is an excellent description of the research projects on semantic domain of color across languages and cultures up to 1974.

25. Brown 149.

26. Paul Kay and Chad K. MacDaniel, "The Linguistic Significance of the Meanings of Basic Color Terms, *Language* 54 (1978): 644. This article is a helpful review of the results of research on color terms across cultures and languages. The research is based upon Brent Berlin and Paul Kay, *Basic Color Terms: Their Universality and Evolution* (Berkeley: U of California P, 1969). Kay and McDaniel also think that this research casts doubt on the theory of discretely contrasting semantic features advocated by scholars such as J. J. Katz.

27. Paul Kay and Willett Kempton, "What Is the Sapir-Whorf Hypothesis?" *American Anthropologist* 86 (1984): 66.

28. Kay and Kempton 66 & 77.

29. Kay and Kempton 67, first italics mine.

30. The positions and disagreements in linguistics are clearly presented in a very important publication of a conference at which most of the leading scholars in the discipline presented papers. See S. R. Harnad, H. D. Steklis and Jane Lancaster, *Origins and Evolution of Language and Speech* (New York: New York Academy Of Sciences, 1976). It would seem to be the case that, ever since Chomsky, linguistic relativism is a lost cause. J. J. Katz's paper in this volume describes the anti-relativist, or "rationalist," position very well in his presentation of what he calls "the effability hypothesis" regarding translation: "Every proposition is the sense of some sentence in each natural language. This means that each of the infinite number of propositions is represented, in each and every language, by means of some sentence" (37). But this hypothesis is clearly opposed by the papers of E. L. Keenan, Paul Kiparsky and Charles Fillmore, all trained in the generative grammar tradition. Also see Ronald Langacker, "Semantic

representations and the linguistic relativity hypothesis," *Foundations of Language* 14 (1976): 307-57. For an excellent argument against the notion that "reality itself is relative to some scheme," see Donald Davidson, "On the Very Idea of a Conceptual Scheme," *Inquiries into Truth and Interpretation* (Oxford: Clarendon, 1985). For an application of Davidson's argument to religion, see Terry F. Godlove, "In What Sense are Religions Conceptual Frameworks?" *Journal of the American Academy of Religion* 52 (1984): 289-306.

31. See Marshal Sahlins, "Colors and Cultures," *Semiotica* 16 (1976): 1-22.

32. Robin Horton, "Professor Winch on Safari," *Archives Europeenes de Sociologie* XVII (1976): 178.

33. Horton, "Professor Winch..." 180.

34. Bartley's analysis of the implications of fideism in theology and philosophy deserves attention in this context. The silence of the Academy of Religion with regard to this book is overwhelming. See William Warren Bartley, *The Retreat to Commitment*, 2nd ed. (La Salle, Ill.: Open Court, 1984).

35. Horton, "African Traditional Thought..." 60.

36. Horton, "African Traditional Thought..." 51.

37. Horton, "African Traditional Thought..." 51.

38. Horton, "African Traditional Thought..." 51.

39. Horton, "African Traditional Thought..." 51.

40. Horton, "African Traditional Thought..." 52.

41. Horton, "African Traditional Thought..." 53.

42. Horton, "African Traditional Thought..." 54.

43. Horton, "African Traditional Thought..." 58.

44. Horton, "African Traditional Thought..." 60.

45. Horton, "African Traditional Thought..." 60.

46. Horton, "African Traditional Thought..." 61.

47. Horton, "African Traditional Thought..." 62.

48. Horton, "African Traditional Thought..." 64.

49. Horton, "African Traditional Thought..." 64.

50. Horton, "African Traditional Thought..." 65.

51. Horton, "African Traditional Thought..." 66.

52. Horton, "African Traditional Thought..." 66.

53. Horton, "African Traditional Thought..." 68.

54. Horton, "African Traditional Thought..." 70.

55. Horton, "African Traditional Thought..." 155.

56. Horton, "African Traditional Thought..." 156.

57. Robin Horton, "Neo-Tylorianism: Sound Sense or Sinister Prejudice?" *Man* 3 (1968): 629 & 630.

58. Horton, of course, is not the only scholar who has taken the "intellectualist" approach to religion. See especially Melford Spiro, "Religion and the Irrational," *Symposium on New Approaches to the Study of Religion* (Seattle: U of Washington, 1964) and "Virgin Birth: Parthenogenesis and Psychological Paternity: An Essay in Cultural Interpretation," *Man* 3 (1968): 242-61; Jarvie, *Concepts and Society*; and Skorupski, *Symbol and Theory*. I should also cite Dan Sperber, *Rethinking Symbolism* (Cambridge: Cambridge UP, 1975); "Is Symbolic Thought Prerational?" *Symbol as Sense*, eds. Mary LeCron Foster and Stanley H. Brandes (New York: Academic P, 1980); and "Apparently Irrational Beliefs." For the opposition's response see John Beattie, "On Understanding Ritual";

Edmund Leach, "Virgin Birth," *Genesis as Myth and Other Essays*; and the heated exchanges between Spiro and Leach in *Man* 3 (1968).

59. Robin Horton, "Lévi-Bruhl, Durkheim, and the Scientific Revolution," *Modes of Thought*, eds. Robin Horton and Ruth Finnegan (London: Faber, 1973).

60. This article should challenge those who think that Durkheim represents our intellectual ancestor in the study of religion as a representation of the sacred. It is also a provocative challenge to all historians and phenomenologists of religion who, far too easily, accept a definition of religion as the distinction between the sacred and the profane. Those scholars who accept this kind of definition are obviously on the contrast/inversion side of the debate on the nature of religious beliefs and actions. This makes it all the more difficult to understand why Horton's challenge has been ignored by the Academy of Religion. Horton's reflections upon why this specific division has become the accepted "theory" of religion is well worth further consideration.

61. Robin Horton, "Tradition and Modernity Revisited," *Rationality and Relativism*.

62. Horton, "Tradition and Modernity..." 226-27.

63. Horton, "Tradition and Modernity..." 216.

64. Horton, "African Traditional Thought..." 51.

65. Suppe 17.

66. Horton, "Neo-Tylorianism..." 625.

67. J. H. M. Beattie, "On Understanding Ritual," *Rationality* 261.

68. I am grateful to Fitz John Porter Poole for this point as well as the example.

69. Achinstein 69.

70. Achinstein 69.

71. See Achinstein, especially Chapters Three and Five for a complete description and critical analysis of these assumptions in logical positivism.

72. Horton, "African Traditional Thought..." 51.

73. Horton, "African Traditional Thought..." 51.

74. "Lévy-Bruhl, Durkheim and the Scientific Revolution," *Modes of Thought* 278.

75. Hilary Putnam, "Beyond Historicism," *Realism and Reason: Philosophical Papers*, vol. 3 (Cambridge: Cambridge UP, 1983) 291.

76. Putnam, "Beyond Historicism" 291.

77. Skorupski, I believe, has also reached the same conclusion, but I am far from certain that he has solved the "unity-in-duality" paradox in Horton, at least as it applies to correspondence rules in scientific theory. See Skorupski 211-13, and also 215-16.

78. Horton, "African Traditional Thought..." 52.

79. Achinstein 72-73. Achinstein formulates the principle as follows: "A theoretical term M, which occurs in a theory T, is significant (meaningful, and so on) if and only if there is within the theory a correspondence rule for M" (72). He then shows that any attempt to revise this principle only produces further difficulties.

80. Horton, "African Traditional Thought..." 53 and "Tradition and Modernity..." 228.

81. Horton, "African Traditional Thought..." 54.

82. Horton, "African Traditional Thought..." 54.

83. See Horton, "African Traditional Thought..." 53. For a description and elaboration of the principles of conjunction, see, Achinstein 74-78.

84. See the first part and "afterward" of Suppe for one of the best analyses of the breakdown of logical positivism. See also Achinstein.

CHAPTER FOUR

FUNCTIONAL EXPLANATIONS OF RELIGION

In this chapter I want to examine functionalist theories as explanations of religion. This examination is also intended to serve as an example of how to demonstrate what is wrong with a theory rather than simply calling those who use it "reductionists." Most of the time, such accusations are warnings to the "faithful," they are encyclicals not critiques.

The status of functionalism and the meaning of the term "function" in the history and phenomenology of religion are unclear. Some scholars, for example, seem to be both for and against functionalism. As we have already noticed, functionalist methods are called reductionistic on the one hand, and auxiliary sciences on the other. In fact, we sometimes read that religion "functions" to express The Sacred.

Let us recall Eliade's assertion about the proper study of religious phenomena: "To try to grasp the essence of such phenomena by means of physiology, psychology, sociology, economics, linguistics or any other study is false; it misses the one unique and irreducible element in it -- the element of the sacred." We must assume that Eliade is not making a metaphorical statement, that what he is asserting is an important methodological principle. But then, what do we make of the following assertion: "I cannot conclude this chapter better than by quoting the classic passages in which Bronislaw Malinowski undertook to show the nature and function of myth in primitive societies."1 The quote which follows this assertion is indeed the classic paragraph from Malinowski's essay "Myth in Primitive Psychology." Eliade quotes it as follows:

Studied alive, myth... is not an explanation in satisfaction of a scientific interest, but a narrative resurrection of primeval reality, told in satisfaction of deep religious wants, moral cravings, social submissions, assertions, even practical requirements. Myth fulfills in primitive culture an indispensable function; it expresses, enhances, and codifies belief; it safeguards and enforces morality; it vouches for the efficiency of ritual and contains practical rules for the guidance of man. Myth is thus a vital ingredient of human civilization; it is not an idle tale, but a hard-worked active force; it is not an intellectual explanation or an artistic imagery, but a pragmatic charter of primitive faith and moral wisdom.... These stories... are to the natives a statement of primeval, greater, and more relevant reality, by which the present life, fates and activities of mankind are determined, the knowledge of which supplies man with the motive for ritual and moral actions, as well as with indications as to how to perform them.2

Since Malinowski is a well-known social anthropologist, often cited as the father of functionalism, which of the two statements by Eliade is true? Which statements are we to take seriously? Has Malinowski grasped the essence of The Sacred in this quotation, or is he describing the psychology of myth among primitives and explaining religion as a function of biological and social needs? If it is the latter, and I do not doubt that it is, then according to Eliade's first assertion, Malinowski's position is false. Yet, we are to take this false statement about myth as the best description of myth that Eliade can find. This kind of confusion, which is widespread, makes it difficult to evaluate just what is being asserted about the proper study of religion.

Malinowski's statement concerning myth simply does not make sense without knowledge of the theory it entails. It is embedded in a theory regarding social institutions and is consistent with his own functionalist position regarding religion. Thus, if we want to avoid confusion, it must be made clear whether we accept his theory or not. If we reject Malinowski's theory of religion and myth as "reductionistic," then it would seem that we would also want to reject his descriptions of the function of myth and religion. Given the decades of methodological confusion, I am not optimistic at all that pointing this out will change anything. Perhaps the best we can hope for is greater recognition that The Sacred and its theological ramifications cannot be disguised, at least not so easily, with the language of functionalism.

Functional explanations of religion have maintained a powerful hold on most of the human sciences. Over the decades, scholars who committed themselves to functional theories of religion have done so because the theory is empirically testable. Moreover, it is also claimed that the theory is able to explain many of the problems older theories could not explain, as well as do more than older theories in terms of explaining social institutions. All these claims and aims are to be applauded as noteworthy examples of the development of a science. The effects of this new theory were revolutionary. Instead of explaining a society by religious traits or units, functional theory reversed the procedure by explaining religion as a variable from within the structure or system of a particular society. The famous slogan became "religion is what it does." The task became one of showing why and how religion functions in a society. Anyone familiar with the development of the theory also knows that its complexity increased in proportion to the problems and criticisms it confronted.

The power of the theory bound together a variety of scholars in the human sciences, even though they disagreed on fundamental issues concerning religion. Three examples suffice to illustrate the point. The first is the lifelong feud between A. R. Radcliffe-Brown and Malinowski concerning ritual and anxiety. For Malinowski, the methodological biologist, anxiety arises in circumstances which human beings cannot control, for example, fishing in the ocean. Although rituals are not technological means which actually control the threat of death on the ocean, they do function to reduce anxiety. For Radcliffe-Brown, the methodological sociologist, it is a society's expectations that produce anxiety, and the performance of rituals is an individual's response to those expectations and the anxiety they generate. Notice that although there is disagreement on what generates anxiety, both use functionalism as an explanation for the existence of rituals. The conflict was finally resolved by Homans in 1941. Homans solved the problem by showing that both are right, that it is not a question of either/or.[3]

The second example is the famous debate between Melford Spiro and Edmund Leach on the belief in virgin birth. Spiro argued that beliefs in the existence of water spirits, and the like, as the cause of pregnancy were to be taken as rational, although false, explanations for pregnancy. Leach argued that there is sufficient evidence to show that most, if not all, societies are well versed in the causes of physiological paternity. Such beliefs, therefore, were not to be taken as mistaken explanations, but as symbolic expressions that reinforce existing social institutions, the marriage bonds for example. The publications of both scholars, however, are excellent examples of functionalism at work in contemporary anthropology.[4]   My final example is the well-known debate between J. Beattie and R. Horton on the proper understanding of ritual and belief. For Beattie, as we have seen, rituals and religious beliefs are expressive; for Horton they are to be explained as cognitive, rational attempts at explanation.5 Once again, we have an example where both scholars are excellent representatives of the functionalist theory at work in the social sciences despite a fundamental disagreement between them about the cognitive status of religious beliefs.

Functionalism can be viewed as the theory for explaining things in the social sciences. Most of the time the theory is never described in any detail but simply assumed as a valid model of explanation. This is especially true of scholars who have become popular in the study of religion. Mary Douglas's book, Purity And Danger, is a good example. The thesis of the book may be summed up as follows. Anomaly creates disturbances of a high level in undifferentiated societies. Such disturbances must be reduced or removed in order for the society to function adequately. Classification systems, taxonomies, and taboo function to reduce anomalies in a society and thus create solidarity by reducing disturbances created by anomalies. Clifford Geertz's elegant essays are clearly located within functionalism, as is Victor Turner's description of the function of "communitas." Festinger's explanation of religious movements based upon "cognitive dissonance" assumes the same functionalist model. All of these scholars have become popular resources for students interested in the study of religion. This is especially true for those who have recognized that the tradition of Otto, van der Leeuw and Eliade has reached a dead end. It is also true for many Biblical scholars who have discovered the importance of the "social context" for interpreting texts.

The theory is very persuasive. You need not really bother about why people hold religious beliefs. All you need do is recognize that the beliefs are relative to a cultural system. As Barnes puts it, "If we ask why an individual believes 'X' the usual answer in all cultures will be that he was told or taught 'X' by a trusted knowledge source. We can then ask why belief 'X' is present in the culture, and that is where functionalism makes claims to provide explanation."6 Indeed it does! The problem is that most scholars who use this model of explanation do not pause to critically reflect on the validity of their claims. Why, then, do they believe it? Well, they were told or taught the theory by a trusted knowledge source! How else do we explain the persistence of such a widespread theory of explanation which is seriously defective.

We can simplify the theory of functionalism as an explanation of religion in the following way: If y (e.g. religion) then z, (e.g. anxiety reduction) where z is a functional requirement of x, (e.g. social maintenance) and y satisfies z. This formula was fully described in 1964 by Melford Spiro. His article, "Causes, Functions, and Cross-Cousin Marriage: An Essay In Anthropological Explanation" makes explicit the claim that functional explanations are causal explanations with an important difference.[7] The difference can be described in the following way. Functional explanations are like causal explanations in that they also want to account for y (religion, for example) in causal terms. The difference, however, is that functional explanations explain y by reference to some condition z, in which z constitutes the contribution of y necessary to the maintenance of some social system x. Thus, the satisfaction of z is the function of y. Religion, for example, is not simply explained as functioning to satisfy social maintenance. Religion functions to reduce anxiety which constitutes the contribution of religion for satisfying a necessary need for the maintenance of a social system. The Kula ritual performed by Trobriand society is explained by reference to reduction of social tensions that must be satisfied for the maintenance of the social system.

The shift here is important. We explain a religion by showing how it satisfies a functional requirement of a social system. The functional requirement is usually expressed as some "need" in the social system. The use of functionalism in psychology focuses on "needs" in the personality system.

I shall not reproduce Spiro's functional explanation for the existence of cross-cousin marriage. I shall, instead, present a simplified model using religion as an example. I do not believe that this simplified model, distorts the claims made about functionalism as an explanation. The simplified version for an explanation of religion can be described as follows:

1. x = a particular social system under a setting of kind c.

2. y = a particular structural unit, (religion or ritual) which is a sufficient condition for satisfying z.

3. z = a functional requirement (let us say family confidence and trust) which is a necessary condition for x, the social system.

In arguing for his more complex model, Spiro makes three things clear. First, functional requirements (z) are necessary, but not sufficient, conditions for the maintenance of a social system. Secondly, structural units (y) may satisfy different functional requirements, and different structural units may satisfy the same functional requirements; in other words, structural units have functional equivalents. Thirdly, within a system it is a joint set of units which is the sufficient condition for satisfying the functional requirement of a system. In conclusion, Spiro is aware that our knowledge of the functional requirements of a social system will not allow us to predict which social units will satisfy the requirements.8

It is important to notice that in the above description the explanation is more complex. Instead of y representing a particular unity (see premise #2 of the simplified model), y represents a set or class of units. As we shall see in a moment, this revision of the model is necessary in order to avoid a conclusion which is invalid.

To complete the description of our model, it is important to point out that a functional explanation must specify the relations between y, z, and x. It does this by stating that the relations are either necessary or sufficient or both necessary and sufficient conditions.

Since the criticism of functional explanations will depend on these logical relations, it is best to describe them before entering into an analysis of the model. To focus on these relations, let us simplify the model and assume that z, the functional requirement, is social maintenance. Let us also assume that y, the explanandum (what we want to explain), is a religious ritual, a particular social unit. We may then write out the following table of necessary and sufficient conditions.

1. Necessary conditions.
a. The absence of social maintenance (z) entails the absence of the ritual (y).
b. The absence of the ritual does not entail the absence of social maintenance.
c. The presence of social maintenance does not entail the presence of the ritual, and
d. The presence of the ritual entails the presence of social maintenance.Social maintenance (z) is then a necessary, but not a sufficient, condition for the presence of the ritual (y).

2. Sufficient conditions.

a. The absence of social maintenance does not entail the absence of ritual.
b. The absence of the ritual entails the absence of social maintenance.
c. The presence of social maintenance entails the presence of the ritual.
d. The presence of the ritual does not entail the presence of social maintenance. The presence of social maintenance (z), then, is a sufficient condition for the presence of ritual (y).

3. Necessary and sufficient conditions.
a. The presence of social maintenance entails the presence of the ritual.
b. The presence of the ritual entails the presence of social maintenance.
c. The absence of social maintenance entails the absence of the ritual, and
d. The absence of the ritual entails the absence of social maintenance.

With the above table in hand, we can move to an analysis of the logic of functional explanations. The model I shall use for this analysis is taken from Hempel's now classic essay on the logic of functionalism.9 I have modified it only slightly, using Spiro's symbols to bring out how religion is explained functionally. I remain convinced that functional theories of religion as presently used in the human sciences can be reduced to this analysis.

Since this assertion has been misunderstood by some of my colleagues, I believe a brief clarification is necessary before the analysis is presented. The first problem arises because of my use of Hempel. Since Hempel is usually identified as a logical positivist, I must also be a logical positivist when I use his analysis of functionalist explanations. This is not bothersome because the accusation is similar to phenomenologists calling scholars they disagree with reductionists.

What is bothersome is a second accusation; that since Hempel's nomological-deductive model for scientific explanations has been devastated along with the logical positivist notions of observational/theoretical language and their relation to correspondence rules, I am using a model that is out of date and irrelevant.10 Let me just say that I am fully aware of the withering attack on logical positivism by contemporary historians and philosophers of science.11 I am also aware that the analysis I am presenting is controversial. It should be, because if it is an accurate description of the logic of functionalism, then this well-known, almost common sense, explanation is in serious trouble regarding its claims as an explanation of religious phenomena; I would extend this to include explanations of any cultural or social phenomena.

The point which needs to be stressed is that I have not invented functionalism as a model for explaining religion. I have not created titles such as Spiro's for an explanation of cross-cousin marriage. I am not interested at the moment in whether "explanation" must be broadened, or revised. The central issue is this; does the history of functionalism in the human sciences, as we know it, fit Hempel's model? I have yet to find one critic who has demonstrated that it does not. In fact, several functionalists I have read explicitly state that this approach to explaining the elements of society and culture is at best a heuristic device and they have reached this conclusion because of Hempel's analysis.12 Once again, it is what functionalists claim they are doing as cultural scientists that is the issue. What the critics will have to demonstrate is that Hempel did not capture this in his analysis of the logic of functional analysis. With this clarification in mind, let us turn to the analysis.

1. At time t, a society x functions adequately in a setting of kind c.

2. x functions adequately in a setting of kind c only if a necessary functional requirement z is satisfied (let z = social maintenance).

3. If unit y were present in x, then, as an effect condition z would be satisfied. (let y = a ritual)

4. Hence, at t unit y is present in x.

Both the logical and empirical requirements of functional explanations are clear in the above model. The first premise gives us, in abbreviated form, the empirical observations of a society at a particular time. It also describes the conditions in which the society is found. It describes rather nicely what we find in the first chapter of many texts which are about societies studied by anthropologists and sociologists. The society is usually placed in its geographical setting, and a full description is given of natural resources, social structure and the like.

The second premise states a necessary condition which must be met in order for the society to function adequately. In our example, it is the necessary requirement of "maintenance" that must be satisfied in order for the society to function adequately. In some explanations this necessary condition is often cited as a "functional prerequisite." Premise three states that if a ritual were present, then, as a consequence, the necessary condition would be satisfied, i.e., the satisfaction of z is the function of y. The existence of the ritual is explained by what it does. The conclusion, however, is invalid. We have not explained why the ritual is present in the society, and this is precisely what it was we wanted to explain. We want to explain why ritual or religion is present in a society. This assertion has often been misunderstood. I am not saying that the conclusion is false. All that has been shown is that the argument is invalid. The conclusion may be true, but the invalid argument does not establish its truth.

The argument is invalid because it commits the fallacy of affirming the consequent. It asserts that "if y then z; z therefore y." It is a simple fallacy which we often commit when we are careless. Here is a clear example of the fallacy: "If John misses his bus he will be late for class; John is late for class. Therefore, he missed the bus." Clearly many other events could have taken place to explain why John was late for class. All we can conclude is that something must have happened to make him late for class and one possibility is his missing the bus. In our table of necessary and sufficient conditions, the conclusion contradicts "c" under necessary conditions.

The above conclusion is the same for functional explanations. Instead of explaining why a particular ritual is present in the society, or persists in the society, all we can conclude is that somehow the necessary condition of maintenance is being satisfied in order for the society to function adequately at time t under the specified conditions c. I believe that most functionalists since Malinowski have seen this problem, and the history of functionalism can be viewed as a history in which revisions were made in an attempt to overcome the problem.

One way of correcting the result is to introduce the notion of "functional equivalents" into the explanation. We may, for example, introduce new terms into the third and fourth premises. Thus, premise one and two would remain the same, but three becomes,

3. If unit y, or its <u>functional equivalent</u>, were present in x, then, as an effect condition z would be satisfied.

4. Hence, at t , y or its <u>functional equivalent</u> is present in x.

The addition of functional equivalents, however, does not help us. In fact, this revision of the model now leaves us with an explanation that is vacuous. It simply asserts that if a society is functioning adequately then something or other must account for that. Once again, this is not enlightening about what it is we wanted to explain; the existence of ritual in the society. The conclusion tells us that somehow the need for social maintenance is being satisfied given the truth of premises one and two.

The addition of "functional equivalents," moreover, makes the explanation more problematic. First, as Hempel has pointed out, what do we mean by "functional equivalents?" How are we to identify the functional equivalents of a religious ritual? Secondly, the introduction of functional equivalents produces serious complications regarding the empirical status of the explanation. If we are free to substitute equivalent units for a particular unit (say, ritual), then the question arises whether we are still observing the same society at t, under the conditions specified.

What is worse, this revision of changing "ritual" to "ritual or its functional equivalent" does not correct the contradiction of requirement "c" in the table of necessary conditions. I find it odd that Hempel did not notice this error in his presentation of the revision. The revised model is invalid on the same basis as the first.

The first model was abbreviated as follows to demonstrate the fallacy: If y then z; z, therefore y. The revised model seems to assert the following: If (y v A v B v C... n) then z. z, therefore, (y v A v B v C... n). Inserting functional equivalents into the argument does not validate the invalid argument.13

There is a third way of correcting the validity of the conclusion. This move is the opposite of the solution we have discussed thus far. Instead of attempting to expand premise three, it tightens it by making premise three a <u>necessary condition</u> for social maintenance. Premise one and two remain the same, but three is changed as follows:

3. Only if unit y were present in x, then, as an effect condition z would be satisfied.
4. Hence, at t, unit y is present in x.

From a logical point of view the change of premise three provides us with a valid conclusion. This is so because when we refer to the tables we find that "d" under "necessary conditions" states that "the presence of the ritual entails the presence of social maintenance."

The problem, however, of turning a cultural unit such as ritual into a necessary condition for the maintenance of a society is a severe one. How are we to maintain that a ritual is indispensable or necessary, to a society? Critics of functionalism, such as Merton, Hempel, Nagel, and Jarvie, have pointed out that the claim of "functional indispensability" for any cultural unit is difficult to sustain on empirical grounds and, in the end reduces functional explanations to a tautology.14

Hempel presents one last possible revision which might satisfy the requirements for a valid explanation. Once again the first two premises remain the same. Premise three is changed as follows:

3. i is the class of empirically sufficient conditions for z in the context determined by x and c, and i is not empty.
4. Hence, some one of the items included in i is present in x at t under conditions c.

The argument as it stands is trivial; some one item is present, but we are not able to specify which item is functioning to satisfy the requirement of social maintenance. Once again, let us recall that functional explanations have been presented as explanations which account for why ritual, myth, or religion is present in a society and why these cultural units persist in a society. On reflecting on this fourth alternative it seems to me that it is no different in its logical construction then the second revision which includes functional equivalents in premise three. Hempel believes that this last revision is valid, although trivial in its conclusion. This seems odd. What we would need, I think, is an additional premise which could be stated as follows:

3. i is the class of empirically sufficient conditions for z in the conditions determined by x and c, and i is not empty.
3.1 The class of empirically sufficient conditions for z constitutes a disjointly necessary condition for z.
4. Hence, some one of the items....

With this revision we are back to a notion of indispensable conditions which are necessary for explaining the presence of ritual in a society. As we have seen, this claim is indeed more plausible since it asserts that some one of a class of items is necessary for z -- if not ritual, then something else. This seems plausible, but it is simply not informative.

Most, if not all, functional arguments do not take the task of specifying an item or unit (religion) as a necessary condition. How could they? Instead they agree with Spiro who asserts that it is a class of structural units which are the sufficient conditions for satisfying the functional requirements of a society. Thus, most functional explanations assert that "it is highly likely," or "it is highly probable," that religion fulfills the requirement. Such conclusions are not only trivial, they are also impossible to confirm or disconfirm. Moreover, this conclusion seems to be invalid given my correction of Hempel's analysis.

It seems to be almost self-evident that religion is what it does until we actually examine the premises which support such a doctrine. If the above analysis is accurate, functionalism fails as a well-formed methodological procedure for explaining religion. It would seem that we are left with heuristic devices and "scholarly guesses" once again.

In an interesting essay on "Religion and the Irrational," Spiro seems to recognize the problem of explaining a religion as included in a class which is the sufficient condition for satisfying a requirement of society. Although his argument is an attempt to show the rationality of religion, the basic theory is functionalist. In arguing for the rationality of religious beliefs and their persistence in a society, Spiro concludes that "Their tenacity in the face of rival scientific beliefs may be simply explained -- scientific beliefs may be functional alternatives for religious beliefs, but they are not their functional equivalents. Religious beliefs have no functional equivalents; being less satisfying, alternative beliefs are rejected as less convincing."15

What is of interest to us in the above quotation is the assertion that there are no functional equivalents to religious beliefs. To make this claim is of course to argue for the function of religious beliefs as a necessary condition for satisfying the functional requirements of a society or the maintenance or integration of personality or both.

Spiro argues that religious beliefs have a cognitive basis. If religious beliefs are attempts at explaining the world, this need not in itself lead us to the conclusion that such beliefs are irrational because they are false. All we need to remember is that there are many scientific theories which have turned out to be false and have been discarded. No one would conclude from this history of science that the falsified theories were, therefore, irrational.

The problem with religious beliefs, according to Spiro is somewhat different. Instead of discarding a religious belief in the face of new discoveries and explanations, it seems that people hold onto their religious beliefs in spite of scientific progress in our knowledge of the world. The question then is not, are religious beliefs irrational, but, why do people continue to persist in holding onto them? This is a problem that most historians and phenomenologists have abandoned long ago. In doing so, we have not solved the problem; in fact, we have left it to be solved by disciplines such as anthropology, clinical psychology and philosophy. Since we claim to be specialists in the study of religion, this is most unfortunate.

Spiro solves the problem by setting both scientific and religious beliefs in the context of systems which satisfy our intellectual needs. Where the two sets or systems differ is on the satisfaction of emotional needs. According to Spiro, religious beliefs satisfy both intellectual and emotional needs. The emotional or motivational basis of religious beliefs thus becomes a partial explanation of their persistence. Religious beliefs, however, cannot be explained as a function of motivation. After all, Spiro notes, there are many religious beliefs which are anything but satisfying. Thus, although it is the case that some religious beliefs are both intellectually and emotionally satisfying and that some religious beliefs may indeed involve empirical support, we must add the importance of "perceptual sets," formed in early childhood, as a strong contributor to the quality of religious conviction and the persistence of the belief system.16

Let us assume that religious beliefs are indeed necessary conditions for the satisfaction of individual and social needs and that "religious beliefs are held not merely from a craving to satisfy intellectual needs, but also from a craving to satisfy emotional needs."17 The additional argument that there are no functional equivalents for religious beliefs is important here. In contrast to what Spiro has written about social units jointly providing the sufficient condition for a functional requirement, we now have one social unit, a religious belief system, can be substituted. Scientific beliefs may well take the place of religious beliefs, but they are not to be understood as providing the identical effects of religious beliefs. If this is not what is meant, then it will be exceedingly difficult to understand the meaning of the statement that, "religious beliefs have no functional equivalent."

Spiro goes on to say that "neither the truth of the beliefs nor the etiology of the conviction by which they are held is relevant to the question of their rationality."18 The criteria of their rationality are dependent on the degree to which religious beliefs satisfy our intellectual, motivational, and perceptual needs. Obviously, the quality of conviction alone will not suffice as a criterion for rationality.

Notice, once again, that Spiro's explanation of the function and rationality of religious beliefs does not reduce the data we are attempting to understand. On the contrary, the theory is offered as a way of solving certain problems that have not been adequately solved by previous theories. The virtue of Spiro's approach is that it attempts to resolve three stubborn problems; the problem of the rationality of religious beliefs, the problem of the truth of religious beliefs and an explanation of the persistence of religious beliefs. It should be satisfying to us all if such a theory succeeds on both logical and empirical grounds. It would advance our knowledge about religion, open new problems for analysis which would in turn provide greater explanatory power and methodological procedures for solving the new problems. In brief, it would provide the "science of religion" with a process for growth in knowledge about religion instead of the stagnant and dogmatic accusation that such an explanation is "reductionistic."

Unfortunately, not even the most sophisticated functionalist theories present us with well-formed arguments for explaining religion. Spiro's "revised" explanation does not commit a logical fallacy. Furthermore, the explanation is not to be taken as a strict causal explanation in the sense that religion is to be explained by its antecedent conditions. Religion is explained by its effect on some consequent condition, which in turn is a necessary condition for the maintenance of a society. Spiro's claim that there are no functional equivalents to religious belief systems also seems to evade the trivial conclusion that "somehow" the requirements of a social system are being satisfied. Nevertheless, serious weaknesses remain, and I believe they are weaknesses of the kind which will not allow us to use the theory as an explanation of religion.

There are at least two basic problems with the example we have used. The first problem has been discussed at some length, and we need not repeat it again. It involves the problem of stating that a religious belief system is a necessary condition for satisfying a functional requirement or set of requirements of a social or personal system. The difficulty here is justifying such an explanation empirically without becoming engaged in circular arguments. What we would have to show is that all the relations between perceptual, motivational, and intellectual needs of a person and their relation to the structure of a society are sustained only if a specific system of religious beliefs is present. No one has succeeded in showing that this is the case. I do not know how it could be shown to be the case without circular argument. The usual option is to argue for functional equivalents or a set of social units taken jointly as a class of sufficient conditions. I have argued that this option does not solve the invalidity of functionalist explanations and the trivial conclusions it ends up with.

There is a second problem with the statement that "religious beliefs have no functional equivalents; being less satisfying, alternative beliefs are rejected as less convincing." At first, such statements may appear to assert the existence of a necessary condition. They are, however, usually qualified in such a way that they become ambiguous as necessary conditions for a functionalist explanation. Just how, for example, are we to interpret the statement that "there are no functional equivalents for religious belief systems because alternative beliefs are less satisfying?" Such qualifications surely do not entail, "only the present belief system satisfies...." What has been introduced is the notion of a range or degree of satisfaction. Some beliefs have a greater power of satisfying certain requirements than others. The difficulties now become compounded. For, to sustain the statement that other beliefs are less satisfying than a religious belief system present in a society, we will have to specify the range or degree of satisfaction as well as a means for measuring the range. If we fail to provide such a scale and the means for calibrating the scale, our statement will remain vague -- not false but simply incapable of being tested or confirmed.

We might also ask whether the statement that "alternative belief systems are less satisfying" means that religious beliefs function as providing maximum satisfaction of a requirement. Once again, we would need some scale which would permit us to measure and test such a maximum. Moreover, the statement "alternative belief systems are less satisfying" does not entail "only this belief system provides maximum satisfaction." It may imply that the religious belief system is more satisfying than alternative belief systems; but, again, this does not entail that the present religious belief system is a necessary condition for satisfying the social requirements.

My argument leads to the following conclusion. A second inspection of Spiro's "revised" explanation of religious beliefs reveals that it will be difficult to create a scale for measuring beliefs which are "more" or "less" satisfying. Nevertheless, such a scale might be created and tested. The deeper problem is that the qualification "more or less" removes the necessary condition of the religious belief system as satisfying a requirement of need in a society. For to say that in the context of a specific social system certain beliefs are "more" satisfying clearly does not exclude the possibility that certain alternative beliefs may become more effective than the beliefs presently held. In brief, we have not explained why the religious belief system is a necessary condition for satisfying the need, and thus we have not shown that there are no functional equivalents for a particular religious belief system in a society.

I believe these problems illustrate the inherent logical difficulties which functionalist theories must resolve before they can be accepted as adequate explanations of religion. If the critique I have presented is not convincing enough, there is a final methodological move which may clinch my argument. This involves the notion that a social system is a self-regulating system.

Both Ernest Nagel and Robert Brown have examined the problems of this model in their analysis of functionalist explanations. According to Nagel, "functional statements are regarded as appropriate in connection with systems possessing self-maintaining mechanisms for certain of their traits, but seem pointless and even misleading when used with reference to systems lacking such self-regulating devices."19

Robert Brown describes a self-maintaining system, a system that has negative feedback in the following way:

A self-persisting system is commonly taken to be a system which maintains at least one of its properties in an equilibrium position despite variations in the other properties, either inside or outside the system, to which the presence of the first property is causally related. This ability to maintain a property in a steady state while its causal factors vary within certain limits depends on the system containing certain devices. These must be self-regulators in the sense that they must register any significant variations in the state of the property which is being maintained and must compensate for these variations in such a way as to preserve the property within a range of permissible values. The simplest example and the one most favored by recent authors, is the thermostat which increases or reduces the heat throttle according to whether its thermometer registers above or below a set value.20

The model for many contemporary theories of religion is something like the above description of a system having negative feedback. This model often permits the functionalist to argue that the criticism of functionalism is basically irrelevant because the argument is directed against attempts to explain the origin or religion. By use of a negative feedback model, many functionalists claim that this is not what functionalism is all about, even though some of the fathers of functionalism made this mistake. The aim of functional theories of religion is not to show why a religious unit comes into existence, but how it functions and persists, what role it plays in a self-regulating system. Religious units in a social system are to be understood as variables in a self-maintaining system. This is an important distinction, but the success of the model for explaining religion is negligible.

Self-regulating systems are often assumed in the explanation of religion. A brief example must suffice to illustrate how the model is used. What we wish to explain is how a particular religious ritual works in the self-regulation of a social system. We assume for example, that both social equilibrium and personal stability are being maintained, since according to our observations both are functioning adequately. The religious ritual is explained if we can show how it functions to satisfy the requirements of equilibrium in the society and the stability in the individual. The religious ritual is explained, then, if we can show the relations of the ritual as reinforcing not only the "perceptual sets" formed in early childhood but also how the satisfaction of intellectual and emotional needs, in turn, reinforces the social structure of the society in which the religious ritual is a unit.

The use of this functionalist model has often been misunderstood. The explanation begins with religion present as a variable and then attempts to explain how it works in providing the self-regulation of the system. Failure to see the significance of this kind of explanation has often led to criticisms which are wide of the mark. The common mistake is to accuse functionalists who use self-adjusting models of not explaining why religion occurs, i.e. they fail to explain what causes religion. This often takes the following form. Let us assume that we have just read a functional explanation which makes it explicit that the model being used is a self-regulating one and that what is to be explained is how religion functions as a variable for providing equilibrium or adjustment as an effect; for example, that the belief in the existence of "Nats" among Burmese Buddhists, or in witchcraft among the Azande, functions to maintain social solidarity. The criticism of such an explanation often states that the belief has not really been explained. After all, the believer in "Nats" or witches is certainly not saying that he has acted in a way which will maintain social solidarity by believing in them or by performing a ritual which will protect him from their evil influences. The reason he believes in them, or performs certain rituals which are related to them is because he believes both that they exist and that they affect his life. If I asked a Shaivite why he believes in Shiva, I would certainly be surprised to hear that he believes in Shiva because Shiva is a symbolic representation of "perceptual sets" formed in early childhood and that, furthermore, such a belief reinforces both emotional and intellectual needs and the social structure as an unintended consequence.

The mistake we make in such critical replies is that the criticism is beside the point. We do not usually travel all the way to India, Africa or Burma, spend our lives reading ancient texts to report what is self-evident, that Azande believe in witches, Burmese Buddhists believe that "Nats" exist, and some Hindu's who belong to the Shaivite tradition believe in the existence of Shiva.

If a functionalist theory is explicit about the aims of the explanation, it should come as no surprise that an Azande or a Hindu does not make the same kinds of functional statements. Most scholars who are interested in explaining the function of religion are interested in the unintended consequences of the beliefs that are held and the rituals that are performed. What the functionalist is interested in is not primarily a report about these beliefs and rituals (as important as they are for an explanation), but the unintended consequences which these beliefs and rituals have for providing feedback into the regulation of the system. And if the functionalist can discover such unintended consequences, then it is surely odd to criticize the explanation because the believer did not report them when asked about the particular beliefs held. Once again, such an explanation would certainly advance our knowledge of religion.

If, however, we wish to take this approach to explain religion as providing feedback in a system of relations which is self-regulating, then it will become necessary to answer several important questions. Robert Brown has come up with three questions which require an answer. The first is, what property is being maintained in a steady state? Secondly, what are the internal variables and can they or their effects be measured? Finally, what are the external conditions which are assumed to be constant?21 No functionalist theory constructed on the model of a feedback system that I know of has come close to meeting the above requirements. In fact, I am not certain about how we could possibly meet them.

Let us imagine, for the moment, that it is conceivable that we could meet the requirements. We could begin by claiming that social solidarity or social equilibrium was the property which was being held in a steady state. We would then have to specify which of the variables or which single variable works to provide the steady state, and we would also have to provide a range of values to determine when the system is in equilibrium. To compound the difficulties, we would also have to specify which external threat of whatever kind could prevent the function of a unit from providing the necessary effects of maintaining the system.

We have discussed the difficulties of establishing whether a religious unit is a sufficient or necessary condition for maintaining a social system. In a self-regulating model, if the unit is a necessary condition for maintaining the system, we will then have to specify the exact relations which it maintains; since it would be most difficult to uphold the notion that a religious belief system, for example, functions to maintain all the relations in a social system. On the other hand, if we state that the unit is a sufficient condition, we then fail to explain exactly how the religious unit functions to satisfy the requirement. If we move to a class of units which jointly function to satisfy the needs of a society, we are reduced to trivial if not invalid conclusions. And no one as far as I know has been able to specify the external conditions which are constant or the degree of variation which will allow a social system to continue to maintain itself. Functionalism is at best a heuristic device, a strategy, for interpreting religion; heuristic devices are neither true nor false, they are in the domain of "your guess is as good as mine."

I believe that this conclusion is fully confirmed by the current debate among Marxists and other social scientists regarding the validity of functionalism in the corpus of publications, ever since Marx, which attempt to "explain" political/economic history.

Jon Elster, for example, offers us the following strong definition of a functional explanation: "On my definition then, an institution or a behavioral pattern X is explained by its function Y for group Z if and only if:

(1) Y is an effect of X;
(2) Y is beneficial for Z;
(3) Y is unintended by the actors producing X;
(4) Y (or at least the causal relationship between X and Y) is unrecognized by the actors in Z;
(5) Y maintains X by a causal feedback loop passing through Z."22

Elster admits that "a closer analysis of purported functionalist explanations shows that in virtually all cases one or more of the defining features are lacking." He then argues that "it is close to impossible to find any cases of functional analysis in sociology where the presence of all features (1)-(5) is demonstrated."23 Given the strong definition entailed in the "if and only if" clause, this is not a surprise. We are back to Hempel's argument. How would anyone claim that an institution or behavioral pattern X is explained by its function Y if and only if "Y is beneficial for Z?" Elster goes on to assert that there is a "naive brand of functional analysis... that from the presence of features (1), (3) and (4) concludes to the presence of feature (2) and often of feature (5). [Moreover,] there exists a more sophisticated brand of functionalism (represented by Merton) that from the presence of features (1)-(4) fallaciously concludes to the presence of feature (5)."24 I think that Elster's argument is correct. Feature (5) is precisely the mechanism, often called a "self-regulating system," which is fallaciously inferred from the presence of the other features.

In other words, functional explanations in the social sciences have turned biological explanations upside-down. Elster's quarrel with Cohen and other functionalists rests on this fundamental point. In his review of Cohen's book Elster asserts that "I believe that I have seen no other mechanism that comes closer to being for sociology what natural selection is for biology, even if this is not, to repeat, to say that it comes very close. Cohen, however, does not even attempt to provide such a mechanism, which is why I believe that his enterprise must be judged a failure."25

What we must not lose sight of in this particular debate is where we began. We began with the problem of why a particular social institution or behavioral pattern exists or persists in a society! In the complex and often confusing debate, this problem seems to disappear. Nevertheless, it remains the central issue, and as far as I can see it has not been answered or explained. As Anthony Giddens puts it, "I agree with most of the elements of Elster's critique of functionalism, and I take as radical a stance as he does in suggesting that functionalist notions should be excluded altogether from the social sciences."26 I think this is good advice.

In the discussion of phenomenology of religion, I pointed out that functionalism is often described as an auxiliary science for the study of religion. Although this claim is often held in contradiction with the claim that such an explanation is reductionistic, we often find anthropology, psychology, and sociology linked up with a phenomenology of religion as useful (and sometimes necessary) for a complete understanding of religion. We can abbreviate this claim by saying that for many phenomenologists of religion a complete study of religion must include both the nature (i.e., the essence) and the function of religion.

This partnership is an illusion. It is an illusion because functionalists do not attempt to explain the "essence" or nature of religion as The Sacred because they want to leave this research to other scholars of religion. The slogan "religion is what it does" is a clear indication that functionalist approaches to religion also involve a rejection of all forms of essentialism.

When biblical scholars, historians and phenomenologists of religion discover the theological roots of their discipline, they are often tempted to become unregenerate or revisionist functionalists. Both Drijvers and Leertouwer among others, seem to have yielded to this temptation. In their "Epilogue" they offer the following advice: "Van Baaren inquires what cultural function of religion still subsists when a great number of persons in the culture no longer feels any emotional or rational tie with religion. This question is not dependent on theological developments, but on the loss of function of the Christian religion in Western culture. In such a situation it becomes urgent to find the function of religion *tout court*."27 If my analysis of functionalism is accurate, I believe there are good reasons for not following this kind of methodological advice.

Given the nature of the problems we have described thus far, it would seem that we have reached a theoretical and methodological impasse in the study of religion. I think we have no one to blame but ourselves for this situation. The utter lack of concern about the methodological issues we face is symptomatic of the present condition in which we find ourselves. It is simply astonishing to discover that an academic discipline, a "science," of religion has little, if any, concern with theory. Perhaps we have been lulled into this slumber because we have become a part of our subject; "we do what we do because in the beginning our ancestors did it that way." If the impasse is of our own making, we can also overcome it. The following chapters are an attempt to describe a way out of theological disguises, the quest for essences, the ideology of neutrality, the bankruptcy of functionalism as a type of causal explanation, and sloppy methodological eclecticism. Please note that I wrote "a way out." There may be other ways that are more adequate -- I have not discovered them.

NOTES.

1. Mircea Eliade, *Myth and Reality*, trans. Willard R. Trask (New York: Harper, 1963) 19.

2. Eliade 20. The passage and its context is taken from Bronislaw Malinowski, *Magic, Science and Religion* (New York: Doubleday, 1954) 101 and 108.

3. See George C. Homans, "Anxiety and Ritual: The Theories of Malinowski and Radcliffe-Brown," *American Anthropologist* 43 (1941): 164-171, for the argument and references.

4. See Edmund Leach, *Genesis as Myth and Other Essays* (London: Cape, 1969) 85-112, for the argument and references. The argument is continued on in several issues of *Man*.

5. See Bryan R. Wilson, ed., *Rationality* (New York: Blackwell, 1971) chaps. 7 and 12, for the relevant arguments and references, and Martin Hollis and Steven Lukes, eds., *Rationality and Relativism* (Cambridge: MIT P, 1982) 201ff., for Horton's return to the issues.

6. Barry Barnes, "The Comparison of Belief-Systems: Anomaly Versus Falsehood," *Modes of Thought*, eds. Robin Horton and Ruth Finnegan (London: Faber, 1973) 193. Italics mine.

7. Melford E. Spiro, "Causes, Functions and Cross-Cousin Marriage: An Essay in Anthropological Explanation," *The Journal of the Royal Anthropological Institute of Great Britain and Ireland* 94 (1964): 30-43. Another useful essay which clearly defines the functional explanations is Melford E. Spiro, "Religion: Problems of Definition and Explanation," *Anthropological Approaches to the Study of Religion*, ed. Michael Banton (London: Tavistock, 1966).

8. Spiro, "Causes..." 34.

9. Carl G. Hempel, "The Logic of Functional Analysis," *Symposium on Sociological Theory*, ed. Llewellyn Gross (New York: Harper, 1959) 271-307. Hempel's essay has been reprinted in many anthologies; it is included in May Brodbeck, ed., *Readings in the Philosophy of the Social Sciences* (New York: Macmillian, 1968) and Carl G. Hempel, *Aspects of Scientific Explanation* (New York: Free, Free Press, 1965).

10. For a good example of this response see Robert N. McCauley and E. Thomas Lawson, "Functionalism Reconsidered," *History of Religions* 23 (1984): 372-381. It should be made clear that I do not disagree with them about the validity of functional explanations in biology. In such explanations, natural selection provides the mechanism which becomes the basis for arguing that beneficial consequences explain their own causes. McCauley and Lawson do not provide us with a similar mechanism in their "reconsideration" of functionalism in the social sciences. It is therefore impossible to determine just what their argument is all about. Appeal to biological explanations which do succeed based on the mechanism of natural selection simply begs the question. An excellent description of this mechanism in biology can be found in Ernst Mayr, *The Growth of Biological Thought* (Cambridge: Harvard UP, 1982), esp. chaps. 11, 12 and 13. I do not regard Herbert Burhenn's attempted revisions an adequate solution to the problems which beset functionalism. He does not make any attempt at defining

functional explanations, and his representation of Hempel is incomplete. Hempel's critique is certainly not concerned with the origin of cultural traits. Burhenn's attempt at revising functionalism from answering a "why" question into a "how-possibly" question seems to entail that he agrees with Hempel that functional explanations fail to answer "why" a cultural trait persists. What he seems to have overlooked is the argument that explanations similar to Dray's "how-possibly" presuppose an answer to the "why" question. Burhenn concludes his essay by stating that he has tried to show that functional explanations have "the possibility of being helpful in understanding religious phenomena...." They may indeed be helpful, heuristic devices. I know of no one who would want to argue the contrary. Once this is admitted, however, it seems clear that we have given up the central claims of functionalism as an explanation in the human sciences. And given the logical problems of this kind of explanation, I think it is only proper to ponder just how "helpful" such an approach really is for studying religion. See Herbert Burhenn, "Functionalism and the Explanation of Religion," *Journal for the Scientific Study of Religion* 19 (1980): 350-60. The quote is taken from page 359.

11. One of the best critiques I have found is Frederick Suppe, ed., *The Structure of Scientific Theories*, 2nd ed. (Urbana: U of Illinois P, 1977). Scholars in the study of religion who have become fascinated with Kuhn and Feyerabend will also find, to their dismay, a thorough critique of their positions in this volume. I have also found Peter Achinstein, *Concepts of Science* (Baltimore: Johns Hopkins UP, 1968) helpful in reflecting on the complexity of theoretical construction. See also Peter Achinstein and Stephen F. Barker, eds., *The Legacy of Logical Positivism* (Baltimore: Johns Hopkins UP, 1969). I think that the question which must be answered by those who are attracted by the notion of heuristic and imaginative devices in scientific discovery is where do hypotheses come from?

12. See I. C. Jarvie, *Functionalism* (Minneapolis: Burgess, 1973). See also I. C. Jarvie, "Limits to Functionalism and Alternatives to it in Anthropology," *Theory in Anthropology*, eds. Robert A. Manners and David Kaplan (Chicago: Aldine, 1968) 196-203 and Piotr Sztompka, *System and Function: Toward a Theory of Society* (New York: Academic, 1974). Sztompka's book is typical of much that has

been written about functional explanations; he mentions Hempel but curiously omits any analysis or criticism of Hempel's description of the logic of functional explanations. This cannot be said about G. A. Cohen's brilliant book *Karl Marx's Theory of History: A Defense* (Princeton: Princeton UP, 1978) esp. chaps. IX and X. I shall turn to the debate Cohen has generated later in this chapter. His thesis is that historical materialism stands or falls with the validity of functionalism as an explanation of history. His criticism of functional explanations in the social sciences and in Marxist writings is excellent. However, I do not believe that he succeeds in overcoming Hempel's basic arguments against the logic of such explanations. For a refutation of Cohen's thesis that "functional explanations in the social sciences can be successful," see Peter Halfpenny, "A refutation of historical materialism?" *Social Science Information* 22 (1983): 61-87.

13. I am indebted to my colleague Merrie Bergmann for this insight as well as other criticisms and suggestions on an earlier draft of the argument.

14. See Robert K. Merton, *Social Theory and Social Structure*, rev. and enl. ed. (Glencoe, Ill.: Free, 1957); E. Nagel, "A Formalization of Functionalism," *Logic Without Metaphysics* (Glencoe, Ill.: Free, 1957); Hempel, "The Logic of Functional Analysis"; and Jarvie, *Functionalism*. For a critique of the argument that religion is a necessary unit for the satisfactions of a need, see also Spiro, "Religion: Problems of Definition and Explanation" 117-121.

15. Melford E. Spiro, "Religion and the Irrational," *Symposium on New Approaches to the Study of Religion*, Proceedings of the 1964 Annual Meeting of the American Ethnological Society, ed. June Helm (Seattle: U of Washington P, 1964) 112-113.

16. Spiro, "Religion and the Irrational" 113. See also Melford E. Spiro, *Buddhism and Society*, 2nd, expanded ed. (Berkeley: U of California P, 1982).

17. Spiro, "Religion and the Irrational" 112.

18. Spiro, "Religion and the Irrational" 114.

19. Nagel 251-252. Also quoted in Robert Brown, *Explanation in Social Science* (Chicago: Aldine, 1963) 111; see also Jarvie, *Functionalism* 28-29.

20. Brown 110-111.

21. Brown 118-119.

22. Jon Elster, *Ulysses and the Sirens: Studies in Rationality and Irrationality* (Cambridge: Cambridge UP, 1979) 28.

23. Elster 28-29.

24. Elster 29.

25. Jon Elster, "Cohen on Marx's Theory of History," *Political Studies* XXVII (1980): 127. For Cohen's response see, G. A. Cohen, "Functional Explanations: Reply to Elster," *Political Studies* XXVII (1980): 129-35. For the current debate see the following articles in *Theory and Society* 11 (1982): Jon Elster, "Marxism, Functionalism and Game Theory" 453-82; G. A. Cohen, "Reply to Elster on 'Marxism, Functionalism and Game Theory'" 483-95; Philippe Van Parijs, "Functionalist Marxism Rehabilitated: A Comment on Elster" 497-511; Johannes Berger and Claus Offe, "Functionalism vs. Rational Choice" 521-26; and Anthony Giddens, "Commentary on the Debate" 527-39. Cohen's 1982 response is a version of G. A. Cohen, "Functional Explanation, Consequence Explanation, and Marxism," *Inquiry* 25 (1982): 27-56. For a revision of Elster's definition, see Russell Hardin, "Rationality, irrationality and functionalist explanation," *Social Science Information* 19 (1980): 755-72. For a critical review of Elster, see Steven Walt, "Rationality and Explanation," *Ethics* 94 (1983-84): 680-700.

26. Giddens, "Commentary on the Debate" 527.

27. Th. P. van Baaren and H. J. W. Drijvers, eds., *Religion, Culture and Methodology* (The Hague: Mouton, 1973) 168.

PART II RESOLUTION

CHAPTER FIVE

STRUCTURE AND LANGUAGE

When I was a graduate student, we did not study structuralism. The name of Lévi-Strauss was seldom heard, when spoken it was usually in the context of "reductionism." When you think about it, you might find it as strange as I do that in 1966 Geertz would open his well-known essay "Religion as a Cultural System" as follows: "Two characteristics of anthropological work on religion accomplished since the Second World War strike me as curious.... One is that it has made no theoretical advances of major importance.... The second is that it draws what concepts it does use from a very narrowly defined intellectual tradition [Durkheim, Weber, Freud, or Malinowski]."1 With a swipe at theologians, who curiously enough find Geertz worth quoting, and a condemnation of what in art is called "academicism," Geertz recommends that we follow Parsons and Shills!2 Those less innocent would surely note the absence of any mention of structuralism or the significant publications of Lévi-Strauss. Let us simply recall that "L'analyse structurale en linguistique et en anthopologie," appeared in Word in 1945. Some twenty years later the same mysterious silence can be found throughout the sixteen volumes of a new encyclopedia of religion.3
    Since most scholars interested in religion, for whatever reasons, have yet to take structuralism seriously, I feel obliged to start from the beginning. This chapter will, therefore, provide a brief description of the work of Saussure, who has become identified as the father of modern linguistics and structural analysis.

As Culler has pointed out, one cannot define structuralism by examining how the word is used. Anthologies on structuralism seem to indicate that structuralism has been around for a long time, that it is nothing new and has been practiced in such diverse disciplines as physics, logic and anthropology. If this is true, then I agree with Culler that an important fact is left unexplained. Although it took several years to arouse attention, it is without doubt Lévi-Strauss that brought structuralism into the academic battlefield.4 It may well be the case that the publications of Lévi-Strauss represented a contemporary vogue in France, but this by itself does not explain the explosion that took place once his work became known in Europe and America. Nor does it explain the controversy, at times bitter, concerning structuralism which has continued for over a decade. Structuralism, or structural analysis cannot be separated from the thought of Lévi-Strauss. After Lévi-Strauss, the study of kinship, totemism, myth and ritual would never be the same again. Kirk, who is anything but satisfied with structural analysis, sums this up as follows: "Yet it has been said that when one turns from Lévi-Strauss to any other attempt to analyze these myths, the results look old-fashioned and unconvincing; and I too find this to be so."5

Lévi-Strauss, however, did not create this new kind of analysis out of the air. Some of his early essays make it clear that his new insights were based on linguistics. Although he states that his primary debts are to Marx, Freud and Geology, it is Ferdinand de Saussure, especially in his Course In General Linguistics, that provided the conditions for a new discipline which Lévi-Strauss would call "structural anthropology."6

What then are the central postulates which define and limit the concept of "structure" as found in the works of Lévi-Strauss? The postulates come from Saussure who raised a basic question which is also crucial for Lévi-Strauss. After many years of intellectual despair concerning the study of language, Saussure asked the following important question: "is a science of language, linguistics, possible?" It is the same question which, as we have seen, was raised by historians and phenomenologists of religion in their quest for a "science of religion." The question, however, is a theoretical one, and Saussure was intensely aware of this fact.

Saussure begins his lectures with a critique of the study of language and quickly concludes that the historical-comparative study of language did not succeed in establishing a science of language. Why? Because, says Saussure, "it failed to seek out the nature of its object of study. Obviously, without this elementary step, no science can develop a method."7 The conceptualization of the object of linguistics entailed such new concepts as the differentiation of language (langue) from speech (parole), form from substance, synchrony from diachrony, and signifier from signified. Saussure's conceptualization of the object of linguistics led to the conclusion that "language then has the strange and striking, characteristic of not having entities that are perceptible at the outset and yet of not permitting us to doubt that they exist and that their functioning constitutes it," that "to be rid of illusions we must first be convinced that the concrete entities of language are not directly accessible."8 In brief, and this is of major importance, the object of linguistics is not immediately given.

I believe that this is a fundamental axiom of structuralism. Once it is fully understood, the necessity for conceptualization follows as a necessary consequence. The production of knowledge, that is, of theory, necessarily requires the conceptualization of the object of knowledge which is not given to us in immediate experience.   Thus, conceptualization of the object of our theory is the production of knowledge. In his analysis of Marx, Althusser states it this way; "To criticize Political Economy cannot mean to criticize or correct certain inaccuracies or points of detail in an existing discipline -- nor even to fill in its gaps, its blanks.... To criticize Political Economy means to confront it with a new problematic and a new object; i.e. to question the very object of Political Economy."9 And what was the object of Political Economy? Althusser answers, Homo Oeconomicus, the subject of needs. But as he points out, to define the object of knowledge in this way simply presupposes the "giveness" of man as the subject of needs. Thus, "it is the need (of the human subject) that defines the economic in economics."10

According to Althusser, Marx thoroughly rejected the "giveness" of the object in either its empirical or idealistic forms."11 The object of economics is not an empirical or ideal subject with a universal essence which is embodied as an attribute or property in each single individual.

The object was identified by new concepts such as forces of production, relations of production, use-value, and surplus value, which in turn were related to different levels of human practice. Althusser is surely correct when he writes that "the identification [of the economic] presupposes the construction of its concept."12 Or, as Lévi-Strauss puts it, "Explanation begins only when we have succeeded in constituting our object," "The mistake of Mannhardt and the Naturalist School was to think that natural phenomena are WHAT myths seek to explain, when they are rather the MEDIUM THROUGH WHICH myths try to explain facts which are themselves not of a natural order but a logical order."13

I cannot think of a more striking contrast between this conceptualization of our task and the approaches to the the study of religion we have gone through in part one. First structuralism does not explain language (or religion) as a "given." As we have seen, the object of study for the history and phenomenology of religion is homo religiosus, an empirical or ideal form which embodies the essence of religion in its "giveness." Structuralism clearly rejects this approach. Second, structural analysis also rejects explanations based on need, regardless of whether the need is described in ontological, sociological or psychological terms. These differences cannot be overemphasized. They are, I believe, the central issues in the debate about structuralism, and we shall be returning to them again in the next chapter.14

Saussure also concluded that linguistics, as a new science, would not succeed if the emphasis continued to be historical research. This conclusion follows from two basic insights. First, any attempt to found linguistics historically would soon encounter the problem that the evidence quickly vanishes as we work backwards; the rest is speculation. Second, a science of language based on history could never be completed for the simple reason that every new utterance would have to be taken into account. From a theoretical point of view, therefore, Saussure realized that linguistics must proceed synchronically.

It is important that we pause here for a moment before describing how Saussure developed his discovery. There is a curious agreement between Saussure's emphasis on the synchronic and the approaches to religion we have discussed in part one. Malinowski's brand of functionalism, for example, was clearly not a diachronic analysis of Trobriand culture. His opposition to this kind of analysis was not simply based upon the fact that his academic discipline studied cultures and societies that did not have written sources for recollecting the tradition. It was only when critics began to attack functionalism for not being able to take account of change that functionalists began talking about history and development; as if history accounted for change!

Historians and phenomenologists of religion have consistently argued against the "quest for origins" as a totally speculative enterprise. Moreover, the best known historians and phenomenologists of religion have not provided us with historical or diachronic descriptions of religion; they have developed an approach to the study of religion which is clearly typological. In fact, what distinguishes "modern" from "traditional" or "archaic" in Eliade's work is precisely what he called "the second fall," that is, "man's fall into history!" This may be as good a place as any to point out that Eliade's notion of "archaic man" is as mythical as "the second fall." Interpretations of Eliade that miss this point seriously distort his work. "Archaic man," the model upon which Eliade's edifice for myth, ritual and religious symbols stand, is an archetype, not an historical period of long ago. It is a powerful image. It is ironic, given this emphasis, that one of the basic criticisms brought to bear on structural studies, by both functionalists and phenomenologists, is that it is synchronic.

How, then did Saussure proceed to describe the object of linguistics? Since the lectures of Saussure, gathered together by his students and published as <u>Cours de linguistique générale</u>, are well known, I shall not review them. It will be necessary, however, to stress four fundamental principles which taken together provide a definition of Saussure's answer to the question, what is language? These principles, in turn, provide the foundation for what has become known as structuralism, or structural analysis.

Before describing the four principles, I think it is important to remember the extraordinary human conditions which confronted this bright intellect in his quest for a science of language. Jonathan Culler has captured it for us in the context of a letter Saussure wrote in 1894.

In Geneva," writes Culler, "his students were fewer and less advanced; he taught Sanscrit and historical linguistics generally. He married, fathered two sons, rarely traveled, and seemed to be settling into a decent provincial obscurity. He wrote less and less, and then painfully, reluctantly. In a letter of 1894, one of the few revealing personal documents we possess, he refers to an article which he has finally surrendered to an editor and continues: 'but I am fed up with all that, and with the general difficulty of writing even ten lines of good sense on linguistic matters. For a long time I have been above all preoccupied with the logical classification of linguistic facts and with the classification of the points of view from which we treat them; and I am more and more aware of the immense amount of work that would be required to show the linguist what he is doing.... The utter inadequacy of current terminology, the need to reform it and, in order to do that, to demonstrate what sort of object language is, continually spoil my pleasure in philology, though I have no dearer wish than not to be made to think about the nature of language in general. This will lead, against my will, to a book in which I shall explain, without enthusiasm or passion, why there is not a single term in linguistics which has any meaning for me. Only after this, I confess, will I be able to take up my work at the point I left off.'15

As we know, Saussure never wrote the book. He worked on Lithuanian and medieval German legends and was assigned to teach a course in general linguistics. He gave the lectures from 1907 to 1911, became ill in the summer of 1912 and died in February 1913 at the age of fifty-six. The famous text, published three years later in 1916, is a synthesis of his lectures made from the notes of his students by two editors (Bally and Sechehaye) who, as far as we know, never attended the course!

Looking at this from a different perspective, Benveniste wrote that "In 1916, amidst the clash of arms, who could have been concerned with a book on linguistics? Nietzsche's saying, that great events arrive on dove's feet, was never truer.... Saussure belongs henceforth to the history of European thought."16

What then is the object of language which would show the linguists "what they were doing?" As Benveniste expresses it, the fundamental principle, the first principle which is the foundation of Saussure's work on general linguistics, is that language, regardless of what approach we take, is always "a double entity, formed of two parts of which the one has no value without the other." This is, says Benveniste, "the center of the doctrine, the principle from which proceeds all the array of notions and distinctions that constitute the published course. Everything in language is to be defined in double terms; everything bears the imprint and seal of an opposing duality:

--the articulatory/acoustical duality;
--the duality of sound and sense;
--the duality of the individual and society;
--the duality of langue and parole;
--the duality of the material and the immaterial;
--the duality of the... paradigmatic and syntagmatic;
--the duality of sameness and opposition;
--the duality of the synchronic and the diachronic, etc.

And, once again, none of these terms thus placed in opposition has value by itself or refers to a substantial reality; each of them takes its value from the fact that it is in opposition to the other."17 Thus, the units of a language system (sounds, words, meanings) are constituted by their relations with other units in the system. Linguistic units as such have no prior or independent existence apart from the relations which define them.

The second principle in Saussure's course in general linguistics follows from the first. Language is a system of signs. A linguistic sign is a double entity. Saussure's notion of 'sign' also entails that language is not a nomenclature, a naming process which somehow connects a list of words with things that the words name. Here is what the Course describes as a linguistic sign: "The linguistic sign unites not a thing and a name, but a concept and a sound-image. The latter is not the material sound, a purely physical thing, but the psychological imprint of the sound, the impression it makes on our sense.... I call the combination of a concept and a sound-image a sign... [and] I propose to retain the word sign [signe] to designate the whole and to replace concept and sound-image respectively by signified [signifié] and signifier [signifiant]; the last two terms have the advantage of indicating the opposition that separates them from each other and from the whole of which they are parts."18 The relation between the signifier and the signified is the signification of the sign.

Saussure's definition of the sign as a double entity constituted by a signifier/signified leads to the important consequence that there are no pre-existent ideas before language; "Language can... be compared with a sheet of paper: thought is the front and the sound the back; one cannot cut the front without cutting the back at the same time; likewise in language, one can neither divide sound from thought nor thought from sound; the division could be accomplished only abstractly, and the result would either be pure psychology or pure phonology."19 It is important to notice as this point that Saussure does not include reference to some external thing as a component of signification. The relation, signifier/signified excludes reference.

This definition of the sign as composed of a relation between signifier/signified as signification leads Saussure to conclude that the nature of the sign is arbitrary. That is to say, the relation between signifier/signified is "unmotivated." The term "unmotivated" is an important one in Saussure's thought and in the development of structural linguistics. As opposed to "motivated," it means that the relation between signifier/signified is not a natural or necessary relation. Here is the example used in Course: "The idea of 'sister' is not linked by any inner relationship to the succession of sounds s-ö-r which serves as its signifier in French; that it could be represented equally by just any other sequence is proved by differences among languages and by the very existence of different languages: the signified "ox" has as its signifier b-ö-f on one side of the border and o-k-s (Ochs) on the other."20

Culler sums up this important point in the following way:

The fact that the relation between the signifier and the signified is arbitrary means, then, that since there are no fixed universal concepts or fixed universal signifiers, the signified itself is arbitrary, and so the signifier. We must then ask, as Saussure does, what defines a signifier or a signified, and the answer leads us to a very important principle; both signifier and signified are purely relational or differential entities."21

Thus, it is the relation between terms, between the signifier and the signified that defines them. | Once again, there is nothing outside, external, to language that determines the connection between a signifiant and a signifié. As Harris points out, this is the "theoretical core of structuralism,

> since Saussurean explanation is "archetypally holistic, and has to be.... The only necessary and sufficient condition for establishing the indentity of any individual sign is that it be distinct from other signs.... Therefore, Saussure accepts that adopting the principle that the linguistic sign is arbitrary forces us to conclude that it can only be the total network of interrelations which establishes individual connexions between signifiants and signifié."22

The third important principle in Saussure's structural linguistics is the distinction between language (langue) and speech (parole). We can easily see the difference between "language" and "speech" if we reflect upon the statement, "I speak a language." We can also say, "I use language to communicate." Thus, "language" is a system; "speech" is "use" of the system, also called "pragmatics." Speech is an act; speaking is behavior of a specific kind. Thus, from a formal point of view speech presupposes language, as in "I speak a language." Saussure's distinction between language and speech is compatible with Chomsky's well-known separation of "competence" from "performance" as a means of specifying the proper object of linguistics.23

For Saussure the distinction between language and speech leads to at least two important consequences. The first leads us into a description of language as a system of forms which are realized in the production of sounds/meanings and speech acts. The second consequence of the distinction is that it allows Saussure to identify the object of linguistics, by identifying the essential features which differentiate the signifying function of language. Culler once again provides us with a good summary of the distinction when he writes that,

> In brief, if the sign is arbitrary then, as we have seen, it is a purely relational entity, and if we wish to define and identify signs we must look to the system of relations and distinctions which create them. We must therefore distinguish between the various substances in which signs are manifested and the actual forms which constitute signs; and when we do this what we have isolated is a system of forms which underlies actual linguistic behavior or manifestation.24

Once the object of linguistics is established as the domain of language rather than speech, it should become obvious why it is the case that Saussure also stressed the importance of synchronic over diachronic analysis. This distinction stresses an analysis of language as a system in a particular state rather than an analysis of the evolution of language through time. Saussure was fond of using chess as an example to drive the point home. First, we do not need to know the history of chess in order to play chess. Second, we do not need to know the history of chess in order to analyze a particular state of a game in progress. But, we do need to know the system of chess in order to describe its history as well as analyze a particular state of the game in progress. These examples also help clarify the differences between, language/speech and competence/performance.

The distinction between synchronic and diachronic and the emphasis on the synchronic in structuralism has caused a great deal of criticism and anger. Given this emphasis, we often read that structuralism can be dismissed because it does not "take history seriously," or that structuralists simply ignore the fact that all cultural phenomena, including language, have a history. Such criticisms, especially in the study of religion, are simply not convincing. They are made in the same polemical context as accusations concerning "reductionism." The target is completely missed when the criticism is used against Saussure's structural theory of language.

First, let us remember that Saussure's search for an adequate theory of linguistics was based on a solid training in the history and comparison of languages. Thus, it is reasonable to assume that Saussure was well aware of the fundamental historicity of language. In fact, given his training, we may assume that history had greater significance for Saussure than it has for most contemporary historians and phenomenologists of religion. Second, it was precisely this awareness that led Saussure to the conclusion that it was necessary to draw a distinction between language as a system and language evolution. The arbitrary nature of the linguistic sign is clearly tied to the contingencies and evolution of history. Saussure well knew that language is subject to change. He knew that there were no essential properties in the nature of the sign which lie outside history. Thus, Saussure knew, far better than critics of synchronic analysis, that it was because language is indeed a historical phenomenon that it becomes necessary to construct a synchronic analysis which will establish the relations which constitute the complex elements of language.

Once again, I cannot improve on what Culler has said concerning why Saussure asserted the priority of synchronic analysis as necessary for an explanation of language. "In modern English," Culler writes,

the second-person pronoun you is used to refer both to one person and to many and can be either the subject or object in a sentence. In an earlier state of the language, however, you was defined by its opposition to ye on the one hand (ye a subject pronoun and you an object pronoun) and to thee and thou on the other (thee and thou singular forms and you a plural form).... Now in modern English you is no longer defined by its opposition to ye, thee and thou. One can know and speak modern English perfectly without knowing that you was once a plural and objective form, and indeed, if one knows this, there is no way in which this knowledge can serve as part of one's knowledge of modern English. The description of modern English you would remain exactly the same if its historical evolution had been wholly different, for you in modern English is defined by its role in the synchronic state of the language.25

Thus, diachronic facts are irrelevant to the analysis of language as a system. My competence, in the full Chomskyian sense of the term, in speaking English does not presuppose any knowledge of the history of the English language. To put it another way, the structure and meaning of the English language is not the sum of the changes that have taken place in the language throughout its history. Synchronic analysis is indeed "ahistorical." To assert this as a criticism of structural linguistics implies that historical analysis could take its place as a more adequate explanation of language as a system of signs. From Saussure's point of view, this is a distortion, if not an error, simply because synchronic and diachronic analysis focus on two different orders or levels of language which must not be confused. "Are facts of the diachronic series of the same class, at least, as facts of the synchronic series?" Saussure answers, "By no means, for we have seen that changes are wholly unintentional while the synchronic fact is always significant. It always calls forth two simultaneous terms. Not Gäste alone but the opposition Gast:Gäste expresses the plural. The diachronic fact is just the opposite: only one term is involved, and for the new one to appear (Gäste), the old one (Gasti) must first give way."26 The stress on the synchronic or the "idiosynchronic" is at the heart of the revolution in linguistics. Saussure's denial of the efficacy or adequacy of historical/comparative linguistics is anchored in the principle that signs are arbitrary.27

All of this suggests that had Lévi-Strauss, to move ahead of ourselves, taken this Saussurian principle seriously he would not have had to hedge his discussion with Ricoeur about his synchronic analysis of myth as dependent on the fact that the myths he examines derive from societies who have no written record, no "history." Lévi-Strauss knows better. He knows, for example, that what we describe as "archaic societies" are actually the result of historical ruptures.

The fourth and final principle I wish to describe is also a consequence of the first principle about the duality of linguistic entities. It is fundamental to structural linguistics because it defines a term which we have been using all along. The term is "relation." The Course in General Linguistics defines relation as either "syntagmatic" or "associative" (now usually called "paradigmatic"). Saussure claimed that language as a system could be defined by these two kinds of relation. Syntagmatic relations define the possible combinations that a linguistic unit may enter with other units. For example, the lexeme "old" is syntagmatically related with the definite article "the" and the noun "cat" in the syntagm, "the old cat." Moreover, the letter "e" is syntagmatically related with "l" and "d" in the lexeme "led." Furthermore, as Culler points out, nouns can be partially defined by the combinations (syntagmatic relations) which they can enter into with prefixes and suffixes, for example, "friendless," "friendship," and "befriend," but not "*friender," or "*overfriend." Saussure claimed that syntagmatic relations define all the possible combinatory relations on all levels of a linguistic system from the phoneme up through syntactic and semantic relations.

Paradigmatic relations define the possible oppositions between units which can be substituted for one another in a syntagm. In our first example, "The old cat," "young," "small" and "sick" are paradigmatically related to "old" since they can be substituted for "old" in the syntagm, just as "man" is paradigmatically related to "cat." Moreover, the phoneme /a/ and /i/ are in paradigmatic relation with /e/ in the lexeme "led."

This all seems straightforward. It is, however, important to stress that it is the syntagmatic and paradigmatic relations, the possible combinatory and contrastive relations, which define the units of language on all levels. "The ultimate law of language," wrote Saussure, "is, dare we say, that nothing can ever reside in a single term. This is a direct consequence of the fact that linguistic signs are unrelated to what they designate, and that therefore, a cannot designate anything without the aid of b and vice versa, or, in other words, that both have value only by the differences between them, or that neither has value, in any of its constituents, except through this same network of forever negative differences."28   It is since the work of Saussure that linguists have recognized that the binary relation of opposition is central to the structure of a language as a system.

What must be remembered is that the foundation of Saussure's development of linguistics is holistic. It is crucial to his thought about language and essential for the development of structuralism. In conclusion, then, we can summarize Saussure's position as follows: "...to consider a term as simply the union of a certain sound with a certain concept is grossly misleading. To define it in this way would isolate the term from its system; it would mean assuming that one can start from the terms and construct the system by adding them together when, on the contrary, it is from the interdependent whole that one must start and through analysis obtain its elements."29 And just in case we missed the significance to this assertion, Saussure drove the point home once again by stating that, "Language is a system of interdependent terms in which the value of each term results solely from the simultaneous presence of the others...."30 It was Lévi-Strauss who recognized that this theory might indeed have important implications for an understanding of culture. We are now prepared to enter this new development in the human sciences.

NOTES.

1. Clifford Geertz, "Religion as a Cultural System," *Anthropological Approaches to the Study of Religion*, ed. Michael Banton (London: Tavistock, 1966) 1.

2. Geertz 2-3.

3. Mircea Eliade, ed., *The Encyclopedia of Religion*, 16 vols. (New York: Macmillan, 1987). As you may recall from the introduction, I mentioned that the article on "myth" mentions Lévi-Strauss in passing but omits him in the bibliography; the article on "myth and history" cites *Mythologiques* in the bibliography but fails to mention this or other works by Lévi-Strauss in the text. And if you want to know the meaning of "damned with faint praise" read the article on "Structuralism" written by Edmund Leach.

4. See Jonathan Culler, *Structuralist Poetics* (London: Routledge, 1975) 3.

5. G. S. Kirk, *Myth: Its Meaning and Function in Ancient and Other Cultures* (Cambridge: Cambridge UP, 1973) 63.

6. See Ino Rossi, "On the Assumptions of Structural Analysis: Revisiting its Linguistic and Epistemological Premises," *The Logic of Culture*, ed. Ino Rossi (South Hadley, Mass.: Bergen, 1982) 3-22; David Pace, *Claude Lévi-Strauss* (Boston: Routledge, 1983) 158ff.; and also Howard Gardner, *The Mind's New Science* (New York: Basic, 1985) 236ff.

7. Ferdinand de Saussure, *Course in General Linguistics*, eds. Charles Bally and Albert Sechehaye with Albert Reidlinger, trans. Wade Baskin (New York: Philosophical Library, 1959) 3.

8. Saussure 197, 110

9. Louis Althusser and Etienne Balibar, *Reading Capital*, trans. Ben Brewster, 2nd ed. (London: NLB, 1977) 158.

10. Althusser and Balibar 163.

11. Louis Althusser, *For Marx*, trans. Ben Brewster (London: NLB, 1977) 228ff.

12. Althusser and Balibar 183.

13. Claude Lévi-Strauss, *The Savage Mind* (Chicago: U of Chicago P, 1966) 250 and 95.

14. For a crisp description of these differences and contrasts, see Ino Rossi, "Lévi-Strauss' Theory of Kinship and Its Empiricist Critics: An Anti-Needham Position," *The Logic of Culture* 42-67.

15. Jonathan Culler, *Ferdinand de Saussure* (New York: Penguin, 1976) 3-5. I shall follow Culler's text in my description of the four principles. I have also found John Lyons, *Semantics*, vol.I (Cambridge: Cambridge UP, 1977) useful; see esp. chap. 8, "Structural semantics I: semantic fields." For an excellent analysis of the text, Saussure's theory and the developments of semiology, see E. F. K. Koerner, *Ferdinand de Saussure* (Braunschweig: Vieweg, 1973). See also Roy Harris, *Reading Saussure* (La Salle, Ill.: Open Court, 1987). Harris' critical commentary of the *Course* should become the standard for future work on Saussure's lectures.

16. Emile Benveniste, *Problems in General Linguistics* (Coral Gables, Fla.: U of Miami P, 1971) 39-40. Benveniste's essay, "Saussure After Half a Century," is an excellent companion piece to Culler's, "The Man and the Course," in the work cited above. Benveniste also quotes from the same letter in more detail which Saussure wrote to Meillet in 1894.

17. Benveniste 35-36.

18. Saussure 66-67.

19. Saussure 113.

20. Saussure 67-68.

21. Culler 14-15. Although Saussure's emphasis on the importance of the arbitrary nature of the sign has been accepted by many linguists, the principle has been rejected by Benveniste in his essay, "The Nature of the Linguistic Sign." According to Benveniste, Saussure slipped, in spite of himself, into thinking that the difference between b-ö-f and o-k-s applied, or referred, to the same "reality." For Benveniste, "Between the signifier and the signified, the connection is not arbitrary; on the contrary it is *necessary*." Benveniste clinches his argument by appealing to Saussure's own statement that "Language can also be compared with a sheet of paper: thought is the front and the sound the back...." (quoted above). See *Problems in General Linguistics*, chap. 4. We shall return to this important essay in the next chapter.

22. Harris 220.

23. I am well aware of the dispute between Chomsky, his students and structuralists. The controversy is confusing because of the difference between "structuralists" of the American Bloomfieldian type and their European counterparts. See John Lyons, *Semantics*, vol. I, especially pages 230ff. for an analysis of the confusion. Lyons asserts that, "What must be emphasized, however, in view of the polemical associations which attach to the term 'structuralism' in the works of Chomsky and other generative grammarians... is that there is, in principle, no conflict between generative grammar and Saussurian structuralism, especially when what we are calling Saussurian structuralism is combined, as it has been in certain interpretations... with functionalism and universalism" (230). This conclusion from a well-known linguist casts serious doubt on the distinction which Ricoeur makes between "structural linguistics" and "generative linguistics" in his analysis of structuralism. See Paul Ricoeur, *The Conflict of Interpretation: Essays in Hermeneutics* (Evanston, Ill.: Northwestern UP, 1974). Ricoeur prolongs the confusion by equating structuralism of the Saussurian type with "taxonomies." Ino Rossi has provided us with an excellent analysis of what he calls "transformational structuralism" in his comparison of Saussure, Lévi-Strauss, Chomsky and Althusser. See Ino Rossi, *From the Sociology of Symbols to the Sociology of Signs* (New York: Columbia UP, 1983).

24. Culler 28.

25. Culler 31.

26. Saussure 85.

27. See Harris for a complete analysis of these concepts and the problems they raise as well as the important correction of the mistaken interpretation of "diachronic" as a synonym for "history."

28. Quoted in Culler 49.

29. Saussure 113.

30. Saussure 114.

CHAPTER SIX

STRUCTURALISM, ANTHROPOLOGY AND LEVI-STRAUSS

Let me begin this chapter by clarifying a possible misunderstanding. I am not claiming that Lévi-Strauss read Saussure and put structural anthropology together from what he read. A great deal of work in linguistics was accomplished between the time the lectures of Saussure were published and the first publications of Lévi-Strauss. Many scholars who have read Lévi-Strauss think that Jakobson had far more influence on his development of structural anthropology than did Saussure.1 This may well be the case. All I wish to claim is that Saussure is always in the background and often comes to the foreground of Lévi-Strauss's thought. Under normal circumstances it would be embarrassing to add that the corpus of his writings is not a theoretical canon. Nevertheless, I do think that the approach Lévi-Strauss takes is well worth defending for the study of religion.

Let us start with Saussure once again. At the beginning of the Course, he had this to say about the place of linguistics in the human sciences (or at least this is what his students wrote in their notebooks):

> Language is a system of signs that expresses ideas and is therefore comparable to a system of writing, the alphabet of deaf-mutes, symbolic rites, polite formulas, military signals, etc. But it is the most important of these systems.
>
> A science that studies the life of signs within society is conceivable; it would be a part of social psychology and consequently of general psychology; I shall call it semiology (from the Greek semion 'sign'). Semiology would show what constitutes signs, what laws govern them. Since the science does not yet exist, no one can say what it would be; but it has a

right to existence, a place staked out in advance. Linguistics is only a part of the general science of semiology; the laws discovered by semiology will be applicable to linguistics, and the latter will circumscribe a well-defined area within the mass of anthropological facts.2

In his inaugural address for the chair of social anthropology at the Collège de France, Lévi-Strauss asked the following question: "What, then, is social anthropology?" He answered as follows:

Although he did not specifically name it, Ferdinand de Saussure came very close to defining it when he introduced linguistics as part of a science yet to be born, for which he reserved the name 'semiology'.... We conceive anthropology as the bona fide occupant of that domain of semiology which linguistics has not already claimed for its own." Four years earlier, he asserted that "From the standpoint with which we are concerned here, linguistics is in a very special position. It is classified as one of the sciences of man, but it is concerned with social phenomenon, for language not only implies life in a society but is indeed the very foundation of that life. What sort of society could there be without language? It is the most perfect and most complex of those communication systems in which all social life consists and with which all the social sciences, each in its special field, are concerned.

Consequently, we may say that any revolution in linguistics is pertinent alike to the social sciences and the sciences of man. Between 1870 and 1920, two basic ideas were introduced into this sphere -- first under the influence of the Russian, Beaudoin de Courtenay, and later under that of the Swiss, Saussure. The first was that language is made up of separate elements, or phonemes; the second, that it is possible, by linguistic analysis, to work out systems or in other words, combinations governed by some law of cohesion, in which, as a result, changes occurring in one part necessarily entail others, that can therefore be foreseen.3

And again, "Anthropology aims to be a semiological science and takes as a guiding principle that of 'meaning.' This is yet another reason (in addition to others) why anthropology should maintain close contact with linguistics where, with regard to this social fact of speech, there is the same concern to avoid separating the objective basis of language (sound) from its signifying function (meaning)."4 It is this inheritance from Saussure which permeates what Levi-Strauss has written. The project is to investigate all levels and aspects of culture as a system of signs.

But this inheritance has a curious, if not important, ambiguity in it. In spite of all that has been written about Lévi-Strauss as a formalist unconcerned with history, it is precisely Saussure's radical opposition between the synchronic and diachronic that bothers him. Lévi-Strauss accepts the description of the synchronic as a relation between "simultaneous elements" and the diachronic as "the substitution of one element for another in time, an event." What he rejects from the Course is the notion that there is nothing in common between the synchronic and the diachronic, or, that they are in radical opposition to each other. "This," says Lévi-Strauss, "is the very aspect of Saussurian doctrine from which modern structuralism, with Trubetzkoy and Jakobson, has most resolutely diverged, and about which modern documents show that the master's thought has at times been forced and schematized by the editors of the Course." He then goes on to assert that "For the editors of Course in General Linguistics, an absolute opposition exists between two categories of fact: on the one hand, that of grammar, the synchronic, the conscious; on the other hand, that of phonetics, the diachronic, the unconscious."5

Now unless the editors of the course got the lectures completely wrong, Lévi-Strauss, I think, must be mistaken in the above description of the Saussurian distinction between the synchronic and diachronic. (As we can see, when we disagree with Saussure we can always blame the editors.) Without entering into the debate about the author vs. his editors, I believe that Lévi-Strauss has distorted what Saussure had in mind in using these important distinctions. We must assume that Saussure did use chess as an example at three different times in the lectures. The first is an excellent example of chess as an analogy of system and the synchronic. The origins of chess, whether we use ivory pieces, toothpicks, or no pieces at all, are irrelevant to chess as a synchronic system based on rules. The elements of the game (the pieces) are defined by the relations they enter into as defined by the rules.

In the second example, Saussure uses chess once again to illustrate the synchronic state in language. First, the respective value of the various pieces depends on their position on the board "just as each linguistic term derives its value from its opposition to all the other terms." Second, "the system is always momentary," and finally, to pass from one synchronic state to the next, only one piece has to be moved, which has an effect on the whole system, including those pieces which are not immediately involved. "In chess, each move is absolutely distinct from the preceding and the subsequent equilibrium. The change effected belongs to neither state: only states matter." Saussure then discovers a glaring weakness in this analogy. He realizes that it is the "chessplayer [who] intends to bring about a shift and thereby to exert an action on the system, whereas language premeditates nothing." He corrects this by asserting, "In order to make the game of chess seem at every point like the functioning of language, we would have to imagine an unconscious or unintelligent player."6 The context tells us that Saussure is describing synchronic states, which as the example demonstrates have nothing to do with "consciousness" or "intentions." In fact, by stressing the weakness of his analogy and correcting it, Saussure is satisfied that the correction, imagining an unconscious player, makes the analogy between chess and language fit at every point of comparison.

Thus, I think that Lévi-Strauss has made a mistake about the nature of the synchronic and diachronic in the Course. There seems to be no doubt that Saussure did mark them as in opposition to each other and that this opposition is absolute. It is this radical distinction between the two domains that Lévi-Strauss rejects and it is this revision of structural linguistics that has important consequences for what Lévi-Strauss has to say about history.

In his response to the criticisms of Haudricourt and Granai, Lévi-Strauss reduced their misunderstandings to two fundamental errors.

The first is that the criticism overemphasized the arbitrary nature of language in contrast to the non-arbitrary nature of other cultural phenomena. The second error is based on an overemphasis on the contrast between the synchronic and the diachronic. Lévi-Strauss attempts to correct both of these errors by appealing to Jakobson who claimed that it was an illusion, both superficial and dangerous, to create a chasm between the synchronic and the diachronic. The first error was corrected by Benveniste who thought that the relation between the signifier and signified was in fact a necessary relation, and therefore, not at all arbitrary.7

I think that anyone who has worked through the literature would agree that it is a mistake to make a radical distinction between the synchronic and the diachronic in an analysis of language. In fact, it might be best to view these terms as methodological devices which are useful in making important distinctions in our analysis of the object of linguistics rather than being inherent features of language. Be that as it may, I am not satisfied with Levi-Strauss's solution to the criticism concerning the arbitrary nature of language. Here, briefly, is his solution to the problem:

> To simplify my argument, I will say that the linguistic sign is arbitrary a priori, but ceases to be arbitrary a posteriori. Nothing existing a priori in the nature of certain preparations made of fermented milk requires the sound-form fromage [cheese], or rather, from (since the ending is shared with other words). It is sufficient to compare the French froment [wheat], whose semantic content is entirely different, to the English word cheese, which means the same thing as fromage, though it utilizes different phonemic material. So far, the linguistic sign appears to be arbitrary.
>
> On the other hand, it is in no way certain that these phonemic options, which are arbitrary in relation to the designatum, do not, once the choice has been made, imperceptibly affect, perhaps not the general meaning of words, but their position within a semantic environment.

This a posteriori influence works on two levels, the phonemic and the lexical.8

Lévi-Strauss sums up this complicated statement with "If we admit, therefore, in accordance with the Saussurian principle, that nothing compels, a priori, certain sound clusters to <u>denote certain objects</u>, it appears probable, nonetheless, that once they are adopted, these sound clusters transmit particular shadings to the semantic content with which they have become associated."9

This reply to his critics makes the same mistake that Benveniste points out that Saussure made when he claimed that language (signs) is arbitrary. Although we have referred to Benveniste's correction in the last chapter, it now becomes necessary to describe it more fully. Benveniste recognizes that Saussure is the source for the idea of the linguistic sign in works on general linguistics and he accepts it as an obvious truth that Saussure thought that the linguistic sign was arbitrary. He also recognizes that this notion has become obvious to everyone else who cites it in publications on linguistics. In his celebrated essay, Benveniste sets out to explain what Saussure meant by the term "arbitrary" and how he went about proving it.

Here are the central points made by Benveniste on Saussure's doctrine of the arbitrariness of the sign.

Saussure took the linguistic sign to be made up of a signifier and signified. Now--and this is essential--he meant by 'signifier' the <u>concept</u>. He declared in so many words that the 'linguistic sign unites, not a thing and a name, but as concept and a sound image.' But immediately afterward he stated that the nature of the sign is arbitrary because it 'actually has no natural connection with the signified.' It is clear that the argument is falsified by an unconscious and surreptitious recourse to a third term which was not included in the initial definition. This third term is the thing itself, the reality.... When he spoke of the difference between b-ö-f and o-k-s, he was referring in spite of himself to the fact that these two terms applied to the same reality. Here, then, is the thing, expressly excluded at first from the definition of the sign, now creeping into it by detour, and permanently installing a contradiction here." He goes on to assert that "One of the components of the sign, the sound image, makes up the signifier; the other, the concept, is the signified. Between the signifier and the signified, the connection is not arbitrary; on the contrary it is necessary. The concept (the 'signified') boeuf is perforce identical in my consciousness with the sound sequence (the 'signifier') böf.... The mind does not contain empty forms, concepts without names.... The signifier is the phonic translation of a concept; the signified is the mental counterpart of the signifier. This consubstantiality of the signifier and the signified assures the structural unity of the linguistic sign.[10]

And then Benveniste appeals to Saussure: "Language can also be compared with a sheet of paper: thought is the front and the sound the back; one cannot cut the front without cutting the back at the same time; likewise in language, one can neither divide sound from thought nor thought from sound; the division could be accomplished only abstractedly, and the result would be either pure psychology or pure phonology."[11] Thus, what is arbitrary is the fact that one sign and no other is applied to a certain object, or thing, in the world. What Saussure demonstrated was that it is not the sign that is arbitrary but "signification," the designatum. If I understand this correctly, reference to an object, to something "in reality," is bracketed in structural linguistics.

The proper reply that Lévi-Strauss should have given his critics is that although the relation, the signification, between a sign and a thing in "reality" is indeed arbitrary this is irrelevant to an analysis of the nature of signs. He seems to assert this when he says that "The meaning of a word depends on the way in which each language breaks up the realm of meaning to which the word belongs; and it is a function of the presence or absence of other words denoting related meanings."[12] The problem of the relation of language to the world is, I believe, yet to be resolved. The early success of linguistics came about because it set aside the problem of semantics. Let us remember that linguistics, the study of signs, did not begin with "signification" as the fundamental object for analysis. This does not mean that "signification" is not a problem, it is as old as Plato's Cratylus and Cratylus has yet to return from the countryside with an answer. As we shall see, Lévi-Strauss remains for the most part consistent with the structuralist focus on the sign, and not signification, as the object of analysis.

He has also remained consistent in maintaining that the synchronic and diachronic are not to be viewed as in radical opposition. The criticism, therefore, that Lévi-Strauss operates purely on a synchronic level, or thinks that the diachronic is simply the synchronic in its transformations through time, misses the mark. To be sure, Lévi-Strauss can become his own worst enemy in creating dense stylistic paragraphs and mind-boggling examples on this subject. In most instances, however, I think that setting his remarks in their proper context helps make his position clear.

The common criticism on Lévi-Strauss' use of synchrony and diachrony is usually set in the context of the suspicion that he is an idealist, a formalist, if not an outright Hegelian.13 In most of such criticisms, these are labels which represent a characteristic unwillingness to take him seriously, defensive walls set up to protect positions he has threatened by his own criticism of historicism, naturalism, phenomenology, and essentialism.

An influential critic of Lévi-Strauss goes after him from a different perspective; Marxism. After describing the Hegelian notion of time and history, Althusser writes:

> I have insisted on the nature of historical time and its theoretical conditions to this extent because this [Hegelian] conception of history and of its relation to time is still alive amongst us, as can be seen from the currently widespread distinction between synchrony and diachrony.... The synchronic is contemporaneity itself, the co-presence of the essence with its determinations, the present being readable as a structure in an 'essential section' because the present is the very existence of the essential structure. The synchronic

therefore presupposes the ideological conception of a continuous-homogeneous time. It follows that the diachronic is merely the development of this present in the sequence of a temporal continuity in which the 'events' to which 'history' in the strict sense can be reduced (cf. Lévi-Strauss) are merely successive contingent presents in the time continuum.14

Nothing could be farther from the truth! Rather than simply stating this and then writing "cf. Lévi-Strauss" in parentheses, as is usually the practice, let us actually take a look at what Lévi-Strauss says. Let us also choose a text, The Savage Mind, which was in print before Althusser published his own book.

In describing "The Logic of Totemic Classifications," Lévi-Strauss writes,

Whenever social groups are named, the conceptual system formed by these names is, as it were, prey to the whims of demographic change which follows its own laws but is related to it only contingently. The system is given, synchronically, while demographic changes take place diachronically, in other words there are two determinations, each operating on its own account and independently of the other. This conflict between synchrony and diachrony is also found on the linguistic plane.... Nevertheless the connection between synchrony and diachrony is not rigid.15

Here is a second example in the context of an analysis of an Osage legend,

The legend suggests twin processes. One is purely structural, passing from a dual to a three-fold system and then returning to the earlier dualism; the other, both structural and historical at the same time, consists in undoing the effects of an overthrow of the primitive structure, resulting from historical events, or events thought of as such: migrations, war, alliance.16

In the same context, Lévi-Strauss quotes M. Roger Priouret's concluding words at a conference (I shall paraphrase for the sake of brevity): "We are faced with two diametrically opposed theories. Raymond Aron thinks there are two basic political attitudes in France, Bonapartist and Orleanist. In moments of crisis France changes its attitude from one to the other. My view is that although actual change is not independent of these constants the change is connected with upheavals which industrialization brings into society." Lévi-Strauss then adds, "The Osage would probably have used these two types of opposition, one synchronic and the other diachronic, as a point of departure. Instead of expecting to be able to choose between them, they would have accepted both on the same footing and would have tried to work out a single scheme which allowed them to combine the standpoint of structure and event."17 In reflecting on "Categories, Elements, Species, Numbers," he writes, "Even if consciously or unconsciously, they apply rules of marriage whose effect is to keep the social structure and rate of reproduction constant, these mechanisms never function perfectly; and they are also endangered by wars, epidemics, and famines. It is thus plain that history and demographic developments always upset the plans conceived by the wise. In such societies there is a constantly repeated battle between synchrony and diachrony from which it seems that diachrony must emerge victorious every time."18

The variations on the Althusserian misunderstanding are so widespread that I shall refer to one more statement from Lévi-Strauss. In "Time Regained" he has this to say about the synchronic and the diachronic in the context of myth and ritual:

It can thus be said that the function of the system of ritual is to overcome and integrate three oppositions: that of diachrony and synchrony; that of the periodic or non-periodic features which either [i.e. historical or mourning rites] may exhibit; and finally, within diachrony, that of reversible and irreversible time, for, although the present and past are theoretically distinct, the historical rites bring the past into the present and the rites of mourning the present into the past, and the two processes are not equivalent.19

We must also keep in mind the larger context which sets the framework for this analysis. There is indeed a polemic running through what Levi-Strauss has to say. In "History and Dialectic" he makes clear what it is he opposes. He rejects those philosophies which attach a special privilege to historical knowledge and the temporal dimension as if "diachrony were to establish a kind of intelligibility not merely superior to that provided by synchrony, but above all more specifically human.... History seems to do more than describe beings to us from the outside, or at best give us intermittent flashes of insight into internalities, each of which are so on their own account while remaining external to each other: it appears to re-establish our connection, outside ourselves, with the very essence of change." He then says, "There could be plenty to say about this supposed totalizing continuity of the self which seems to me to be an illusion sustained by the demands of social life -- and consequently a reflection of the external on the internal -- rather than the object of an apodictic experience." After an analysis of the claim that historical knowledge is somehow privileged, Lévi-Strauss concludes that historical facts are no more given than any others.20 This argument is similar to his rejection, throughout all of his publications, of claims such as those made by Levy-Bruhl that the mentality of "primitives" is different than ours or that, through some kind of historical evolution of stages, it is we who have reached the summit of rationality.

It would seem that Lévi-Strauss is closer to Althusser than he is to Hegel. Let us return to the last quotation in the above paragraph. What more could be said about the supposed totalizing continuity of the self which seems to Lévi-Strauss to be an illusion, "sustained by the demands of social life -- and consequently a reflection of the external on the internal -- rather than an object of an apodictic experience?" The first thing that can be said is that Lévi-Strauss in this passage is clearly rejecting the Cartesian cogito as well as all phenomenological notions of a transcendental subjectivity or ego. Secondly, he is also rejecting all forms of idealism. He was well aware of the fact that given what he wrote about society and culture he would be accused of idealism. He was right.

I do not wish to misunderstood. I am not mounting a defense of Lévi-Strauss against his critics.21 There is sufficient evidence to confirm that he is capable of defending himself. The task at present is to clarify structural analysis by an examination of its beginnings in the work of Lévi-Strauss. This is important simply because it is not an uncommon practice to read critiques or reviews instead of the actual text. A good example which should confirm or disconfirm the above accusation is the subject of ideology. What then has Lévi-Strauss actually said about ideology and its place in history and philosophy?

He has said that, "I do not at all mean to suggest that ideological transformations give rise to social ones. Only the reverse is true. Men's conception of the relations between nature and culture is a function of modifications of their own social relations."22 And he repeats this claim several pages later:

> Here again I do not mean to suggest that social life, the relations between man and nature, are a projection or even result, of a conceptual game taking place in the mind.... Without questioning the undoubted primacy of infrastructures, I believe that there is always a mediator between praxis and practices, namely the conceptual scheme by the operation of which matter and form, neither with any independent existence, are realized as structures, that is as entities which are both empirical and intelligible. It is to this theory of superstructures, scarcely touched on by Marx, that I hope to make a contribution. The development of the study of infrastructures proper is a task which must be left to history -- with the aid of demography, technology, historical geography and ethnography.... All that I claim to have shown so far is, therefore, that the dialectic of superstructures, like that of language, consists in setting up constitutive units (which, for this purpose, have to be defined unequivocally, that is by contrasting them in pairs) so as to be able by means of them to elaborate a system which plays the part of a

synthesizing operator between ideas and facts, thereby turning the latter into signs.23

In a note to his analysis of "The Story of Asdiwal," he reminds us once again that, "From the very beginning the myth seems governed by one particular opposition which is more vital than the others... that between earth and water which is also the one most closely linked with methods of production and the objective relationships between men and the world. Formal though it be, analysis of a society's myths verifies the primacy of the infrastructures."24

Ten years earlier he put it this way:

All the models considered so far, however, are 'lived-in' orders: they correspond to mechanisms which can be studied as part of objective reality [i.e. infrastructures]. But no systematic studies of these orders can be undertaken without acknowledging the fact that social groups, to achieve their reciprocal ordering need to call on orders of different types, corresponding to a field external to objective reality and which we call the 'supernatural.' These 'thought-of' orders [i.e. superstructures] cannot be checked against the experience to which they refer, since they are one and the same as this experience. Therefore, we are in the position of studying them only in their relationships with the other types of 'lived-in' orders.25

It is within this context, I think, that Lévi-Strauss' famous definition of myth can be fully understood. "The purpose of myth," says Lévi-Strauss, "is to provide a logical model capable of overcoming a contradiction (an impossible achievement if, as it happens, the contradiction is real), a theoretically infinite number of slates will be generated, each one slightly different from the others."26 Overcoming a contradiction will be an impossible achievement if, as it happens, the contradiction is "real," that is to say, if the contradiction is inherent in the infrastructure, the objective conditions of existence, the "lived-in" order of human existence. In brief, "existence is not determined by consciousness, but consciousness by existence."27

These passages should confirm that Lévi-Strauss's brand of structuralism is not a philosophically transformed extension of Hegelian or Kantian idealism. But, it must also be noted that it is not an extension of "vulgar" Marxism either! From a personal point of view, I think that when a new approach appears in the history of the human sciences that is attacked by both phenomenological idealism and Marxian materialism, as well as from the side of British and American empiricist/functionalism, then it might just be the case that this new approach deserves careful attention. Lévi-Strauss must be doing something right!

Personal opinion aside, Lévi-Strauss is vulnerable precisely because of the position he takes. Scholars from different disciplines who are sympathetic with what he has accomplished have pointed out in one way or the other that what has not been resolved is the precise relations between the infrastructure and the superstructure, between the "lived-in" and "thought-of" orders of life. Lévi-Strauss cannot evade this issue by stating that the one belongs to ethnography and the other to ethnology, or that one belongs to history, the other to psychology. But, Lévi-Strauss is also aware of the fact that an analysis of the relation between the material conditions (infrastructure) of existence and ideology (superstructure) cannot simply be solved by a return to functionalism, even though at times he does seem to slip back into this type of explanation. He is also aware of the fact that the history of social infrastructures and superstructures does not explain anything; it is the history that needs to be explained. Although I shall not make an attempt to solve this crucial problem, I think that specialists in the study of religion could provide competence and knowledge which would be an important contribution towards resolving it.28 I am not optimistic that this contribution will be forthcoming. If my critique of the history and phenomenology of religion is accurate, then it should become apparent that these disciplines are moving in the opposite direction in the attempt, as yet unsuccessful, to establish their own autonomy.29

The remainder of this chapter will demonstrate how structural method has been applied by Lévi-Strauss to explain three well-known subjects of study in anthropology; kinship, totemism, and myth. Before turning to this, however, it is important to set straight a final, but important, misunderstanding involving the meaning of the terms "structure" and "structural system" as these terms are used by Lévi-Strauss.

When we read through the corpus of Lévi-Strauss' publications it becomes obvious that he is conscious of this misunderstanding; from "Social Structure" (1952) to "Structure and Form" (1960) and The Raw And The Cooked (1964), Lévi-Strauss has repeatedly returned to a clarification of these terms.

One use of "structure" is consistently rejected by Lévi-Strauss: the widespread British-American assumption that structure is the order which explains the observable relations between individuals or units of a social system. Structures from this point of view are relations that can be observed directly and empirically. Once we have described the principles or the arrangement by which individuals enter into institutional relations, we have also established the structure of these relations. In brief, structures are visible relations, and the construction of models of these relations represents the actual behavior of individuals within institutionalized relations.

Lévi-Strauss has made it clear that structural analysis is not an empirical description. Here is what he says,

> Passing now to the task of defining 'social structure', there is a point which should be cleared up immediately. The term 'social structure' has nothing to do with empirical reality but with models that are built up after it. This should help one to clarify the difference between two concepts which are so close to each other that they are often confused, namely, those of social structure and of social relations. It will be enough to state at this time that social relations consist of the raw materials out of which the models making up the social structure are built, while social structure can, by no means, be reduced to the ensemble of the social relations to be described in a given society.30

Although it might have been enough to state it this way at the time, it did not prevent misunderstandings. Eight years later and with apparent frustration, Lévi-Strauss once again tried to clarify his point in a reply to Maybury-Lewis;

> To sum up, may I point out to what extent my critic remains the prisoner of the naturalistic misconceptions that have so longed pervaded the British school. He claims to be a structuralist.... But he is still a structuralist in Radcliffe-Brown's terms in that he believes the structure to lie at the level of empirical reality and to be a part of it. When therefore, he is presented a structural model which departs from empirical reality, he feels cheated in some devious way. To him, social structure is like a kind of jigsaw puzzle, and everything is achieved when one has discovered how the pieces fit together. But, if the pieces have been arbitrarily cut, there is no structure at all. On the other hand, if -- as is sometimes done -- the pieces were automatically cut in different shapes by a mechanical saw, the movements of which are regulated by a camshaft, the structure of the puzzle exists, though not at the empirical level (since there are many ways of recognizing the pieces which fit together). Its key lies in the mathematical formula expressing the shape of the cams and their speed of rotation. This information does not correspond in any perceptible manner to the puzzle as it appears to the player, but it alone can explain the puzzle and provide a logical method to solve it.31

Lévi-Strauss closes his reply with the following example:

> The ultimate proof of the molecular structure of matter is provided by the electronic [sic.] microscope, which enables us to see actual molecules. This achievement does not alter the fact that henceforth the molecule will not become any more visible to the naked eye. Similarly, it is hopeless to expect a structural analysis to change our way of perceiving

concrete social relations. It will only explain them better. If the structure can be seen, it will not be at the earlier, empirical level, but at a deeper one, previously neglected; that of those unconscious categories which we may hope to reach by bringing together domains which, at first sight, appear disconnected.32

The above quotation is reasonably clear but open to serious misunderstanding. We can for example stop after reading that social structures have nothing to do with empirical reality since they have to do with models. That is to say, models we construct, that are in our heads, that explain, in some sense of explain, the empirical reality we have observed. I think that this interpretation of Levi-Strauss is mistaken since it would place him squarely within the empiricist/positivist tradition he has rejected. Part of the problem is due to Lévi-Strauss himself. First of all, it does not help the reader to discover that Lévi-Strauss refers approvingly to Leach in the passage quoted above. Secondly, the passage is ambiguous in that "structure" and "model" seem to be the same. What is clear is that Lévi-Strauss makes a distinction between "social relations" and "social structures." Social relations are the raw material from which models are built that make manifest the social structure itself.33

Structuralism is not a form of behaviorism or empiricism.34 The object for study is not to be confused with the observations, as rigorous as we can make them, of actual human behavior wherever we find it. The distinction between language and speech, social structure and social relations implies that we must not confuse the evidence with the object of our study. What I think Lévi-Strauss is saying in the above statement is that we use "the raw material" of social relations as evidence for the rules which constitute the social structure. To suppose that the rules are rules of empirical social relations is to think that the evidence is the object of study. I believe this interpretation of Lévi-Strauss can be demonstrated by turning to what he actually does in his analysis of kinship, totemism and myth. In turning to these three examples I do not intend to describe the details Lévi-Strauss uses in his analysis. What I am interested in is how he goes about establishing the analysis and the results.

Kinship, let us recall, was at one time the central object of study in anthropology. It had also become a central problem. For it seemed to be the case that there was an inverse relation between the increase in data and the established definition of "kinship" as a cultural universal. Put in other terms, there seemed to be a breakdown in the relation between the established definitions of kinship and the increasing number of accounts of "kinship" in various societies. Lévis-Strauss examined this problem in a significant article entitled "Structural Analysis in Linguistics and Anthropology" published in 1945. I believe this is the earliest essay in which structural linguistics is explicitly used as a theory for explaining anthropological data.35

He cites structural linguistics as a revolution and describes its methodology by referring to Troubetzkoy: "First, structural linguistics shifts from the study of _conscious_ linguistic phenomena to study their _unconscious_ infrastructure; second, it does not treat _terms_ as independent entities, taking instead as its basis of analysis the _relations_ between terms; third, it introduces the concept of _system_... finally, structural linguistics aims at discovering _general laws_, either by induction 'or... by logical deduction, which would give them an absolute character.'"36 He notes that the final aim is nothing less than the capacity to formulate necessary relations by means of the first three rules. It is important to focus on this final aim simply because functionalists, as we have seen, reached for it without success. We must also notice that although Troubetzkoy's methodology involves hypothetico/deductive operations it is not causal in its mode of explanation.

Lévi-Strauss, I believe, is the first scholar in the human sciences to appropriate this set of methodological procedures for resolving an important problem. He is also careful to point out that we cannot simply move from a structural analysis of phonemes to an analysis of kinship systems. There are important differences, yet, the four rules are applicable: "Although they belong to _another order of reality_, kinship phenomena are _of the same type_ as linguistic phenomena." Thus, contrary to many interpretations of Lévi-Strauss, he has never asserted that kinship or myth, are synonymous with language. All he wishes to point out is that there are significant relations and analogies between them.

Lévi-Strauss found at least two fundamental errors in his review of various attempts to resolve the problem mentioned above. The first is an attempt to resolve the problem historically; kinship terminology and rules are based on specific customs. If this is true, then how do we explain the regularity of kinship? How do discrete, historical customs explain an apparent universal institution across cultures? One way to do it is to assert that a specific element of a kinship system is the survival or residue of a previous custom now lost. Thus, the importance of the mother's brother in many kinship systems is "explained" as a survival of matrilineal descent or the consequence of several distinct customs now lost. This, of course, is sheer speculation which generates more problems than it attempts to solve.

The second error was to attempt to explain kinship by an analysis of the biological family; father, mother, children. Once we begin by focusing on this unit of kinship the avunculate remains external to the system and cannot be explained. Although Radcliffe-Brown made a great step forward in proposing that the problem of the avunculate could be solved by demonstrating that it involves two antithetical systems of attitudes (authority/familiarity) determined by either patrilineal or matrilineal descent, the problem remained unresolved. The avunculate, for example, does not occur in all patrilineal or matrilineal societies and is present in some societies that are neither matrilineal nor patrilineal. The problem with Radcliffe-Brown's solution is that it remained on the surface of social relations, arbitrarily restricting the "structure" to two sets of terms, father/son, maternal uncle/nephew.37

As we know, Lévi-Strauss proposed what he called the "atom of kinship" as composed of the following set of relations; brother/sister, husband/wife, father/son, maternal uncle/nephew. And it is this set of relations which also accounts for the three constituent kinship relations; affinity, consanguinity, and filiation.38 Furthermore, this set of relations is the result of "the universal presence of the incest taboo." Lévi-Strauss concludes by asserting that "This is really saying that in human society a man must obtain a woman from another man who gives him a daughter or a sister. Thus we do not need to explain how the maternal uncle emerged in kinship structure: He does not emerge -- he is present initially. Indeed, the presence of the maternal uncle is a necessary precondition for the structure to exist. The error of traditional anthropology, like that of traditional linguistics, was to consider the terms, and not the relation between the terms."39

This is indeed a striking illustration of a procedure which first constructs a model consisting of a set of relations and then makes manifest the structure as it actually exists in societies. It is a deductive operation, not observable on the empirical level and surely not in the consciousness of an informant. The explanation is also not causal, but rather a set of necessary relations in which the relations function as definitions of the terms. It is also theoretically possible to construct such a symmetrical structure in which the sexes would be reversed.

And what about the problem Lévi-Strauss laid at the foot of Radcliffe-Brown, the fact that we have the avunculate in systems which are neither patrilineal nor matrilineal and so on? First, not all societies are regulated by kinship. But, second, we may construct more complex systems in which the avunculate relation may be present but submerged. For example, "we can conceive of a system whose point of departure lies in the elementary structure but which adds, at the right of the maternal uncle, his wife, and at the left of the father, first the father's sister and then her husband."40 In brief, what Lévi-Strauss is asserting is that this construction is based on a set of relations which are syntagmatic.

The structure of kinship is not founded on the biological family, it is, to use a term from structural linguistics "unmotivated." It would seem to be the case, therefore, that the elements of kinship have no intrinsic value, their value is established by the relationships into which they enter.

Let us now turn to Lévi-Strauss's analysis of totemism. It is important to first point out that totemism, like kinship, had been the focus of study for many scholars. Totemism was identified as the origin of culture and religion, totemism was the primitive institution. We need only recall the importance of totemism in the works of such scholars as

Durkheim, Freud and Radcliffe-Brown as a reminder that this subject was thought by many to be the key that would unlock the mystery of the origins of culture and religion. For many years the journal Anthropos reserved a special section in each of its volumes for continued work on the subject.

The history of this intellectual enterprise is fascinating in itself when we remember the attention given to the subject for almost one hundred years. The subject, as we now know, was primarily created in the minds of scholars who then went in search of it among societies. The history of the study of this intellectual creation called "totemism" did not suddenly collapse but endured for many years in spite of the internal problems which were fully recognized by various scholars. Why it endured for as long as it did is an interesting topic in itself.

I shall resist the temptation to answer this question. Let me just point out that by 1910 Alexander Goldenweiser, inspired by Boas, had proved convincingly that there was no such thing as universal totemism resulting from a single historical or psychological origin. And yet, once having shown the diversity and heterogeneity of the features identified as totemism, Goldenweiser continued to insist on a "totemic complex" which included exogamy, a mystical relation between man and nature, and a set of social units which are equivalent, as universal features. The task, then, was to find a general formula which would explain these three features as constituting totemism.

By 1954 we are no longer reading about totemism, but totemisms. For A. P. Elkin the issue was no longer a quest for an institution known as totemism, but placing totemism back into the cultures where it was originally found. Once we place totemism back into its particular social context, he believed, we can solve the problems by making a distinction between social totemism and cult totemism. The first is associated with kinship, the regulation of marriage, and the differentiation of social groups. The second, cult totemism, is associated with explaining group origins, the maintenance of custom, and certain rituals related to the maintenance of the social group.

Four years earlier Piddington after studying what had been written about totemism wrote, "It will seem that the term 'totemism' has been applied to a bewildering variety of relationships between human beings and natural species or phenomena. For this reason it is impossible to reach any satisfactory definition of totemism, though many attempts have been made to do so.... All definitions of totemism are either so specific as to exclude a number of systems which are commonly referred to as 'totemic' or so general as to include many phenomena which cannot be referred to by this term."41 The study of totemism was in disarray. No one had taken Lowie seriously when about forty years earlier he raised the question whether it might not be best to pause and "first inquire whether... we are comparing cultural realities or merely figments of our logical modes of classification."42

Given this most remarkable chapter in the history of the human sciences, Lévi-Strauss did heed the call of Lowie and turned to an investigation of this peculiar problem and its history.43 The problem is made very clear by Lévi-Strauss. "If totemism is defined," he writes, "as the joint presence of animal and plant names, prohibitions apply[ing] to the corresponding species and the forbidding of marriage between people of the same name and subject to the same prohibition, then clearly a problem arises about the connection of these customs. It has however long been known that any one of these features can be found without the others and any two of them without the third."44

Lévi-Strauss proceeds to resolve the problems by means of a method that is strikingly similar to the one used in explaining what he called the atom of kinship. Here is how he begins:

> Let us try to define objectively and in its most general aspects the semantic field within which are found the phenomena commonly grouped under the name of totemism. The method we adopt, in this case as in others, consists in the following operations:
> (1) define the phenomenon under study as a relation between two or more terms, real or supposed;
> (2) construct a table of possible permutations between these terms;
> (3) take this table as the general object of analysis which, at this level only, can yield the necessary connections, the empirical phenomenon considered at the beginning being

only one possible combination among others, the complete system of which must be reconstructed beforehand.45

Lévi-Strauss arbitrarily chooses the terms "natural" and "cultural" to cover relations which are posited ideologically between two series. He then chooses "categories" and "particulars" as terms which comprise the natural series, and "groups" and "persons" as terms which comprise the cultural series.

Thus, we have the following set of relations between two or more terms, real or supposed:

NATURE:	Category	Particular
CULTURE:	Group	Person

By constructing a table of possible permutations between these terms, we get the following set of relations which exists between the two series:

	1	2	3	4
NATURE:	Category	Category	Particular	Particular
CULTURE:	Group	Person	Person	Group

Lévi-Strauss then moves on to demonstrate that the four combinations correspond to observable data among various societies. It will be best to quote his correlations. Australian totemism fits the first combination, since,

> under 'social' and 'sexual' modalities, [it] postulates a relation between a natural category (animal or vegetable species, or class of objects or phenomena) and a cultural group (moiety, section, sub-section, cult-group, or the collectivity of members of the same sex). The second combination corresponds to the 'individual' totemism of the North American Indians, among whom an individual seeks by means of physical traits to reconcile himself with a natural category. As an example of the third combination we may

take Mota, in the Banks Islands, where a child is thought to be the incarnation of an animal or plant found or eaten by the mother when she first became aware that she was pregnant.... The group-particular combination is attested from Polynesia and Africa, where certain animals (guardian lizards in New Zealand, sacred crocodiles and lion or leopard in Africa) are objects of social protection and veneration.46

The "totemic illusion" is the result of distorting the semantic field by focusing on the first two combinations, abstracting them from a system of logical relations which are, in fact, equivalent transformations of the same set. And once this abstraction takes place, we cannot account for either the remaining combinations, or the presence or absence of certain "totemic features" in the societies we examine.

But, there is more to this analysis than the creation of a set of relations which constitute a structure in which, among other things, totemic features can be placed and explained. The principles of this method show why it was a fatal error to seek certain properties of a totem as the key for its selection and use. It remains a popular notion that totems are symbols. Thus, a society may have the lion as totem because it symbolizes courage. Or, the bear becomes a totem for a clan because of its strength, the eagle because of its swiftness, and so on. Apart from the difficulty of demonstrating the semantic relations between lion/courage or bear/strength (why not lion/lazy, bear/stink), there is another difficulty that has not been solved. What does the fly, the mosquito, vomit, or the wind "symbolize" as a totem in certain societies? We have now entered the realm of creative imagination rather than explanation.

What we must clearly grasp is that totems as elements in a system have no intrinsic significance as such. They are to be analyzed as "signs" in a system. "There is no such thing as the real totem," writes Lévi-Strauss, "the individual animal plays the part of the signifying, and the sacredness attaches neither to it nor to its icon but to the signified, which either can stand for."47

Once this is fully understood, it becomes obvious that when we think about the enormous amount of raw material that could be selected from the world about us it is possible that an indefinite number of systems could be created that would be just as coherent as the structures we actually find in different societies. Thus, there is no particular system that is necessary, or originally given, as the structure for all societies. As Lévi-Strauss puts it,

> The operative value of the systems of naming and classifying commonly called totemic derives from their formal character; they are codes suitable for conveying messages which can be transposed into other codes, and for expressing messages received by means of different codes in terms of their own system. The mistake of classical ethnologists was to try to reify this form and tie it to a determinate content when in fact what it provides is a method for assimilating any kind of content. Far from being an autonomous institution definable by its intrinsic characteristic totemism, or what is referred to as such, corresponds to certain modalities arbitrarily isolated from a formal system, the function of which is to guarantee the convertibility of ideas between different levels of social reality.48

The axiomatic principle, as Lévi-Strauss calls it, of the totemic concept can be described as follows: it is "an homology not between social groups and natural species, but between differences existing, on the one hand within the social system, and on the other within the natural system. Two systems of differences are conceived as isomorphic, although one is situated in nature, and the other in culture." The structure can be schematized as follows, with vertical lines indicating relations of homology:

NATURE: species 1 + species 2 + species 3 + species n

          | | | |

CULTURE: group 1 + group 2 + group 3 + group n. 49

The schema is to be read as follows; group 1 : group 2 :: species 1 : species 2, or clan 1 differs from clan 2 as eagle differs from bear. The point is that we must refuse to look on the so-called totemic features in a society as first of all animals who resemble each other because of their overall behavior and then social groups which resemble each other. As Lévi-Strauss says, "The resemblance presupposed by so-called totemic representations is between these two systems of differences."50

Before turning to the example of myth, I think it best to pause here in order to illustrate how structural analysis differs from functionalism. As we have seen, structuralism does not explain social relations by using a type of causal explanation. On the contrary, it rejects this attempt by moving to an explanation which although deductive in nature is primarily interested in the function of terms as a logical set of relations. And Lévi-Strauss, rather than using a type of Hempelian criticism of functionalism comes up with another argument against it. In closing his critique of functionalist theories of totemism which is based on need and emotion, he says,

As affectivity is the most obscure side of man, there is the constant temptation to resort to it, forgetting that what is refractory to explanation is ipso facto unsuitable for use in explanation. A datum is not primary because it is incomprehensible: this characteristic indicates solely that an explanation, if it exists, must be sought on another level. Otherwise, we shall be satisfied to attach another label to the problem, thus believing it to have been solved.... Actually, impulses and emotions explain nothing: they are always results, either of the power of the body or of the impotence of the mind. In both cases they are consequences, never causes. The latter can be sought only in the organism, which is the exclusive concern of biology, or in the intellect, which is the sole way offered to psychology, and to anthropology as well.51

He therefore, concludes with the well-known phrase, "totems are not good to eat, they are first of all good to think." We have first of all to know our world before it becomes useful to us. In brief, totemism is not a matter of utilitarian satisfactions of need, but of epistemology!52

Let us now turn briefly to a description of Lévi-Strauss's structural analysis of myth. Lévi-Strauss once again begins with a problem; the chaotic situation in the study of mythology. This is how he described the situation in 1955: "Precisely because the interest of professional anthropology has withdrawn from primitive religion, all kinds of amateurs who claim to belong to other disciplines have seized this opportunity to move in, thereby turning into their private playground what we have left as a wasteland."53 The cause of this wasteland is attributed to an early attempt at explaining myth from a psychological approach, which when discredited, was turned into an attempt to explain myths as a function of affectivity, "inarticulate emotional drives." We may note that this is precisely his criticism of the attempts to explain "totemism."

As a result, the situation remains chaotic. "Myths are still widely interpreted in conflicting ways: as collective dreams, as the outcome of a kind of esthetic play, or as the basis of ritual. Mythological figures are considered as personified abstractions, divinized heroes, or fallen gods. Whatever the hypothesis, the choice amounts to reducing mythology either to idle play or to a crude kind of philosophic speculation."54 Or, we might add, myths become an ontological quest for being, with Plato as the first philosopher to decipher the symbolic meaning of myth.

Given this situation, what does Lévi-Strauss think is the fundamental problem, and how does he attempt to solve it? The problem seems to be an inherent contradiction; myths themselves seem to be chaotic. In myth anything goes, everything becomes possible. Yet, anyone who has studied mythology also knows that there is a striking similarity between myths from diverse regions of the world. Lévi-Strauss resolves this apparent "antinomy" by moving directly to Saussure and structural linguistics.

The misconception in the study of mythology is based on the notion that myth like language links a particular sound to a particular meaning. Thus, there are "sun", "lunar", "water," "earth" and "sky" myths and patterns or archetypes which possess a certain meaning. The error is comparable to thinking that similar or identical sounds across languages entail similar or identical meanings. But this is contradicted by our knowledge that although there may be identical sounds across languages, the meanings related to the sounds may be entirely different. The contradiction is resolved by an analysis which demonstrates that it is not sounds, but the combination of sounds which is significant, and that linguistic signs are arbitrary as vehicles of signification.

Lévi-Strauss applies this development in structural linguistics in the following way:

> (1) If there is a meaning to be found in mythology, it cannot reside in the isolated elements which enter into the composition of a myth, but only in the way those elements are combined. (2) Although myth belongs to the same category as language, being, as a matter of fact, only part of it, language in myth exhibits specific properties. (3) These properties are only to be found above the ordinary linguistic level, that is, they exhibit more complex features than those which are to be found in any other kind of linguistic expression.55

Myths, then, like language are made up of "constituent units" which Lévi-Strauss calls "mythemes." Lévi-Strauss is quite aware of the hypothetical nature of this construction, but the guidelines are clear.

> How shall we proceed," he writes, "in order to identify and isolate these gross constituent units or mythemes? We know that they cannot be found among phonemes, morphemes, or sememes, but only on a higher level; otherwise myth would become confused with any other kind of speech. Therefore, we should look for them on the sentence level. The only method we can suggest at this stage is to proceed tentatively, by trial and error, using as a check the principles which serve as a basis for any kind of structural analysis: economy of explanation; unity of solution,

and ability to reconstruct the whole from a fragment, as well as later stages from previous ones."56

This hypothesis together with the methodological guidelines has been consistently followed by Lévi-Strauss throughout his work on myth. It is this approach that has produced a radical change in the study of mythology. Let us briefly review some of the important features of this change.

First of all, it is important to notice that a structural analysis of myth puts an end to the quest for the "original" myth. It is simply useless to speculate about which myth is the more "genuine." A myth consists of all its versions, there simply is no preferred myth which discloses the meaning of myth. "Properly speaking, there is never any original: every myth is by its very nature a translation [or, transformation of other myths] and derives from another myth belonging to a neighboring, but foreign, community, or from a previous myth belonging to the same community or from a contemporaneous one belonging to a different social sub-division."57 Second, remaining true to the development of structural linguistics with regard to the nature of the "sign," we must view the "constituent" elements of a myth as essentially without content, without signification. Following Jakobson, Lévi-Strauss asserts that a mytheme "is a purely differential and contentless sign." It may well be the case that in ordinary language, the sun is the star of the day, but,

in and of itself, the mytheme "sun" is meaningless. Depending on the myths that one chooses to consider, "sun" can cover the most diverse ideal contents. Indeed, no one who finds "sun" in a myth can make any assumptions about its individuality, its nature, or its function there. Its meaning can emerge only from its correlative and oppositive relations with other mythemes within the myth. This meaning does not really belong to any of the mythemes; it results from their combination.58

What follows from the above hypothesis is that myths have no obvious practical function. And as Lévi-Strauss has convincingly shown, it is very dangerous if not erroneous to view myths as symbolic representations of actual social realities or of some cultural psyche, whatever that may mean. Furthermore, it is also a mistake to study myths as concealing some hidden "mystical" meaning. The meaning of a myth is given in its concrete relations with other versions. Thus, it is clearly a misunderstanding to call this type of analysis reductionistic. Lévi-Strauss has consistently claimed that the meaning of myth must be sought on its own level. Thus, myths disclose their own meaning, and we must "resign ourselves to the fact that the myths tell us nothing instructive about the world order, the nature of reality or the origin and destiny of mankind. We cannot expect them to flatter any metaphysical thirst, [sic.] or to breathe new life into exhausted ideologies." And yet, the structural analysis of myth does teach us a great deal about the societies from which they originate, and most important of all, "they make it possible to discover certain operational modes of the human mind, which have remained so constant over the centuries, and are so widespread over immense geographical distances, that we can assume them to be fundamental...."59

At this point, I think it best to allow Lévi-Strauss to summarize what he is doing. The lengthy quotation from an interview given below serves four purposes. First, it allows Lévi-Strauss to speak for himself, since he has often complained that he has been misunderstood. Second, it demonstrates that no description of his structural analysis of myth can be given without some ethnographic detail. Third, it also highlights how structural analysis of myth is not an explanation of the function of myth as providing social cohesion or maintenance, but an analysis which explains the meaning of myth as a translation or transformation of relations that are to be found at different levels from within the myth. Finally, it might help put an end to popular assertions that the analysis is the result of Lévi-Strauss' creative imagination; thus, structural analysis, like myth itself, is dramatic, expressive, an art, not a science which can be disconfirmed.

Lévi-Strauss points out in the interview that the initial situation which confronts us as we study myth is one of total arbitrariness, and confusion. He then states that myth instead of formulating abstract relationships, sets one element against another, sky and earth, earth and water, man and woman, light and darkness, raw and cooked, fresh and rotten. He is then asked to give an example and here is his reply.

The Salish-speaking peoples who inhabited North America between the Rocky Mountains and the Pacific Ocean near the fiftieth parallel often speak in their myths of a deceitful genie who, whenever a problem puzzles him, excretes his two sisters imprisoned in his bowels, whereon he demands their advice by threatening them with a torrential downpour; they, being excrement, would disintegrate. The tale seems like a clownish farce without any basis, defying all interpretation except, some would argue, through psychoanalysis. But this wouldn't get you very far for the simple reason that the storytellers' individual psychic constitutions are not a causal factor. Rather, an anonymous tradition has thrust these stories on them.

As in the previous instance, one may well ask himself if the apparent absurdity of the motif is not a result of our having arbitrarily isolated it from a much larger ensemble in which it would represent one possible combination among others produced as well, so that there would be no meaning to each one taken alone, but only in its relation to the others. Now, in Salish myths, the same genie creates for himself two adaptive daughters, out of raw salmon roe. When they are fully grown, he desires them. Testing his position, he pretends to call them by mistake 'my wives' instead of 'my daughters.' They promptly take offense and leave.

Finally, the Salish tell of a third pair of supernatural women. These women are married and are incapable of expressing themselves in articulate speech. They live at the bottom of natural wells and, on request, send up dishes of hot, well-cooked food to the surface.

These three motifs cannot be understood apart from one another. On the other hand, once you compare them, you notice their common origin. All the women are related to water: either, as in the case of the well-women, to stagnant water, or to running water for the two other pairs.

The later are distinct from one another in that the salmon-roe daughters come from a positive, earthly source of water -- salmon streams -- and the excrement-sisters are threatened with destruction by a negative, heavenly source of water -- the disintegrating rain. That's not all: the salmon-roe daughters and excrement-sisters are the products of either raw (in the first case) or cooked (in the other) food, while the well-women are themselves producers of cooked food. Further, the well-women, if you permit me, are 'marrying-types' as wives and good cooks. The other two pairs are 'non-marrying types' whether because they are labeled as sisters or because they avoid incestuous marriage with their foster father. Finally, two pairs of women are endowed linguistically: one for their wise counsel, the other because they catch on to a half-spoken, improper hint. In this way they contrast with the third pair, the well-women, who cannot speak.

Thus from three meaningless anecdotes you extract a system of pertinent oppositions: water, stagnant or moving, from the earth or sky; women created from food or producing it themselves, raw or cooked food; women accessible or opposed to marriage depending on linguistic or non-linguistic behavior. You arrive at what I'd call a 'semantic field' which can be applied like a grill to all the myths of these populations, enabling us to disclose their meaning.

And what is this meaning? "You realize that the Salish myths compose a vast sociological, economical and cosmological system establishing numerous correspondences between the distribution of fish in the water network, the various markets where goods are exchanged, their periodicity in time and during the fishing season, and finally exogamy; for, between groups, women are exchanged like foodstuffs.60

This long quotation is the best summary I have come across which describes what Lévi-Strauss is doing in the monumental four volume work on mythology. The analysis attempts to show that there is a differential, oppositional logic which is inherent in myths. The analysis begins by demonstrating the structure, the grill, of this logic in a particular myth, and then proceeds to establish the meaning of myth as this structure is translated or transformed into other myths. This logic shows that it is the differences, not the resemblances, which are significant. I might add that this is precisely the opposite of most historians' and phenomenologists' interpretations of myths.

Lévi-Strauss has consistently described this inherent logic in mythology by the following formula, A : B :: C : D. He has also described it by.the following algebraic formula:

$$f_x(a) : f_y(b) :: f_x(b) : f^{(a-1)}(y)$$

The formula is explained as follows: "Here, with two terms, a and b, being given as well as two functions, x and y, of these terms, it is assumed that a relation of equivalence exists between two situations defined respectively by an inversion of terms and relations, under two conditions: (1) that one term be replaced by its opposite (in the above formula, a and a-1); (2) that an inversion by made between the function value and the term value of two elements (above y and a)."61

This formula has been used by Lévi-Strauss in his study of myth and is clearly at work in his analysis of "The Story of Asdiwal" which, as we will recall, begins with a mother and daughter in a valley and ends with a father and son on a mountain, as well as the various oppositions of the various sociological, geographical, economic and cosmological levels.62 The formula can also be seen at work in the four volumes on mythology in South and North America.

The major problem I have with this analysis is not that it is speculative, that there is no way we can falsify what he is doing, or that only Lévi-Strauss can perform this kind of magic. None of this kind of criticism is true. The major problem is to be found in Lévi-Strauss' notion that it is the transformations of the myths into different sets of oppositions that is the meaning of the myths. It simply is not clear to me how such transformations can generate meaning. Nor am I satisfied with his notion that such meanings are hidden; it is the structural grill which "discloses" the meaning of the myths. There is not doubt about the fact that myths pick up aspects of culture and nature as elements to be woven into the myths. Thus, we usually find social, economic, and political relations as well as geographical and cosmological elements in the stories. "Case III," in the following chapter will provide a good example of this. We have learned, thanks in part to Lévi-Strauss, however, that it is very dangerous to interpret the myths as symbolic representations of social or natural structures. Often we find that it is just the opposite which is the case; the myth represents a matrilocal system, the society is partrilocal. Forced into the corner we are then tempted to look for the hidden meaning of myth. I agree with Sperber that we should try this response as an answer of last resort. One of the difficulties with the notion of hidden meanings is the answer we must give to, "why all these hidden meanings?" Why do so many societies insist upon speaking in a cryptic language which we must decode? The usual response to these questions leads us straight into the mine-field of functionalism.63

It is precisely this synchronic structure of oppositions, of differences, which has caused the most criticism of his analysis of myth. What his critics want is precisely what he refuses to give them; an empirical and causal explanation of myth based on need or an interpretation of myth as symbolic of a metaphysical reality. Since, as we have seen, both of these approaches have led to a theoretical impasse, Lévi-Strauss is quite correct in his refusal to move down these pathways. He has offered his hypotheses and methodological principles as tentative, open to falsification. His procedures have been by trial and error. His theory may well turn out to be wrong, but I know of no more adequate place to begin than from the place Lévi-Strauss started from, i.e., linguistics.64

NOTES.

1. Lévi-Strauss states that "[I] knew almost nothing about linguistics, and I had never heard of Roman Jakobson," before 1942, when he met Jakobson in New York. See Claude Lévi-Strauss, "The Lesson of Linguistics," *The View from Afar*, trans. Joachim Neugroschel and Phoebe Hoss (New York: Basic, 1985) 138. This essay was originally the preface to Roman Jakobson, *Six Lectures on Sound and Meaning* (Cambridge: MIT P, 1978). The lectures and preface were originally published in Paris in 1976.

2. Ferdinand de Saussure, *Course in General Linguistics*, eds. Charles Bally and Albert Sechehaye with Albert Reidlinger, trans. Wade Baskin (New York: Philosophical Library, 1959) 16.

3. Claude Lévi-Strauss, *Structural Anthropology*, vol. II (New York: Basic, 1976) 9-10 and "The Mathematics of Man," *UNESCO International Social Science Bulletin* VI (1954): 581-82.

4. Claude Lévi-Strauss, *Structural Anthropology*, vol. I (New York: Basic, 1963) 364-65.

5. Lévi-Strauss, *Structural Anthropology*, vol. II 16.

6. Saussure 88-90. For the first example see pages 22-23. The third use of chess demonstrates the significance of "value," see page 110.

7. Emile Benveniste, "The Nature of the Linguistic Sign," *Problems in General Linguistics* (Coral Gables, Fla.: U of Miami P, 1971) 45.

8. Lévi-Strauss, *Structural Anthropology* 91.

9. Lévi-Strauss, *Structural Anthropology* 92, italics mine.

10 Benveniste.43-45.

11. Benveniste 45.

12. Lévi-Strauss, *Structural Anthropology*, vol. I 93.

13. For the most recent denial of this type of criticism, see Lévi-Strauss, *The View from Afar* 102ff.

14. Louis Althusser and Étienne Balibar, *Reading Capital* (London: NLB, 1977) 95-96.

15. Claude Lévi-Strauss, *The Savage Mind* (Chicago: U of Chicago P, 1966) 66-67.

16. Lévi-Strauss, *The Savage Mind* 69.

17. Lévi-Strauss, *The Savage Mind* 70.

18. Lévi-Strauss, *The Savage Mind* 155.

19. Lévi-Strauss, *The Savage Mind* 237. We could continue this mode of citation indefinitely by moving on to the four volume work on mythology. Throughout this massive study, Lévi-Strauss brings history (the diachronic) into his analysis again and again: maps, geographical distributions, and the like. For example, "In an area where the exponents of the historical method try to discover contingent links and traces of a diachronic *evolution*, I have uncovered an

intelligible synchronic system. Where they itemize terms, I focus on relations. Where they put together unrecognizable fragments or haphazard assemblages, I have pointed out significant contrasts. In so doing, I have simply been putting into practice one of Ferdinand de Saussure's teachings.... Nevertheless, it is impossible to evade the historical problem, since it is no doubt true that we must ask what things consist of before we can reasonably ask ourselves how they came to be what they are...." Claude Lévi-Strauss, *The Origin of Table Manners*, trans. John and Doreen Weightman (London: Cape, 1978) 263-64. Italics mine.

20. Lévi-Strauss, *The Savage Mind* 256-57.

21. There are, of course, very good defenses of his position. See, for example, Ino Rossi, "On the Assumptions of Structural Analysis: Revisiting its Linguistic and Epistemological Premises," and "On the 'Scientific' Evidence for the Existence of Deep Structures and Their 'Objective' and Mathematical Nature," *The Logic of Culture*, ed. Ino Rossi (South Hadley, Mass.: Bergen, 1982) 3-22; 265-93; and Jean-Marie Benoist, *The Structural Revolution* (New York: St. Martin's, 1978). On the comparison of Lévi-Strauss with Althusser, see Ino Rossi, *From the Sociology of Symbols to the Sociology of Signs* (New York: Columbia UP, 1983).

22. Lévi-Strauss, *The Savage Mind* 117.

23. Lévi-Strauss, *The Savage Mind* 130-131.

24. Lévi-Strauss, *Structural Anthropology*, vol. II 196, note 19.

25. Lévi-Strauss, *Structural Anthropology*, vol. I 312-313. Maurice Godelier has attempted to develop the notion of "lived-in" and "thought-of" orders in "Myth and History." See Maurice Godelier, *Perspectives in Marxist Anthropology*, trans. Robert Brain (Cambridge: Cambridge UP, 1977) 204ff. Although the essay is very interesting, it eventually fails because of the functionalist premises which are inherent in Marxism.

26. Lévi-Strauss, *Structural Anthropology*, vol. I 229.

27. Lévi-Strauss, it should be noted, also views art in a similar if not identical way. In describing the complex art of body painting among the Caduveo, he concludes,

"They therefore, never had the opportunity of resolving their contradictions or at least concealing them by means of artful institutions. But the remedy they failed to use on the social level, or which they refused to consider, could not evade them completely.... And since they could not become conscious of it [i.e., the contradictions] and live it out in reality, they began to dream about it." Claude Lévi-Strauss, *Tristes Tropiques*, trans. John and Doreen Weightman (New York: Atheneum, 1974) 196.

28. For an excellent contribution towards resolving some of the problems, see G. A. Cohen, "Base and Superstructure, Power and Rights," *Karl Marx's Theory of History: A Defense* (Princeton: Princeton UP, 1978) 216-48. Although I have found Maurice Godelier's work on this problem interesting, I do not find it persuasive. Godelier attempts to resolve the problem by bringing functionalism back into his argument. See Maurice Godelier, "Myths, Infrastructures and History in Lévi-Strauss," *The Logic of Culture* 232-61.

29. I have found the following publications very useful in reflecting about the problem: Maurice Godelier, *Rationality and Irrationality in Economics* (New York: Monthly Review P, 1972), especially the "Forward" to the English edition, as well as his collection of essays, *Perspectives in Marxist Anthropology* (Cambridge: Cambridge UP, 1977). As I have already noted, Godelier thinks that the solution is to join structuralism with Marxist functionalism. I do not think that this is a solution because of the weaknesses in functionalism as a causal theory of explanation. See also Miriam Glucksmann, *Structuralist Analysis in Contemporary Social Thought: A Comparison of the Theories of Claude Lévi-Strauss and Louis Althusser* (London: Routledge, 1974). Glucksmann produces a very good analysis of why, given Lévi-Strauss's own work, he has been accused of idealism and formalism and thinks that he has ignored "the productive nature of man, replacing it with an unchanging homo sapiens. The autonomy of the superstructures is so great that there is no need even for investigation of the relationships between the social formation and its cultural products" (93). Given the numerous quotations from Lévi-Strauss on this issue, I believe that this is at best an over-simplification of his position and seems to contradict the author's convincing conclusion that Lévi-Strauss and Althusser are very close in the theoretical positions they hold. See also Fredric Jameson, *The Prison-House of*

Language: A Critical Account of Structuralism and Russian Formalism (Princeton: Princeton UP, 1972) for what I think is a profound as well as clear description of the various positions and problems. The only text I have found that confronts the functionalist premises in Marx's thought can be found in G. A. Cohen, *Karl Marx's Theory*.... Although I judge the book to be an excellent piece of analysis, I do not believe that Cohen has overcome the Hempelian critique of functionalism. See esp. chaps. IX and X for Cohen's argument.

30. Lévi-Strauss, *Structural Anthropology*, vol. I 279.

31. Lévi-Strauss, *Structural Anthropology*, vol. II 79-80.

32. Lévi-Strauss, *Structural Anthropology*, vol. II 80.

33. I am well aware of the fact that the article "Social Structure" was first published in English in 1953. The French edition of *Structural Anthropology*, however, reads as follows: "Le principe fondamental est que la notion de structure sociale ne se rapporte pas à la réalité empirique, mais aux modèles construits d'après celle-ci.... Les *relations sociales* sont la matière première employée pour la construction des modèles qui *rendent manifeste* la *structure sociale* elle-même." *Anthropologie Structurale* (Paris: Plon, 1958) 305-306. Penultimate emphasis mine.

34. For a very good comparison of these positions with structuralism, see Ino Rossi, *From the Sociology of Symbols to the Sociology of Signs.*

35. Lévi-Strauss, *Structural Anthropology*, vol. I 31-54.

36. Lévi-Strauss, *Structural Anthropology*, vol. I 33.

37. For an excellent analysis and defense of Lévi-Strauss' theory of kinship, see Ino Rossi, "Lévi-Strauss' Theory of Kinship and its Empiricist Critics: An Anti-Needham Position," *The Logic of Culture.*

38. Compare "Structural Analysis in Linguistics and Anthropology" with "Reflections on the Atom of Kinship" which was published 28 years later. See Lévi-Strauss, *Structural Anthropology*, vol. II 82ff.

39. Lévi-Strauss, *Structural Anthropology*, vol. I 46.

40. Lévi-Strauss, *Structural Anthropology*, vol. I 48.

41. Quoted in Claude Lévi-Strauss, *Totemism*, tran. Rodney Needham (Boston: Beacon, 1962) 9.

42. Lévi-Strauss, *Totemism* 10.

43. The results of his research appeared in three separate publications which deal with totemism from slightly different angles. The first was *Totemism*, in 1962, referenced above. The second was *The Savage Mind*, also 1962, trans. into English in 1966, and the third was "The Bear and the Barber," *The Journal of the Royal Anthropological Institute* XCIII (1963): 1-11. Reprinted in William A. Lessa and Evon Z. Vogt, eds. *Reader in Comparative Religion*, 2nd ed. (New York: Harper, 1965) 289ff.

44. Lévi-Strauss, *The Savage Mind* 97.

45. Lévi-Strauss, *Totemism* 16.

46. Lévi-Strauss, *Totemism* 17.

47. Lévi-Strauss, *The Savage Mind* 239.

48. Lévi-Strauss, *The Savage Mind* 75-76.

49. Lévi-Strauss, "The Bear and the Barber," *Reader in Comparative Religion* 292 and *The Savage Mind* 115. In both of these essays, Lévi-Strauss experiments with a second hypothesis which would transform the totemic structure into a caste structure. Although I think it is a significant hypothesis for anyone interested in caste systems, or systems in which a specific group is a "giver" of kings, teachers, barbers, and the like, I will resist entering into a discussion of this possibility here. There is however, an important point made by Lévi-Strauss that must be highlighted. In concluding his essay "The Bear and the Barber" he says, "Thirdly, as we have seen, the tremendous differences existing between totemic groups and caste systems, in spite of their logical inverted similarity, may be

ascribed to the fact that castes are right and totemic systems are wrong, when they believe that they provide real services to their fellow groups. This should convince us that the 'truth-value' is an unavoidable dimension of structural method. No common analysis of religion can be given by a believer and a non-believer, and from this point of view, the type of approach known as 'religious phenomenology' should be dismissed" (297).

50. Lévi-Strauss, *Totemism* 75.

51. Lévi-Strauss, *Totemism* 69 and 71. I think that this statement can also be directed to the historian's and phenomenologist's approach to religion as well. All we need to do is substitute "the sacred" for "affectivity" and we notice that the critique hits the target.

52. Although I cannot analyze the texts in this chapter, it is important to point out that Lévi-Strauss makes the same point in an essay that is often overlooked. In his study of shamanistic cures he says, "The cure would consist, therefore, in making *thinkable*, a situation originally existing on the emotional level and in rendering acceptable to the mind pains which the body refuses to tolerate." Lévi-Strauss, *Structural Anthropology*, vol. I 197. Emphasis mine. The English translation unfortunately translates "pensable" as "explicit," thus, "The cure would consist, therefore, in making explicit a situation...." Here is the text: "La cure consisterait donc à rendre pensable une situation donnée d'abord en termes affectifs: et acceptables pour l'esprit des douleurs que le corps se refuse à tolérer." *Anthropologie Structurale* (Paris: Plon, 1958) 217.

53. Lévi-Strauss, *Structural Anthropology*, vol. I 206

54. Lévi-Strauss, *Structural Anthropology*, vol. I 207.

55. Lévi-Strauss, *Structural Anthropology*, vol. I 210.

56. Lévi-Strauss, *Structural Anthropology*, vol. I 211.

57. Claude Lévi-Strauss, *The Naked Man: Introduction to a Science of Mythology*, vol.4, trans. John and Doreen Weightman (New York: Harper, 1971) 644.

58. Lévi-Strauss, *The View From Afar* 145.

59. Lévi-Strauss, *The Naked Man* 639.

60. "Interview: Claude Lévi-Strauss," *Diacritics* (Fall, 1971): 48-49.

61. Lévi-Strauss, *Structural Anthropology*, vol. I 228. It is important to note that Lévi-Strauss did not drop this "algorithm" for the study of myth. In fact, six years later he asserts that "It was necessary to quote it at least once more as proof of the fact that I have never ceased to be guided by it since that time." Claude Lévi-Strauss, *From Honey to Ashes*, trans. John and Doreen Weightman (New York: Harper, 1973) 249. See also N. Ross Crumrine, "Transformational Processes and Models: with Special Reference to Mayo Indian Myth and Ritual," *The Logic of Culture* 68-87.

62. See Lévi-Strauss, *Structural Anthropology*, vol. II 146ff. The analysis of "The Story of Asdiwal" first appeared in English in Edmund Leach, ed., *The Structural Study of Myth and Totemism* (London: Tavistock, 1967). It was originally published in *L'annuaire 1958-1959 de l'Ecole Pratique des Hautes, VI Section*, and reprinted in *Les Temps Modernes*, #179. This text was faithfully reproduced in Leach. However, its republication in *Structural Anthropology*, vol. II, reverses two of the oppositions in the "Integration Schema" (compare Leach 19 with *Les Temps Modernes* 1099 and *Structural Anthropology*, vol. II 163). The schema in vol. II is obviously the right one even though the author and the translator do not alert us about the change.

63. One of the best critiques of the notion of "hidden meaning" from a linguistic approach is Dan Sperber, *Rethinking Symbolism* (Cambridge: Cambridge UP, 1975) chap. 2, "Hidden Meanings."

64. For a more recent example, see Harvey Rosenbaum, "Verification in Structural Theory: A Linguist's Point of View," *The Logic of Culture* 88-110.

CHAPTER SEVEN

STRUCTURE AND RELIGION

There are several lessons we can learn from the success of structuralism in the human sciences. First of all, we must remember Saussure's central rule: never consider a religious element or term in isolation from the system of which it is a part. For, "to define it in this way would isolate the term from its system; it would mean assuming that one can start from the terms and construct the system by adding them together when, on the contrary, it is from the interdependent whole that one must start and through analysis obtain its elements." Or, to put it in other terms, it is the relation of the elements, not the elements or symbols themselves, that is important for explaining religion. Religion, from this approach, "is a system of interdependent terms in which the value of each term results solely from the simultaneous presence of the others." Repeating these quotes from Course, might well raise the comment, "So what else is new?" This response is very familiar to me. The answer must be blunt; most of the work done in the history, phenomenology and anthropology of religion has been a gross violation of the above rule. As we have seen, most studies of religion are attempts to describe religion as a manifestation of The Sacred, or as a quasi-historical development of some kind, or as a particular satisfaction of some need. None of the above approaches to the study of religion begin with the "interdependent whole."

Rather than repeat what has already been written I would like to present three cases which I believe will demonstrate the strengths of structuralism for the future study of religion. The first two cases are major steps forward in our understanding of two important religions. I do not think that these steps could have been taken without the development of structural analysis. The third case is my own attempt at producing a structural explanation of a cycle of myths which I do not believe has been seriously studied.

CASE I.

The consequence of the errors I have discussed is serious since they produce a misunderstanding of religion. A good example, one with which I am most familiar, is the study of South Asian religion. Pick up any text on Hinduism, and you will find a quasi-historical description of this religion which usually begins with the Vedas, then the Upanishads and ends with the Bhagavad Gita or something like it. In addition, most of these descriptions of Hinduism place primary emphasis on the ascetic tradition; the yogi or sanyasin. The essence of Hinduism, or normative Buddhism, is defined as the teaching of the ascetic. With the exception of a few volumes, The Sacred Books Of The East is a good example of this one-sided emphasis. One of the many problems that arises is how to explain the presence of others who identify themselves as Hindu or Buddhist but are not ascetics. The response usually fragments the religion into a "great" and "little" tradition, "elite" and "folk" religion, "philosophical" and "popular" religion, "orthodox" and "heterodox" Hinduism.

Here is the most recent example I have found in what must be taken to be a definitive description of religion. Hinduism begins with the Indus Valley, then come Vedism, Brahmanism, the Upanishads, Classical Hinduism as a synthesis, a brief detour into Varnashramadharma, and then Classical Bhakti, Tantra, Advaita and Smarta Orthodoxy, Sectarian Hinduism (Vaishnavism, Krishnaism, and Shaivism) and finally Popular Hinduism.1 Once this kind of fragmentation of a religion occurs, we begin to wonder whether the term "religion," or "Hinduism," has any meaning at all! Hinduism from this point of view is nothing more than a collection of historical episodes in India which do not have any intrinsic connection. Hinduism is arbitrary, irrational history.

We should have noticed long ago that there is something quite wrong with this approach to Hinduism. First, as structuralism has taught us, the history of a religion is not its meaning, just as the history of English is not the meaning of English. Second, even if there are such religions as Vedism and Brahmanism, it seems odd that they are always placed at the beginning of books on Hinduism. Exactly how Vedism and Brahmanism form part of Hinduism is never made clear -- the answer seems to be that they don't. It may be very useful, for comparative purposes, to know the antecedent languages of English. Once again, however, this knowledge is not necessary for explaining the structure, the syntax or the semantics of English. Why is the study of religion any different? Finally, labelling certain aspects of Hinduism as "orthodox" and "heterodox," or "sectarian," is a good example of using labels that may make sense for describing the development of Christianity but make little sense at all when attached to Hinduism. The distortion that results from the use of these labels is clearly recognized in the maxim that Hinduism is not concerned with "orthodoxy" but rather "orthopraxis." In other words, it doesn't matter what you believe as long as you do it properly! Given this maxim, just how you go about "doing it properly" without belief is never explained without involving ourselves in contradiction.

The caste system is another good example of a distortion due to concentration on elements of the system rather than the "interdependent whole." The absence of any analysis of caste as an important part of Hinduism in most, if not all, handbooks and texts on religion is astonishing. In reviewing such texts published in both the United States and in Europe, I have not been able to find a single description of the significance of the caste system in Hinduism. Why has this been omitted? Because, as R. N. Dandekar sums it up, "Hinduism as a religion must be distinguished from Hinduism as a social organization."2 But, as is usually the case when such divisions are made, Dandekar soon contradicts himself when he admits that one of the distinctive features of Hinduism is the "belief in the ideological complex of karma-samsara-moksa on the metaphysical plane and the acceptance of the caste system on the socio-ethical plane."3 In other words, Hinduism does encompass both. The problem, of course, is that it is very difficult to explain the caste system as a manifestation of The Sacred! Nevertheless, preoccupation with The Sacred as the essence of religion prevented most scholars in the study of religion from realizing how important caste is for an adequate understanding of Hinduism.

Caste was simply left to the social sciences which not only attempted to explain caste from typical political/economic models but also ignored the classical Indian literature on caste; this literature was viewed as religious, and ideological and thus irrelevant. But the caste system resists explanations that are political/economic, that approach the system as a variation on the division of labor. As usual in such cases, instead of taking a hard look at the theory and methodology the call went out for more data. What we needed were more detailed studies of caste in India!

The solution, of course, is not more data -- we have more than we can use but more critical reflection on what we are doing, a realization that we cannot "start from the [elements] and construct the system adding them together" one by one. Most studies of the caste system are analogous to an explanation of chess by an empirical study of the pawn or knight.

It was Louis Dumont who convincingly demonstrated why purely economic or political explanations of caste were bound to fail. The reason for the failure is due to a significant error -- the failure to recognize that ritual status is not congruent with the division of labor. Dumont finds three fundamental errors throughout the history of the study of caste. The first entails the "reduction" of religion to the non-religious. The second problem involves a methodology which takes the part for the whole. The third problem involves the failure to understand the importance of hierarchy.4

In brief, Dumont discovered that the caste system is constituted by ritual! He begins his analysis with a fresh set of principles taken from structural analysis. The principles can be described as follows. First, explicate the units in the caste system as a set of relations which are complementary. Second, discover the form or structure of the system rather than concentrate on the visible relations of a particular caste. Finally, separate for theoretical purposes, caste as a system from caste as individual behavior on the part of individuals.5

If the results of Dumont's analysis are right, and I think they are, then the dominant superstructure in Hinduism is the ideology of pollution. The basic set of oppositions which constitute the system is a ritual complementary relation between the pure and the impure. The structural schema of the binary oppositions of the caste system based upon the rule of pure/impure can be given the following diagramatical form:

The Religious System Of India

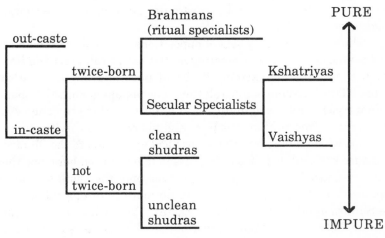

Figure 1

The structure as portrayed in Figure 1 is an obvious illustration of the classical fourfold caste system called varna: Brahman, Kshatriya, Vaishya, Shudra. The schema can be used to illustrate the following points. Caste in India is a religious system based upon ritual purity/impurity. The basic set of oppositions which constitute the system is the opposition between pure and impure. Thus, we can begin to read the structure as the pure is to the impure as twice-born is to not twice-born. What must be emphasized is that we cannot adequately account for the caste system by focusing on one or more of its elements. In order to fully explain the system, we must analyze the set of relations which comprise or define the various elements in the system.

The first point, that caste is essentially religious, overturns at least three decades of scholarship on caste. It opens up a complete set of new problems and issues that need to be studied and resolved. The system of relations which defines caste is based upon the primary relation between pure and impure, which is the principle of pollution. The principle of pollution constitutes the <u>form</u> of the system in both theory and practice. It is precisely the opposition between pure and impure that defines the elements in the system. For example, Brahmans are vegetarians, Shudras eat meat.

The complementary sets of oppositions can be analyzed on several levels. One of the more interesting is that both Brahmans and Shudras, which constitute the extreme limits of pure and impure, are service castes. This extreme set of relations encompasses both the "political" (Kshatriya) and "economic" (Vaishya) castes in the system. Furthermore, the Brahman is pure and his rituals purify <u>because</u> of the relations which define him in hierarchical opposition to the Shudra, who is impure and pollutes. There is a lesson to be learned here, one that has been overlooked. If your goal is to overcome the caste system as an oppressive ideology you will have to do more than upgrade or rename the Shudra or other "untouchable" castes. You will have to rupture the relation between Brahman and Shudra. That is to say, the relation pure/impure must be broken. It is interesting to note that neither Buddhism, the Bhagavad Gita nor Gandhi was willing to go that far.

Finally, there is nothing external, or "outside" the system, which fixes or determines it -- the elements in themselves are arbitrary. Dumont extracts the following ontological consequence from this conclusion: "To say that the world of caste is a world of relations is to say that the particular caste and the particular man have no substance: they exist empirically, but they have no reality in thought, no Being."6

It should be clear from this brief analysis that a structural approach to religion does not search for "essences" or integrate symbols into some kind of final "coincidence of opposites" which might manifest The Sacred. It also avoids the problems functionalism encounters when explaining ritual or religion as symbolic representations of the political, economic and psychological needs of individuals and society.

Our very brief analysis of the caste system, however, is only a partial explanation of Hinduism. To leave it here would produce a distortion of Hinduism similar to those studies that identify the "wisdom of the East" with the Yogi or Buddhist monk. We must also account for the ascetic tradition in our explanation. Following Dumont, we discover that a structural account of the ascetic tradition in Hinduism is as elegant as it is surprising. The ascetic, the renouncer, is in opposition to caste, he is an outcaste. The ascetic tradition in India is a transformation of a hierarchical system of relations based upon the opposition "pure/impure" into its opposite, "neither pure/impure." The new set of relations is now pure/impure in opposition to neither pure nor impure. We can describe the total structure of Hinduism as follows:

The Structure Of Hinduism

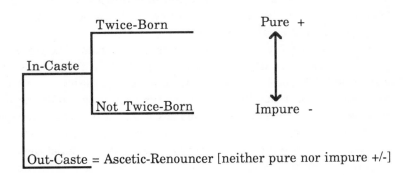

Figure 2

Figure 2 illustrates the point that the ascetic is literally an outcaste, one who has renounced caste. P. V. Kane's monumental work, The History Of Dharmashastra, provides substantial evidence which supports this conclusion in classical Hinduism. Anyone in caste may become a renouncer. By renouncing caste the ascetic gives away all of his goods and looses all rights to family property and inheritance. He draws his fire into himself, that is to say, he completes his own funeral ceremony. The ascetic renounces one of the most important rituals in all of the Hindu rites of passage -- marriage. It is marriage that links the past with the future as the birth of sons provides for the continued well-being of the ancestors through ritual. The ascetic is not touched by purity or impurity. If the classical texts can be trusted, Shankara, one of the great ascetic-philosophers of Hinduism argued that if twice-born the ascetic should give up the sacred thread. Thus, it is not only marriage that is renounced but also the ritual which every twice-born is obligated to perform. (It is worth remembering that twice-born [dvija] in Hinduism is defined as one who has performed the Upanayana ritual during youth. It is this rite of passage that is the necessary condition for marriage.) The ascetic in India is an outcaste. An outcaste is one who has renounced caste. Thus, asceticism in Hinduism, as well as in Indian Buddhism, is an inverse relation to caste. Caste as a set of relations constituted by the opposition pure/impure affirms karma. The ascetic, having renounced caste, seeks to eliminate karma altogether. Notice the remarkable consistency, the rationality in the wonder that is Hinduism. There is nothing mysterious, or mystifying, in the position taken by the ascetic. To understand the ascetic in Hinduism involves placing this religious phenomenon back where it belongs -- in opposition to caste. In the final analysis, we find that although the ascetic is in opposition to caste the ascetic tradition does not contradict caste. In fact the two poles are complementary. If caste is a hierarchical set of relations in which the individual is not, then the yogi in opposition to caste and hierarchy affirms the same thing in the achievement of liberation. If the advaitan tradition, that most popular of all Hindu ascetic philosophical systems, asserts anything at all, it is that the individual is not. Both the world and the individual are maya; that is, they are neither real or unreal. And Buddhism, born in India as one of the great caste renouncing systems, places the doctrine of "no self," and "pratityasamutpada" (the doctrine of causation) at the center of its teachings.7

We are now prepared to give a complete definition of Hinduism. Hinduism is the religion which is defined by the significance of the oppositional relation caste/ascetic. This definition also serves as a litmus test for books and articles on Hinduism. If the description breaks the oppositional relation or emphasizes one element of the relation, we may suspect a distortion of Hinduism. One of the consequences of this approach to religion entails rewriting most of the handbooks and essays on Hinduism. Furthermore, we now have good reasons for thinking that it may be the case that descriptions and explanations of other religions are also defective. Buddhism comes to mind rather quickly because of its birth in India.

CASE II.

Instead of staying within the field of the historian and phenomenologist of religion, let us move to anthropology for an example for our second case. Melford Spiro's work on Burmese Buddhism is an excellent example of a problem that has bewitched Buddhist studies for decades. The problem is disclosed in the title of Spiro's book; Buddhism And Society: A Great Tradition and Its Burmese Viscissitudes.8 The words "Great Tradition" are what I want to focus on. Once again, a religious system is split into two: great and little tradition, or normative and popular Buddhism. Spiro corrects the long-standing notion that Buddhism is a religion of nihilism and pessimism but then divides Buddhism into three systems. "Buddhism is best viewed as comprising not one, but three separate if interlocking systems: two soteriological (one normative and one nonnormative) and one nonsoteriological" primarily concerned with protection from illness and danger.9 Spiro calls these three systems Nibbanic, (nirvana), Kammatic, (karma) and Apotropaic Buddhism. The first is a normative soteriological system, the second is soteriological but not normative, and the third is neither soteriological nor normative. What used to be a dualistic religious tradition, ascetic-canonical vs. popular-folk Buddhism has now developed into a triad. This means that the Buddhist tradition is becoming more schizoid as we try to understand it. The problem, of course, has to do with how we begin. Once we start with the Buddhist monk and the sangha as defining "true" Buddhism or normative

Buddhism we bump into an immediate problem -- what to do with those Buddhists who are obviously not following the ascetic path to nirvana and are, in fact, contradicting that path in their lives as householders.

We do not have to go to Burma or Thailand to discover this. The Theravada canon itself recognizes two kinds of Buddhists -- monks and laypersons. Once the relation between the two is ruptured the pieces of the Buddhist puzzle never fit together again, and the outcome of our study always seems to make Buddhism incoherent, if not irrational. Here we have a clear example, once again, of starting with one of the elements and constructing the system by adding them together one by one, rather than viewing the system as an interdependent whole. I must add that Spiro's view of Buddhism is not unique; it follows what has become the standard approach to Buddhism -- normative Buddhism is synonymous with the monk.

The ideology of the Buddhist "Eightfold Path," the ascetic community (the sangha), is usually identified as the essential element for defining Buddhism. This definition clearly produces a distortion of the religion.

Structural analysis, holistic in its approach, allows us to describe and explain this religion more adequately. Buddhism, as well as Hinduism, always was and will be a religion which is constituted by the relation renouncer/householder or monk/layperson. And it is this relation which is normative! Anyone familiar with Indian Buddhist texts, including the Pali canon known as the Tripitaka, knows that this relation is consistently affirmed throughout the history of Buddhism in India and elsewhere in South Asia.

This relation can be described somewhat differently by using the king as the householder or layperson. It is to Tambiah's great credit that he saw this as crucial for an understanding of Buddhism. He saw this because of the structuralist approach he used for analyzing this religion. The title of one of his books, World Conqueror and World Renouncer, is right on target.10 The great Buddhist stupas and temples in India, Burma and Sri Lanka confirm the fact that the great ascetic is continually thought of in royal terms. One thing seems certain; there simply is no such thing as Buddhism without the relation ascetic/layperson. And that relation is one of opposition. Thus, it should come as no surprise that the layperson does not seek nirvana but seeks a better life in the next world through service to the monk and the sangha. The reciprocity between the sangha and the layperson is as rational as can be; the giving of gifts yields merit in return. And the monk is literally dependent on the householder for his existence -- a point that is as obvious as it is significant for an understanding of Buddhism.

Since Tambiah has thoroughly documented this reciprocal relation in another study of Thai Buddhism, I shall not repeat it here. Toward the end of this rare structural analysis of Buddhism, Tambiah demonstrates the synchronic structure of what he calls "the religious field."11   It can be rewritten in the following way:

The Structure Of Thai Buddhism.

A :	B ::	C :	D
Buddha	Life Spirits	Guardian Spirits	Bad Spirits
Monk	Ritual Elder	Intermediary	Exorcist
Collective Merit	Rites of Passage	Agricultural Rites	Rites of Affliction
Total Community	House/ Neighbor	Total Community	Patient
Good Death/ Rebirth	Good Life	Protective/ Fertility	Bad Death/ Rebirth
Pali Spoken	Local Language	Local Language	Pali Spoken

Figure 4

Each column in this formal structure represents a set of persons, functions, and rituals. Thus, column A begins with the Buddha and the monk whose ritual performances are essentially for collective merit, although the monk is also engaged for blessing the home and at funerals. He is not engaged however, in what we usually call individual rites of passage such as marriage rituals. The ritual for collective merit is for a good death and rebirth and the language of the ritual is in Pali, a language which the layperson does not understand.

Column B represents the life spirits and their rituals. They are performed by elders of the village who perform the rituals in the local language. The guardian spirits are usually called upon for protection and fertility and are involved in important agricultural rituals. The bad or malevolent spirits, the Phii cause bad death and rebirth and are confronted by exorcists who are trained in their profession by teachers who use secret mantras. The language they use for the rituals of exorcism is Pali. What this analysis highlights that might not otherwise be noticed is the inverse relation between the monk and exorcist even though they both use Pali.

There is much in Tambiah's work that is new and worth reflecting upon for further development. The results of his research are good examples of structuralist theory at work. There is, however, one basic problem that needs to be worked out. Tambiah thinks that the collective merit rituals, chanted in Pali, that he has analyzed are primarily communication systems. The problem is, we are never told just what is being communicated. Whatever the answer is, we could then ask, but why are they communicating in this strange way when they could just speak to each other? When we recall, as is the case in many religions, that when the monks utter Pali Sutras most if not all of the community do not understand them, the mystery of communication deepens.

I am afraid that the notion that ritual is primarily a communication system is in deep trouble. The idea that ritual is a "performative utterance" is a good one, but it is an oversimplification of the complexity of ritual. If there is a "code" that is hidden in ritual, then it must be made clear just what the code and the message is. And as I have already pointed out, when that is made explicit we must also have an answer for why people communicate in this way since we have just demonstrated that the message can be put into ordinary langauge.12

CASE III.

A great deal of successful work has been accomplished in the structural study of myth. Unfortunately, Hinduism has not received its share of attention. I suspect that the reason for this lack of attention is due to the continuing influence of the 19th century on the study of the religions of Asia. The assumptions that myths are false, or that they are proto-philosophy, or the product of folk religion are basic to much that has been published about Hinduism. These approaches to myth also help explain the assumption that the essence of Hinduism is to be found in Indian asceticism. How else do we explain the fact that one of the richest mythological mines in the history of religion has been left unexplored in texts on Hinduism.13

You will recall that in the introduction I defined myth as a story that has a beginning, middle and end, that we have good reason to believe is or was transmitted orally and the story is about the acts of superhuman beings. This clarification of the term "myth" clearly leaves us with an enormous corpus to study. With this precise meaning for the term in mind I shall follow Lévi-Strauss and assert that the purpose of myth is to provide a logical model of overcoming a contradiction, an impossible achievement if, as it happens, the contradiction is real. That is to say, myths will not achieve their purpose if there is an inherent contradiction in the material conditions of existence. This does not in any way deny the logical structure of myth nor does it reduce myth to the infrastructures of existence. I shall bracket or suspend the question whether myths assume or entail truth conditions. This is a crucial question which I shall attempt to resolve at another time.

The Puranic literature is indeed huge. The myths contained in them are often quite bizarre and violent. This makes it quite difficult for scholars to convince us that they are symbolic expressions of The Sacred. Nevertheless, this great corpus of mythology is a crucial part of Hinduism. Let us, then, follow the lead of structuralists and apply this analysis to a cycle of myths that, as far as I know, have not been studied from a structuralist approach. The cycle of myths I have chosen can be found in the second section of the Shiva Purana called the Rudrasamhita (i.e. the tradition of Rudra/Shiva).14 The Samhita is divided into five books, or sections, of about one thousand pages of translated narrative.

The story, as usual, begins with the creation of the cosmos by Brahma the creator god. The point of the myths is usually given at the end of each cycle. For example, after telling a myth, Brahma concludes by saying, "Whoever reads, teaches, listens to or narrates this story derives all desires.... A sick man becomes free from sickness, a frightened man becomes free from fear, no one will be harassed by spirits, a brahmin derives splendor, a Kshatriya becomes victorious, a Vaishya prospers and a Shudra attain equality with the good. It confers salvation and reveals Shiva and increases devotion to Shiva."15 The main point of the myths is obvious -- Shiva is the best of all deities.

Before producing a brief synopsis of the cycles of the myth, I think it might be wise to provide the basic structure of Hindu mythology to those not familiar with it. Although the gods do relate to man (Krishna in the Bhagavad Gita is a good example), their primary activity is in relation to the Asuras who are their opponents. The term "Asura" is often translated as "demon." This is correct if taken in the classical sense, that is, a demon is an opponent of a deity. Thus, we can translate "Asura" as "demon," as long as we do not imply that these beings are essentially evil in nature. In brief, the gods are in opposition to the demons. To complete the structure, let me point out that the cosmologies of Hinduism provide us with a fourfold classification of beings. Brahma, the four-faced creator god, creates the cosmos together with its cardinal directions. The cosmological domain of the gods is in the east, that of the demons is in the west. Thus, most Hindu temples are entered from the east. Man is situated in the north and is in opposition to the ancestors which are located in the south. According to the ritual texts, when a young boy performs the ritual of the sacred thread (the twice-born ritual) he stands north of the fire facing west. At the moment of his rebirth he faces east.16 The point of this brief digression is that it is important to notice that such instructions are not accidental or incoherent. Let us now turn to the cycles of the myth of Shiva as narrated in the Rudrasamhita of the Shiva Purana.

The Samhita begins with several chapters on the relations between Shiva, Vishnu and Brahma; the various modes of worshiping Shiva; and the deception of Narada. After creating the cosmos, Brahma creates a host of beings, including the famous seven sages, who are mind-born. He also creates daughters and gives them in marriage to the sages, his sons! One of the offspring of these marriages is Kubera, "ill-shaped," with three legs and jagged teeth. He practices extreme asceticism reducing himself to skin and bone. Because of his single-minded devotion, Shiva grants him divine vision. Given this vision, Kubera sees Parvati, Shiva's wife, and desires her. Parvati becomes quite irritated about this and complains to Shiva, "Why does this wicked ascetic look at me and often say, 'you make my penance shine!'" Shiva laughs and replies, "He is your son." He then turns to Kubera and says, "Come on, this is your mother, fall at her feet with delighted heart." Parvati then says, "You shall be called Kubera (deformed body) since you jealously looked at me." Shiva and Parvati then depart for their dwelling place. Shiva eventually arrives on Mt. Kailasa without Parvati but, with a huge entourage, is crowned king and lives happily together with Kubera on Mt. Kailasa. Kubera becomes the keeper of Shiva's treasury.

The second cycle repeats the story of Brahma creating the sages and adds that one of Brahma's daughters is Sandhya. Both father Brahma and his sons desire her, and out of Brahma's mental desires Kama is born. (Kama is the cupid of Hinduism.) Kama is cursed by Brahma and later in the cycles is burned to death by Shiva, then restored on the request of Kama's wife. Shiva notices that Brahma desires his own daughter and says, "Oh Brahma, how is it that you were so overwhelmed with lustful feeling on seeing your own daughter? Sister, brother's wife and daughter are like one's own mother." (II.3.39-45)

Brahma is now in distress. Rebuked and insulted by Shiva, he begins to perspire, and from the drops of sweat a woman, Rati, is born. (The text states that it is Daksha who gives birth to Rati.) Kama, restored, meets Rati and marries her, and they all return to their proper abodes. Sandhya, meanwhile, is renamed as Arundhati and marries Vasishtha, Brahma's (or Daksha's) son. Sandhya, therefore, has married her brother! In this cycle it is very clear that Brahma thinks that Shiva is his son.

Daksha, one of the sages and original mind-born sons of Brahma begins the third cycle which is a duplicate of cycle two. Daksha begets sons that are also mind-born and twice produces sons through intercourse with his wife Virini. The sexually produced sons are instructed by their father to go West to do penance in order to produce progeny. They head west and meet Narada who tells them that they should first seek the end of the earth. They follow his instruction into extinction. Daksha curses Narada for this. He then creates daughters, including Sati.

Sati wins Shiva who falls in love with her because of her strict vows of meditation. Shiva pleads with Brahma to make Daksha accept him as a son-in-law. Brahma then acts as a go-between and his scheme finally succeeds. A marriage is planned by the pleased parents of Sati, and Brahma is the chief ritualist, or Brahmin (purohita), at the wedding. On seeing the feet of the bride, Brahma is overcome with desire and spills his semen on the ground. Shiva, seeing this, threatens to kill him, but Vishnu points out that they are all one. The wedding ends happily, and Shiva and Sati go to Mt. Kailasa to live.

A fourth cycle now takes place. A great sacrifice is about to be performed at Prayoga, which is on the north bank of the Ganges river at the confluence of the Ganges and the Yumna. It is below the mountains on the plain. All the sages and gods are there. Daksha appears, and all salute him as the patriarch of Brahmans; all, that is, save Shiva who stays seated. Daksha is furious; gravely insulted, he curses Shiva saying, "How is it that this shameless frequenter of cremation grounds does not bow to me? He is devoid of rituals. He has cast off the rituals. Besides, he is always engrossed in the love of his wife." (II.26.14-18)

Sometime later Daksha, begins to perform another sacrifice to which Sati and Shiva are not invited. Sati descends from the mountain, is received respectfully, and begins to argue with her father Daksha. In anger she throws herself into the fire of the sacrifice and burns herself to death. Shiva appears and cuts off Daksha's head. He then restores Daksha to life by replacing his head with the head of a goat. Daksha praises Shiva and invites him to the ritual performance.

The fifth cycle is the beginning of the third section of the Rudrasamhita. Once again, cycles two and three are duplicated. Here we find Himavat (Lord of the Mountain) and Mena, his wife, dwelling on a mountain. Mena is the daughter of Svadha, Svadha is one of Daksha's daughters; thus, Brahma is her grandfather. Himavat and Mena are childless. A son is born. Then Parvati is mind-born and placed in Mena's womb. The birth is miraculous, and it is predicted that Parvati will marry a naked ascetic who is without father or mother.

Himavat introduces Parvati to Shiva, and Shiva rebukes him for doing this. Parvati falls head over heals for Shiva and departs for the forest to practice asceticism in order to win Shiva over against the strong commands of her mother not to do so. Separated from Shiva, Parvati practices yoga for over 3,000 years. Finally, Shiva is persuaded to marry her, for only his son can kill the terrible demon Taraka (an Asura) who has appeared in this cycle.

Mena, Parvati's mother, is absolutely beside herself about Parvati's choice of a husband. The chief of Brahmins reminds them that Shiva is not a suitable husband; he is a naked ascetic, his age is unknown, he cannot support her, and he has no kinsmen. (III.31.44-52) Finally, when Mena does see Shiva she faints. Upon recovery she threatens to kill herself. Parvati, she tells the assembled group, has made a laughing stock out of the whole family. She reminds them once again that Shiva "has neither a mother nor a father, no brother or kinsmen. He has no beauty, no skill, not even a house of his own." (III.44.68-70)

Mena finally and grudgingly consents to the marriage. It takes place with Brahma once again at the head of the ritual. And once again upon seeing the bride, Brahma is overcome with desire and spills his semen on the earth. Brahma of course, is Parvati's grandfather! Once again, Shiva sees what has happened and threatens to kill Brahma. He is persuaded not to, and the cycle closes with Shiva and Parvati happily travelling to Mt. Kailasa.

The sixth cycle now takes place. Although Shiva and Parvati are happily married and make passionate love for over 1,000 years, Parvati has yet to give birth to a son. The demon Taraka is still alive. The gods are shaken by their strenuous lovemaking, and Agni is sent to plead with them to slow down for the whole earth is trembling. Interrupted at love, Shiva ejaculates his sperm, and Agni swallows it before it has a chance to hit the ground. Parvati naturally becomes quite agitated by the interruption and curses the gods to remain barren as she is. Agni, in the meantime, cannot contain the sperm he has swallowed because of its heat (tapas). He is advised to place it in a woman. Meanwhile the Krittikas, the six wives of the original mind-born sages, have gone to the Ganges for a bath. Chilled, they draw near to a fire, which is Agni. Agni disperses Shiva's sperm into all of the wives through the pores of their skin. All six are now pregnant, and when their husbands find out about it they are anything but happy. The six wives cannot contain the sperm either, they throw it up, form a foetus, and deliver it to Himavat. Himavat, in turn cannot contain the foetus either and throws it up into the Ganges. (If you have followed the story thus far, let me just complicate it a little more by adding the information that the Ganga is indeed a river, but Ganga is also a daughter of Daksha. Thus, Himavat has just thrown up his son-in-law's sperm into the womb of his wife's mother's sister.)

Ganga cannot contain the sperm and throws it up into the reeds. Skanda is born in the reeds and is adopted by the six wives of the sages. Now, let me remind you that the six wives, the Krittikas, are also daughters of Daksha; they were married to Daksha's brothers, the original mind-born sons of Brahma. Thus, Brahma is indeed the grandfather of them all.

Skanda, reed born, is finally adopted by Shiva and Parvati. He is crowned chief of Shiva's troops, and he does eventually kill the demon Taraka in an incredibly bloody conflict. He returns to Mt. Kailasa victorious and lives with Shiva and Parvati. One of his main duties is to guard the door of Shiva and Parvati's bedroom to prevent anyone from interrupting their lovemaking.

The seventh cycle at the end of book four of the Rudrasamhita finds Parvati alone taking a bath. Shiva interrupts her, obviously wanting to make love. She becomes irritated with him and kicks him out of the bathroom. Barren all of this time, adopting Skanda as their only child, Parvati takes the dirt from her bath and creates a son called Ganesha. (In some versions she creates Ganesha out of her sari.) She requests of Ganesha that he should become the guardian of her door, replacing Skanda. His duty is to keep Shiva out! Ganesha does his job very well and Shiva is furious. All of Shiva's troops fight Ganesha and fail to overcome him. Finally, Shiva himself takes over and kills Ganesha. He cuts off Ganesha's head and later restores Ganesha to life by replacing his head with that of an elephant. He becomes a devoted son of Shiva and Parvati. Ganesha marries two daughters of Visvarupa, a brother of Daksha. He has two sons, one from each of his wives.

Skanda, in the meantime, is very upset because he believes he has been tricked. Both Skanda and Ganesha were told by their parents, Shiva and Parvati, that whoever first walked around the earth would win the daughters of Visvarupa. Skanda immediately started off on the journey. Reflecting on the instructions, however, Ganesha simply walks around his parents. Upon returning, Skanda finds that Ganesha has married the two women each of whom have given birth to a son. Skanda is deeply hurt. He tells his parents that he is leaving for Mt. Kraunca. They forbid it, but Skanda replies, "Oh parents, I shall not stay here for a moment when deception has been practiced as affection." (IV.20.25) Skanda leaves and even to this day remains a bachelor on the mountain.

The fourth book ends here, but the story continues in the fifth book of the Rudrasamhita which contains five major cycles. The first involves the famous story of how Shiva destroyed the three great cities of three powerful Asuras through deception and with a single arrow. The second concerns the birth, marriage and battles of Jalandhara who is born in the ocean from the brilliance of Shiva's third eye. The third cycle is the birth, marriage, death and restoration by Shiva of Shankhacuda. The fourth is the story of the birth of Andhaka from the sweat of Shiva which is produced during sexual intercourse with Parvati. Andhaka, blind, deformed and black in color, is given to the head of the demons and is eventually killed by Shiva then restored and adopted by Shiva and Parvati. Shiva then swallows Bhargava who is emitted as Shiva's semen and renamed Shukra. In the final episode, Vidala and Utpala are slain by Shiva because of their passion and attempted abduction of Parvati. The gods rejoice and return to their abodes. Shiva and Parvati also return to their dwelling on the mountain. The samhita ends with the following advice, "the Rudrasamhita yields enjoyment here and liberation hereafter. The man who reads this Samhita that wards off harassment from enemies shall attain all desires. Thereafter he shall attain liberation." (V.59.39-49)

Let us now turn to the analysis of the myth. It should be obvious that the myth I have described cannot be read as a symbolic representation of Indian social life! In fact this myth confirms Lévi-Strauss' finding that myths often express just the opposite structure of social life. The myth also disconfirms the notion that all myths are to be imitated as models of The Sacred. The myth is not imitated simply because it is so seemingly bizarre, but because we as human beings cannot imitate the acts of superhuman beings. The main business of the gods has to do with the demons with which they are in direct opposition. The text makes it crystal clear that the point is not "imitate me," that is, practice yoga as I do and you will achieve all your desires. It states over and over again, if you hear the myth, or read it, you will find liberation. Although there are undoubtedly different versions of the myth in the Hindu tradition, it is unnecessary if not impossible, to search for the original or an "urmyth" which we could use as a code to decipher the cycles as they appear in the Shiva Purana. I shall adhere to the hypothesis that the history of a myth is not to be confused with its meaning.

What we need is a synchronic analysis of the cycles. The diagram below (Figure 5) is based upon the first model Lévi-Strauss used in his 1958 analysis of the Oedipus myth. From my study of Lévi-Strauss, I have concluded that this model is the most successful. The analysis should also demonstrate once again that the widespread criticism that it is impossible to follow Lévi-Strauss, or that you cannot verify what he is doing, is simply false. This does not imply that this model is not in need of revision or that someone could not come up with a more adequate model. I shall simply follow the 1958 version as the most intelligible.

THE SYNCHRONIC STRUCTURE OF THE MYTH OF SHIVA

| A | : | B | :: | C | : | D |

| ASCETICSIM | : | EROTICISM | :: | DESTRUCTION | : | CREATION |

A	B	C	D
1. Kubera Meditates (grandson of Brahma)	Kubera desires Parvati his mother	Kubera looses an eye	Dwells on Mt. Kailasa with Shiva
2.Brahma creates sons & daughters (all mind born)	Brahma & sons desire Sandhya	Shiva condemns Brahma curses	Sandhya & Kama marry
3.Daksha creates sons & daughters Sati practices yoga	Brahma desires Sati	Shiva threatens to kill Brahma	Sati marries Shiva & they dwell on Mt.
4.[a great sacrifice takes place at the Ganges and Yumna rivers]		Daksha curses Shiva, Sati burns herself to death Shiva kills Daksha	Daksha restored & Shiva attends great. ritual
5.Himavat and Mena create Parvati Parvati meditates	Brahma desires Parvati	Shiva threatens to kill Brahma	Shiva & Parvati marry & live Mt. Kailasa
6.-----------------------	Shiva spills seed, Agni swallows it	Parvati curses gods to be barren as she is	Skanda is born and adopted by Shiva & Parvati
7.-----------------------	----------------------	------------------------	Ganesha born from Parvati's bath water
8.-----------------------	Strong bonds between Ganesha and Parvati	Shiva kills Ganesha	Ganesha restored and marries, has two sons
9.Skanda leaves for Mt. forever a bachelor	-----------------------	------------------------	----------------------

Figure 5

Although a great deal of the narrative has been left out of my synopsis, I do not think I have distorted the story itself. Given the narrative, I do not think I have manufactured a false or deceptive diagram or forced the myth into an illegitimate form.

The diagram can be read in two ways. The first is syntagmatic or diachronic from left to right, top to bottom. When read this way, we find the sequence of events and the cycles of the myth unfolding as they are given in the text. We can also read the text synchronically and paradigmatically, reading each column one at a time from top to bottom, right to left. Using the formula A : B :: C : D we may write the synchronic structure of the myth as follows: Asceticism is to Eroticism as Destruction is to Death. Or, Asceticism : Eroticism :: Death : Life.

The myth is a striking example of what Lévi-Strauss has called the methodological opposition of nature/culture; am I from one or am I from two, from nature or culture? With two exceptions, to which I shall return, all the births are either mind-born, produced through meditation, or generated through sweat, dirt, or by swallowing semen. That is to say, none are natural births. Moreover, and this is especially the case with the artificial births Shiva produces, the offspring must first be killed and then restored to life, or given a new name. Thus, biological reproduction and incest are denied; superhuman beings are "mind-born."

The two exceptions are quite interesting. The first appears in the third cycle. Virini, Daksha's wife gives birth to thousands of sons and sixty daughters. Daksha instructs the sons to go West; doing so, they are told by Narada to seek the end of the earth before procreating. They head out into extinction! The daughters are given to various sages.

The second exception is the natural birth of two daughters from the union of Ganesha and his two wives in cycle seven.17 What is of interest here is that in both instances it is not sons, but daughters who have a natural birth and survive.

The myths obviously contradict the social and religious world of Hinduism. Shiva is quite correct in his condemnation of Brahma's incestous desires -- "you should not covet your daughter, sister or brother's wife for they are like ones mother." The classical texts on caste obligations (Dharma) insist on death for those who commit incest.

Mena is also quite right in her outrage at Parvati's choice for a husband. Shiva is an ascetic. Hindu asceticism is in opposition to caste. More concretely, Hindu asceticism is in opposition to the householder (grihastha). All of the authors of the various texts on Dharma (Dharma Shastras) glorify the householder and are hostile to asceticism. Some of the oldest texts claim that there is only one status or stage (ashram) in human life, the householder. Manu, one of the well-known classical texts, praises the householder as the most important, since without the householder the other classical stages of Hinduism, student, hermit, ascetic, would be impossible.18

Mena states it very well. She says, "what an awful bridegroom. He has neither father nor mother, he has no kinsmen, no skill, not even a house, he is not learned." Shiva is in opposition to Hindu dharma which the authors of the Dharma Shastras sum up as a threefold debt that must be paid; to the sages, the study of the Veda, to the gods the performance of ritual, and to the ancestors the founding of a family. Thus, Shiva's marriage is condemned from the very beginning.

It is a mistake to concentrate on Shiva as the central element or symbol which gives meaning to the myth. The basic tension, if not contradiction, which runs throughout all of the cycles is based upon the opposition between asceticism/eroticism, destruction/creation, death/life. And this basic set of oppositions is fully represented in Shiva/Parvati. Shiva dwells on a mountain as an ascetic. Parvati, mountain born, begins her life in a household and leaves home to become an ascetic in order to win Shiva. The cycle which contains the story of Sati is obviously an inverse duplicate of the Parvati cycle. One of the interesting aspects of her story in cycle three is that Shiva is painfully in love with Sati and pleads for her hand. In the Parvati cycle Shiva rebukes Himavat, her father, for bringing Parvati to him. On meeting them, Shiva says, "Oh Himavat, I forbid you to bring her near me again. I am an ascetic, ascetics should not have any relations with women, they are the root of all attachments." (III.12.28-33) Moreover, we must remember that Brahma himself, as well as his offspring, is, in turn, an ascetic and an erotic figure. Shiva is not unique in the myths. We must also notice that in the Sati cycle the parents are pleased with the proposals for marriage. Mena in the Parvati cycle bitterly opposes the marriage; nevertheless, the wedding takes place, and the marriage endures. The marriage of Sati and Shiva ends in disaster. Sati burns herself to death in the ritual fire.

Hinduism, as do most, if not all, religions, has explicit rules regarding the avoidance of incest. In classical Hinduism such rules are known as sapinda. They describe the degree of distance required from common ancestors for legitimate marriages. The rules are quite complex, and there seems to be no agreement in the Dharma Shastras regarding the exact number of degrees. Lingat sums up the primary sources as follows: "She should not be related to her future husband through an ancestor nearer than six degrees on the father's side or four degrees (counting exclusively on the intended spouse) on the mother's side... or six degrees in both lines...."19

It is as clear as can be that in every instance the rule of sapinda has been violated in the Shiva cycle described above. Brahma creates mind-born sons and daughters who marry each other. Daksha and Virini are brother and sister and so are Kama and Rati. Sandhya, renamed Arundhati, marries either her brother or her uncle. Shiva is the son of Brahma and marries either his sister or niece, Parvati. A close examination of the myth reveals that the sixty daughters of Daksha are given to his brothers and a nephew. This should come as no surprise. Incest is an inevitable consequence of the creation of the cosmos from a single principle or person.

What is surprising is that Shiva knows the law of sapinda very well. Recall that he rebukes Brahma saying, "Sister, brother's wife and daughter are like one's own mother!" In the very next cycle Shiva will marry his brother's daughter. And that marriage will end in a disaster.

What about the wedding and married life of Shiva and Parvati? The marriage is never consummated -- their passionate love-making is always interrupted. It is not the case that Parvati is in bed with Shiva just for the fun of it. The aim throughout the cycles is to have children. Recall that when their love-making is interrupted by Agni, Parvati curses the gods to remain as barren as she is. Their marriage contradicts the law of sapinda, and this contradiction will not be resolved through the "natural" reproduction of children. It is also important to remember that Shiva is an ascetic, and this only compounds the contradiction.

Let us take a brief look at the three "offspring." Shiva tells Parvati that Kubera is her son, but it seems as if she knows better. Kubera is told to bow down to his mother. She does not really accept him as a son and goes off to live by herself. Shiva moves in with Kubera on Mt. Kailasa, and they become close "friends." In the sixth cycle Shiva's semen is swallowed by Agni, the final result being the "birth" of Skanda among the reeds. He is adopted by Shiva and Parvati and will end up on a mountain as a bachelor. Next, Ganesha is born from the dirt of Parvati, becomes her door keeper to keep Shiva out, is killed by Shiva, given the head of an elephant, and then marries two wives. In the fifth book of the Samhita, the birth stories are completely reversed once again. Andhaka is born as the result of the sweat from Parvati's hands which wet Shiva's third eye during their love-making. Here, very clearly, the roles are reversed; it is Parvati who "inseminates" Shiva! (It is important to remember that sweat is also linked to meditation; the yogin becomes heated, literally sweats, when meditating. But, the act of meditation is not synonymous with the sexual act; no character that I am aware of in the Siva cycles produces offspring through the sweat of meditation; Parvati creates Ganesha from her dirt, not the sweat of her meditation.)

Andhaka is also born deformed as Kubera and blind. Emperor of all the Asuras, he also passionately desires Parvati! Viraka, another adopted son, is the guardian of her door and keeps Andhaka out. Andhaka is eventually impaled on Shiva's trident. Thus, Ganesha is the only "child" born without Shiva's participation and seems to be the only "son" who lives out a "normal" life -- his sons are not the consequence of a violation of sapindaship. This is what should be expected. Ganesha though born miraculously does not resolve the contradiction between the ascetic/erotic, nor is his birth a violation of the law against incest.

It seems clear that we could continue this analysis indefinitely. There are numerous sets of oppositions and reversals within the cycles which I have not mentioned. Once we compare these cycles with the mythical cycles of other Puranas, the task becomes almost endless.20 Nevertheless, I believe I have demonstrated that there is a specific structure to the cycles. We can conclude by displaying the structure in the following way:

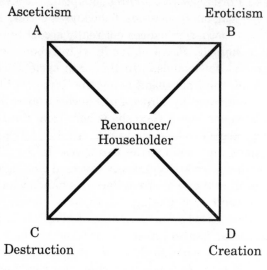

Figure 6

Figure 6 represents the form of the cycles. The basic oppositions remain the same, A : B :: C : D. Moreover, we can now see the inversions quite clearly: A is the inverse of D -- Kubera, deformed and meditating is the inverse of Ganesha married with sons. Or, if you would rather start with what I have marked as the second cycle, we get, Brahma creating mind-born sons and daughters is the inverse of Ganesha married with sons. We also have a second set of inversions, C - D. Kubera dwelling on a mountain with Shiva and Parvati is the inverse of Skanda on a Mt. forever a bachelor; or the marriages of Sandhya and Kama as the inverse of Skanda the bachelor. These sets of oppositions together with the contradictions they generate are mediated by Shiva and Parvati. Both are ambiguous. It is true that Shiva is an ascetic who becomes a householder and Parvati is within a household and becomes an ascetic, but both are fertile and fail to produce children together. Shiva has long been known as the ascetic whose phallus is always erect. Shiva, however, is only one element in the system; it is the oppositional relation which defines who he is. As we have seen, the opposition is with the householder, more specifically, with Parvati. Parvati can be described as forever a passionate lover, and she is an ascetic.

We can now repeat some of the conclusions that were reached by Lévi-Strauss. First, we can see how mistaken approaches to myth are that assume that myths are attempts to explain natural phenomena. Second, we can also see how mistaken the reaction is to explain the essence of myth as a moralizing about some aspect of human life, such as love, death, suffering, or courage. I shall not, however, take the final step that Lévi-Strauss took and ask to "what final meaning these mutually significative meanings are referring -- since in the last resort and in their totality they must refer to something...."21 His answer is well known, the totality of meaning refers to the mind. We need not take this problematic step simply because the meaning of myth may not refer to anything at all!

After showing us where the mistake was made, Lévi-Strauss seems to fall back into it. The mistake, as we have seen, is to think that myths refer to nature, or to some aspect of human nature (love, suffering, etc.). Lévi-Strauss is surely correct in thinking that this approach simply trivializes myth. Structuralism has underscored the problem of the meaning of myth; it has not solved it. We must take great care in our attempts to resolve this problem to remember that the solution does not necessarily imply that in the end myths must refer to something. If this turns out to be the case, that the meaning of myth is not referential, then we will indeed have demonstrated something that both historians and phenomenologists of religion have argued all along; myths are autonomous, their meanings cannot be "reduced" to nature or society. The cost, of course, also entails cashing in any reference to The Sacred. I think that the gain of an adequate semantics for myth is well worth the cost.

NOTES

1. "Hinduism," *Encyclopedia of Religion*, ed. Mircea Eliade, vol. 6 (New York: Macmillan, 1987).

2. R. N. Dandekar, "Hinduism," *Historia Religionum*, eds. C. J. Bleeker and Geo Widengren, vol. II (Leiden: Brill, 1971), 239.

3. Dandekar 241.

4. See Louis Dumont, *Homo Hierarchicus: The Caste System and its Implications*, complete revised English ed. (Chicago: U of Chicago P, 1980) 32. (The original French edition appeared in 1966.) My account of the problem and the solution of the caste puzzle is heavily indebted to Dumont's research.

5. See Dumont, chap. 2.

6. Dumont, 272.

7. A great deal has been written about Dumont's theory. Since the theory places ritual at the foundation of caste, Marxists in particular have been especially caustic in their criticism. For constructive comments and revisions of the theory see Veena Das, *Structure and Cognition*, (Delhi: Oxford UP, 1977) esp. chap. 2; Richard Burghart, "Renunciation in the Religious Traditions of South Asia," *Man* 18 (1983): 635-53; "Symposium: The Contributions of Louis Dumont," *Journal of Asian Studies* XXXV (1976) and *Way of Life: King, Householder, Renouncer, Essays in honour of Louis Dumont, ed. by T. N. Madan (Delhi: Vikas Publishing House, 1982)*..

8. Melford E. Spiro, *Buddhism and Society: A Great Tradition and Its Burmese Viscissitudes*, 2nd, expanded ed. (Berkeley: U of California P, 1982).

9. Spiro 12. Since I have discussed functionalism I shall not take up Spiro's definition of religion as "a symbolic expression of a restricted set of needs,

fantasies, wishes conflicts, aspirations and so on which are deeply rooted in a universal human nature." Spiro 14.

10. S. J. Tambiah, *World Conqueror and World Renouncer* (Cambridge: Cambridge UP, 1976). It is indeed strange that neither this work nor Tambiah's early book on *Buddhism and the Spirit Cults in North-East Thailand* (Cambridge: Cambridge UP, 1970) are cited in the bibliography of the second edition of Spiro's book. Had he done so, he might have corrected the mistaken comment in note 2 of the first chapter that Tambiah "deliberately ignore[s] canonical Buddhism as a self-conscious methodological stance" (4). Spiro does mention Tambiah in the preface to the second edition but only as confirmation of his findings concerning Burmese Buddhism. The two studies of Buddhism, however, are as different theoretically as night and day. What is of interest here is that the data being used from Thailand and Burma are almost identical and this makes an excellent case study for theoretical comparison.

11. Tambiah, *Buddhism and the Spirit Cults* 338.

12. The notion of "code" appears late in the works of Lévi-Strauss. The basic issue for Lévi-Strauss is the analysis of transformations and comparison of systems, not communication. See Umberto Eco, *Semiotics and the Philosophy of Language* (Bloomington: Indiana UP, 1986) 166-68.

13. Anthologies on the mythology of Hinduism taken from the Puranas have appeared only recently. See Wendy Doniger O'Flaherty, trans., *Hindu Myths* (Baltimore: Penguin, 1975) and Cornelia Dimmitt and J. A. B. van Buitenen, trans. and eds., *Classical Hindu Mythology* (Philadelphia: Temple UP, 1978). Madeleine Biardeau, "Etudes de Mythologie Hindoue," (I) and (II), *Publications de l'Ecole Francaise d'Extreme Orient* LIV-LV (1968) is as outstanding as it is unique in its concentration on the Puranas via structuralism. Wendy O'Flaherty has also concentrated on Puranic literature. Thanks to her research and linguistic competence no one can plead ignorance concerning the mythology of Shiva. See *Asceticism and Eroticism in the Mythology of Shiva* (New York: Oxford UP, 1973).

14. *The Siva Purana*, 4 vols. (Delhi: Banarsidass, 1970) The references refer to this translation of the *Purana* with minor revisions.

15. IV 20, 40-45. The reference refers to the fourth book of the *Rudrasamhita*, chapter 20, verses 40-45.

16. Several years ago I wrote a paper on the cosmological structure of the ritual of becoming twice-born. I believe that this structure can be found in other rites of passage in Hinduism. See Hans H. Penner, "Creating a Brahman: A Structural Approach to Religion," *Methodological Issues in Religious Studies*, ed. Robert D. Baird (Chico, Cal.: New Horizons, 1975); see also Das, esp. chap. 4, "Concepts of Space."

17. Those familiar with the text may want to argue that there is a third exception: the birth of Sati (Shiva/Parvati). As I have already indicated, it is clear that this birth is a miraculous one. The mother goddess of the universe "incarnates" herself into the womb of Daksha's wife.

18. See *The Laws of Manu* (*Sacred Books of the East*, vol. XXV) VI 89-90 and III 77-80; P. V. Kane, *History of*

Dharmasastra, 2nd ed., vol. II, part 1 (Poona: Bhandarkar Oriental Research Inst., 1968) 424ff.; and Robert Lingat, *The Classical Law of India*, trans. J. Duncan M. Derrett (Berkeley: U of Californi P, 1973) 49-50.

19. Lingat 56, see also 156ff. Derrett is less cautious. "The degrees are counted inclusively by ascent *and* descent; thus, the father's father's father's son's son's son is, according to the Hindu method of computation, a *sapinda* in the *fourth* degree. A mother's mother's mother's mother's ancestor's descendent, however near or remote by any method of computation is not a *sapinda*, being beyond the fifth degree." J. Duncan M. Derrett, *Religion, Law and the State in India* (London: Faber, 1968) 17, also 105. For an analysis of the classical literature on *sapinda*, see P. V. Kane, *History of Dharmasastra*, vol. II, part 1 452ff.

20. Much of the work has been done by O'Flaherty. Those who wish to continue this analysis will find both Appendix F, "Index of Motifs," and Appendix G,

"Index of Characters," very useful in locating the specific mythical details in the various Puranas. See O'Flaherty, *Asceticism and Eroticism in the Mythology of Shiva*. Although the sources are not always cited, Vettam Mani, *Puranic Encyclopaedia* (Delhi: Banarsidass, 1975) when used carefully, is a useful resource for identifying the various characters.

21. Claude Lévi-Strauss, *The Raw and the Cooked*, trans. John and Doreen Weightman (New York: Harper, 1969) 341.

BIBLIOGRAPHY OF WORKS CITED

Achinstein, Peter. *Concepts of Science.* Baltimore: Johns Hopkins UP, 1968.

Achinstein, Peter, and Stephen F. Barker, eds. *The Legacy of Logical Positivism.* Baltimore: Johns Hopkins UP, 1969.

Adorno, T. *Zur Metakritik der Erkenntnistheorie: Studien über Husserl und die Phänomenologischen Antinomien.* Stuttgart: Kolhammer, 1956.

Ager, Tryg A., Jerrold L. Aronson, and Robert Weingard. "Are Bridge Laws Really Necessary?" *Nous* VIII (1974): 119-134.

Allen, Douglas. "Edmund Husserl." Eliade, *Encyclopedia.*

---. "The Phenomenology of Religion." Eliade, *Encyclopedia.*

Althusser, Louis. *For Marx.* Trans. Ben Brewster. London: NLB, 1977.

Althusser, Louis, and Etienne Balibar. *Reading Capital.* Trans. Ben Brewster. 2nd ed. London: NLB, 1977.

Banton, Michael, ed. *Anthropological Approaches to the Study of Religion.* London: Tavistock, 1966.

Barnes, Barry. "The Comparison of Belief-Systems: Anomaly Versus Falsehood." Horton and Finnegan 193.

Bartley, William Warren. *The Retreat to Commitment.* 2nd ed. La Salle, Ill.: Open Court, 1984.

222

Beattie, J. H. M. "On Understanding Ritual." Wilson 240-68.

---. "Ritual and Social Change." *Man* 1 (1966): 60-74.

Benoist, Jean-Marie. *The Structural Revolution*. New York: St. Martin's, 1978.

Benveniste, Emile. *Problems in General Linguistics*. Coral Gables, Fla.: U of Miami P, 1971.

Berger, Johannes, and Claus Offe. "Functionalism vs. Rational Choice." *Theory and Society* 11 (1982): 521-26.

Berlin, Brent, and Paul Kay. *Basic Color Terms: Their Universality and Evolution*. Berkeley: U of California P, 1969.

Biardeau, Madeleine. "Etudes de Mythologie Hindoue." (I) and (II). *Publications de l'Ecole Francaise d'Extreme Orient* LIV-LV (1968): (I) 2-45; (II) 5-105.

Bleeker, C. J. *The Rainbow: A Collection of Studies in the Science of Religion*. Leiden: Brill, 1975.

Brodbeck, May, ed. *Readings in the Philosophy of the Social Sciences*. New York: Macmillan, 1968.

Brown, Robert. *Explanation in Social Science*. Chicago: Aldine, 1963.

Brown, Roger. "Reference: In memorial tribute to Eric Lenneberg." *Cognition* 4 (1976): 125-53.

Burghart, Richard. "Renunciation in the Religious Traditions of South Asia." *Man* 18 (1983): 635-53.

Burhenn, Herbert. "Functionalism and the Explanation of Religion." *Journal for the Scientific Study of Religion* 19 (1980): 350-60.

Cohen, G. A. "Functional Explanation, Consequence Explanation, and Marxism." *Inquiry* 25 (1982): 27-56.

---. "Functional Explanations: Reply to Elster." *Political Studies* XXVII (1980): 129-35.

---. *Karl Marx's Theory of History: A Defense*. Princeton: Princeton UP, 1978.

---. "Reply to Elster on 'Marxism, Functionalism and Game Theory.'" *Theory and Society* 11 (1982): 483-95.

Crumrine, N. Ross. "Transformational Processes and Models: with Special Reference to Mayo Indian Myth and Ritual." Rossi 68-87.

Culler, Jonathan. *Ferdinand de Saussure*. New York: Penguin, 1976.

---. *Structuralist Poetics*. London: Routledge, 1975.

Dandekar, R. N. "Hinduism." *Historia Religionum*. Eds. C. J. Bleeker and Geo Widengren. Vol. II. Leiden: Brill, 1971. 237-345.

Das, Veena. *Structure and Cognition*. Delhi: Oxford UP, 1977.

Davidson, Donald. *Inquiries into Truth and Interpretation*. Oxford: Clarendon, 1985.

Derrett, J. Duncan M. *Religion, Law and the State in India*. London: Faber, 1968.

Dimmitt, Cornelia, and J. A. B. van Buitenen, trans. and eds. *Classical Hindu Mythology*. Philadelphia: Temple UP, 1978.

Dreyfus, Hubert L., and Paul Rabinow. *Michel Foucault: Beyond Structuralism and Hermeneutics*. 2nd ed. Chicago: U of Chicago P, 1983.

Dumont, Louis. *Homo Hierarchicus: The Caste System and its Implications*. Complete revised English ed. Chicago: U of Chicago P, 1980.

224

Eco, Umberto. *Semiotics and the Philosophy of Language.* Bloomington: Indiana UP, 1986.

Eliade, Mircea, ed. *Encyclopedia of Religion.* 16 vols. New York: Macmillan, 1987.

---. *Myth and Reality.* Trans. Willard R. Trask. New York: Harper, 1963.

---. *Patterns in Comparative Religion.* Trans. Rosemary Sheed. New York: World, 1958.

---. *The Quest.* Chicago: U of Chicago P, 1969.

Eliade, Mircea, and Joseph M. Kitagawa, eds. *The History of Religions: Essays in Methodology.* Chicago: U of Chicago P, 1959.

Elster, Jon. "Cohen on Marx's Theory of History." *Political Studies* XXVII (1980): 127.

---. "Marxism, Functionalism and Game Theory." *Theory and Society* 11 (1982): 453-82.

---. *Ulysses and the Sirens: Studies in Rationality and Irrationality.* Cambridge: Cambridge UP, 1979.

Evans-Pritchard, E. E. "The Intellectualist (English) Interpretation of Magic." *Bulletin of the Faculty of Arts.* Vol. I, part 2. Cairo: U of Egypt, 1933. 1-27.

---. "Lévi-Bruhl's Theory of Primitive Mentality." *Bulletin of the Faculty of Arts.* Vol. II, part 1. Cairo: U of Egypt, 1934. 1-36.

---. *Nuer Religion.* Oxford: Oxford UP, 1956.

Fink, Eugene. "Die Phänomenologische Philosophie Edmund Husserl in der Gegenwärtigen Kritik." *Kantstudien* 38 (1933): 319-383.

Føllesdal, Dagfinn. "Husserl's Notion of Noema." *The Journal of Philosophy* 66 (1969): 680-87.

Foster, Mary LeCron, and Stanley H. Brandes, eds. *Symbol as Sense*. New York: Academic P, 1980.

Foucault, Michel. *The Archaeology of Knowledge*. New York: Pantheon, 1972.

Gardner, Howard. *The Mind's New Science*. New York: Basic, 1985.

Geertz, Clifford. "Religion as a Cultural System." Banton 1-46.

Gellner, Ernest. *Cause and Meaning in the Social Sciences*. London: Routledge, 1973.

Giddens, Anthony. "Commentary on the Debate." *Theory and Society* 11 (1982): 527-39.

Glucksmann, Miriam. *Structuralist Analysis in Contemporary Social Thought: A Comparison of the Theories of Claude Lévi-Strauss and Louis Althusser*. London: Routledge, 1974.

Godelier, Maurice. "Myths, Infrastructures and History in Lévi-Strauss." Rossi 232-61.

---. *Perspectives in Marxist Anthropology*. Trans. Robert Brain. Cambridge: Cambridge UP, 1977.

---. *Rationality and Irrationality in Economics*. New York: Monthly Review P, 1972.

Godlove, Terry F. "Interpretation, Reductionism, and Belief in God." *Journal of Religion* 69 (1989): 184-198.

226

---. "In What Sense are Religions Conceptual Frameworks?" *Journal of the American Academy of Religion* 52 (1984): 289-306.

Gurwitsch, Aron. *Studies in Phenomenology and Psychology*. Evanston, Ill.: Northwestern UP, 1966.

Hacking, Ian. *Why Does Language Matter to Philosophy?* Cambridge: Cambridge UP, 1975.

Halfpenny, Peter. "A refutation of historical materialism?" *Social Science Information* 22 (1983): 61-87.

Hardin, Russell. "Rationality, irrationality and functionalist explanation." *Social Science Information* 19 (1980): 755-72.

Harnad, S. R., H. D. Steklis, and Jane Lancaster. *Origins and Evolution of Language and Speech*. New York: New York Academy of Sciences, 1976.

Harris, Roy. *Reading Saussure*. La Salle, Ill.: Open Court, 1987.

Helm, June, ed. *Symposium on New Approaches to the Study of Religion*. Proceedings of the 1964 Annual Meeting of the American Ethnological Society. Seattle: U of Washington P, 1964.

Hempel, Carl G. *Aspects of Scientific Explanation*. New York: Free, 1965.

---. "The Logic of Functional Analysis." *Symposium on Sociological Theory*. Ed. Llewellyn Gross. New York: Harper, 1959. 271-307.

Hiltebeitel, Alf. "Hinduism." Eliade, *Encyclopedia*.

Hollis, Martin, and Steven Lukes, eds. *Rationality and Relativism*. Cambridge: MIT P, 1982.

Holmes, Richard H. "An Explication of Husserl's Theory of the Noema." *Research in Phenomenology* 5 (1975): 143-53.

Homans, George C. "Anxiety and Ritual: The Theories of Malinowski and Radcliffe-Brown." *American Anthropologist* 43 (1941): 164-171.

Horton, Robin. "African Traditional Thought and Western Science." *Africa* XXXVII (1967): 50-71; 155-187.

---. "Lévi-Bruhl, Durkheim, and the Scientific Revolution." Horton and Finnegan.

---. "Neo-Tylorianism: Sound Sense or Sinister Prejudice?" *Man* 3 (1968): 625-34.

---. "Professor Winch on Safari." *Archives Europeenes de Sociologie* XVII (1976): 157-80.

---. "Tradition and Modernity Revisited." Hollis and Lukes 201-60.

Horton, Robin, and Ruth Finnegan, eds. *Modes of Thought*. London: Faber, 1973.

Hubbeling, H. G. "Theology, Philosophy and Science of Religion and their Logical and Empirical Presuppositions." van Baaren and Drijvers 9-34.

Husserl, Edmund. *Cartesian Meditations*. Trans. Dorian Cairns. The Hague: Nijhoff, 1960.

---. *Die Krisis der europäischen Wissenschaften und die transzendentale Phänomenologie*. Den Haag: Nijhoff, 1954.

---. *Ideen zu einer reinen Phänomenologie und phänomenologischen Philosophie*. vol. I. Den Haag: Nijhoff, 1950.

---. *Ideen zu einer reinen Phänomenologie und phänomenologischen Philosophie*. vol. II. Den Haag: Nijhoff, 1952.

---. *Logische Untersuchungen*. 5th ed. Tübingen: Mohr Verlag, 1968.

"Interview: Claude Lévi-Strauss." *Diacritics* (Fall, 1971): 48-49.

Jakobson, Roman. *Six Lectures on Sound and Meaning.* Cambridge: MIT P, 1978.

Jameson, Fredric. *The Prison-House of Language: A Critical Account of Structuralism and Russian Formalism.* Princeton: Princeton UP, 1972.

Jarvie, I. C. *Concepts and Society.* London: Routledge, 1972.

---. *Functionalism.* Minneapolis: Burgess, 1973.

---. "Limits to Functionalism and Alternatives to it in Anthropology." *Theory in Anthropology.* Eds. Robert A. Manners and David Kaplan. Chicago: Aldine, 1968.

Jarvie, I. C., and Joseph Agassi. "The Problem of the Rationality of Magic." Wilson 172-93.

Kane, P. V. *History of Dharmasastra.* 2nd ed. Vol. II. Part 1. Poona: Bhandarkar Oriental Research Inst., 1968.

Katz, Steven T., ed. *Mysticism and Religious Traditions.* Oxford: Oxford UP, 1983.

Kay, Paul, and Willett Kempton. "What Is the Sapir-Whorf Hypothesis?" *American Anthropologist* 86 (1984): 65-79.

Kay, Paul, and Chad K. MacDaniel. "The Linguistic Significance of the Meanings of Basic Color Terms. *Language* 54 (1978): 610-46.

King, Ursula. "Historical and Phenomenological Approaches." *Contemporary Approaches to the Study of Religion, Vol. I: The Humanities.* Ed. Frank Whaling. The Hague: Mouton, 1983. 29-164.

Kirk, G. S. *Myth: Its Meaning and Function in Ancient and Other Cultures.* Cambridge: Cambridge UP, 1973.

Kitagawa, Joseph M., ed. *The History of Religions: Essays on the Problem of Understanding.* Chicago: U of Chicago P, 1967.

Koerner, E. F. K. *Ferdinand de Saussure.* Braunschweig: Vieweg, 1973.

Kristensen, W. Brede. *The Meaning of Religion.* The Hague: Nijhoff, 1960.

Kuhn, Thomas S. "Second Thoughts on Paradigms." Suppe 459-82.

Langacker, Ronald. "Semantic representations and the linguistic relativity hypothesis." *Foundations of Language* 14 (1976): 307-57.

Langsdorf, Lenore. "The Noema as Intentional Entity: A Critique of Føllesdal." *The Review of Metaphysics* 37 (1984): 757-84.

Leach, Edmund. *Genesis as Myth and Other Essays.* London: Cape, 1969.

---, ed. *The Structural Study of Myth and Totemism.* London: Tavistock, 1967.

Lessa, William A., and Evon Z. Vogt, eds. *Reader in Comparative Religion.* 2nd ed. New York: Harper, 1965.

Lévi-Strauss, Claude. *Anthropologie Structurale.* Paris: Plon, 1958.

---. "The Bear and the Barber." *The Journal of the Royal Anthropological Institute* XCIII (1963): 1-11.

---. *From Honey to Ashes.* Trans. John and Doreen Weightman. New York: Harper, 1973.

---. "The Mathematics of Man." *UNESCO International Social Science Bulletin* VI (1954): 581-82.

---. *The Naked Man: Introduction to a Science of Mythology*. Vol.4. Trans. John and Doreen Weightman. New York: Harper, 1971.

---. *The Origin of Table Manners*. Trans. John and Doreen Weightman. London: Cape, 1978.

---. *The Raw and the Cooked*. Trans. John and Doreen Weightman. New York: Harper, 1969.

---. *The Savage Mind*. Chicago: U of Chicago P, 1966.

---. *Structural Anthropology*. Vol. I. New York: Basic, 1963.

---. *Structural Anthropology*. Vol. II. New York: Basic, 1976.

---. *Totemism*. Trans. Rodney Needham. Boston: Beacon, 1962.

---. *Tristes Tropiques*. Trans. John and Doreen Weightman. New York: Atheneum, 1974.

---. *The View from Afar*. Trans. Joachim Neugroschel and Phoebe Hoss. New York: Basic, 1985.

Lingat, Robert. *The Classical Law of India*. Trans. J. Duncan M. Derrett. Berkeley: U of California P, 1973.

Lyons, John. *Semantics*. Vol.I. Cambridge: Cambridge UP, 1977.

Madan, T. N. ed. *Way Of Life: King, Householder, Renouncer, Essays in honour of Louis Dumont*. Delhi: Vikas Publishing, 1982.

Malinowski, Bronislaw. *Magic, Science and Religion*. New York: Doubleday, 1954.

Mani, Vettam. *Puranic Encyclopaedia*. Delhi: Banarsidass, 1975.

Marcuse, Herbert. "Zum Begriff des Wesens." *Zeitschrift für Socialforschung* 5 (1936).

Mayr, Ernst. *The Growth of Biological Thought*. Cambridge: Harvard UP, 1982.

McCauley, Robert N., and E. Thomas Lawson. "Functionalism Reconsidered." *History of Religions* 23 (1984): 372-381.

Merton, Robert K. *Social Theory and Social Structure*. Rev. and enl. ed. Glencoe, Ill.: Free, 1957.

Müller, Wolfgang H. *Die Philosophie Edmund Husserls*. Bonn, 1956.

Nagel, Ernest. *Logic Without Metaphysics*. Glencoe, Ill.: Free, 1957.

---. "The Meaning of Reduction in the Natural Sciences." *Science and Civilization*. Ed. Robert C. Stauffer. Madison: U of Wisconsin P, 1949. 131.

---. *The Structure of Science*. New York: Harcourt, 1961.

O'Flaherty, Wendy Doniger. *Asceticism and Eroticism in the Mythology of Shiva*. New York: Oxford UP, 1973.

---, trans. *Hindu Myths*. Baltimore: Penguin, 1975.

Orth, Ernst Wolfgang. *Bedeutung, Sinn, Gegendstand: Studien zur Sprach Philosophie Edmund Husserls und Richard Höningswald*. Bonn: Bouvier, 1967.

Otto, Rudolph. *The Idea of the Holy*. Oxford: Oxford UP, 1957.

232

Oxtoby, Willard. "The Idea of the Holy." Eliade, *Encyclopedia.*

Pace, David. *Claude Lévi-Strauss.* Boston: Routledge, 1983.

Parijs, Philippe Van. "Functionalist Marxism Rehabilitated: A Comment on
Elster." *Theory and Society* 11 (1982): 497-511.

Peel, J. D. Y. "Understanding Alien Belief-Systems." *British Journal of
Sociology* 20 (1969): 55-74.

Penner, Hans H. "Creating a Brahman: A Structural Approach to Religion."
Methodological Issues in Religious Studies. Ed. Robert D. Baird. Chico,
Cal.: New Horizons, 1975. 49-66.

Penner, Hans H., and Edward A. Yonan. "Is a Science of Religion Possible?" *The
Journal of Religion* 52 (1972): 107-33.

Proudfoot, Wayne. *Religious Experience.* Berkeley: U of California P, 1985.

Putnam, Hilary. *Mind, Language and Reality: Philosophical Papers.* Vol. 2.
Cambridge: Cambridge UP, 1975.

---. *Realism and Reason: Philosophical Papers,* Vol. 3. Cambridge: Cambridge
UP, 1983.

Ricoeur, Paul. *The Conflict of Interpretations: Essays in Hermeneutics.*
Evanston, Ill.: Northwestern UP, 1974.

---. *Freud and Philosophy: An Essay on Interpretation.* New Haven: Yale UP,
1970.

Rorty, Richard. *Philosophy and the Mirror of Nature.* Princeton: Princeton UP,
1980.

Rosenbaum, Harvey. "Verification in Structural Theory: A Linguist's Point of View." Rossi 88-110.

Rossi, Ino. *From the Sociology of Symbols to the Sociology of Signs*. New York: Columbia UP, 1983.

---, ed. *The Logic of Culture*. South Hadley, Mass.: Bergen, 1982.

Ryle, G. "Phenomenology." *Aristotelian Society Supplement* 11 (1932): 68ff.

Sahlins, Marshal. "Colors and Cultures." *Semiotica* 16 (1976): 1-22.

Said, Edward W. *Orientalism*. New York: Pantheon, 1978.

de Saussure, Ferdinand. *Course in General Linguistics*. Eds. Charles Bally and Albert Sechehaye with Albert Reidlinger. Trans. Wade Baskin. New York: Philosophical Library, 1959.

Schellings Werke. Sechster Band. Müchen: Beck, 1928.

Schneider, David. "Notes Toward a Theory of Culture." *Meaning in Anthropology*. Eds. Keith Basso and Henry A. Selby. Albuquerque: U of New Mexico P, 1976. 197-220.

Schwab, Raymond. *The Oriental Renaissance*. Trans. Gene Patterson-Black and Victor Reinking. New York: Columbia UP, 1984.

Seebohm, T. M. *Die Bedingungen der Möglichkeit der Transzendentalephilosophie*. Bonn: Bouvier, 1962.

Sharp, E. *Comparative Religion: A History*. 2nd ed. La Salle, Ill.: Open Court, 1986.

The Siva Purana. 4 vols. Delhi: Banarsidass, 1970.

Skorupski, John. *Symbol and Theory*. Cambridge: Cambridge UP, 1976.

Sokolowski, Robert. "Intentional Analysis and the Noema." *Dialectica* 38 (1984): 113-129.

Solomon, Robert C. "Husserl's Concept of the Noema." *Husserl: Expositions and Appraisals*. Eds. Fredrick A. Elliston and Peter McCormick. Notre Dame: U of Notre Dame P, 1977. 168-81.

Sperber, Dan. "Apparently Irrational Beliefs." Hollis and Lukes 149-80.

---. "Is Symbolic Thought Prerational?" Foster and Brandes 25-44.

---. *Rethinking Symbolism*. Cambridge: Cambridge UP, 1975.

Spiegelberg, Herbert. *The Phenomenological Movement: A Historical Introduction*. 2 vols. The Hague: Nijhoff, 1960.

Spiro, Melford E. *Buddhism and Society: A Great Tradition and Its Burmese Viscissitudes*. 2nd, expanded ed. Berkeley: U of California P, 1982.

---. "Causes, Functions and Cross-Cousin Marriage: An Essay in Anthropological Explanation." *The Journal of the Royal Anthropological Institute of Great Britain and Ireland* 94 (1964): 30-43.

---. "Religion and the Irrational." *Symposium on New Approaches to the Study of Religion*. Seattle: U of Washington, 1964. 102-15.

---. "Religion: Problems of Definition and Explanation." Banton 85-126.

---. "Virgin Birth: Parthenogenesis and Psychological Paternity: An Essay in Cultural Interpretation." *Man* 3 (1968): 242-61.

Suppe, Fredrick, ed. *The Structure of Scientific Theories*. Urbana: U of Illinois P, 1977.

"Symposium: The Contributions of Louis Dumont." *Journal of Asian Studies* XXXV (1976): 579-650.

Sztompka, Piotr. *System and Function: Toward a Theory of Society*. New York: Academic, 1974.

Tambiah, S. J. *Buddhism and the Spirit Cults in North-East Thailand*. Cambridge: Cambridge UP, 1970.

---. *World Conqueror and World Renouncer*. Cambridge: Cambridge UP, 1976.

Taylor, Charles. "Rationality." Hollis and Lukes 87-105.

Todorov, Tzvetan. *Theories of the Symbol*. Ithaca: Cornell UP, 1982.

van Baaren, Th. P. "Science of Religion as a Systematic Discipline: Some Introductory Remarks." van Baaren and Drijvers 35-56.

van Baaren, Th. P., and H. J. W. Drijvers, eds. *Religion, Culture and Methodology*. The Hague: Mouton, 1973.

van der Leeuw, G. *L'Homme Primitif et la Religion*. Paris: Presses U de France, 1940.

---. *Phänomenologie Der Religion*. Tübingen: Mohr Verlag, 1933.

---. *Religion in Essence and Manifestation*. London: Allen, 1938.

Waardenburg, J. D. J. *Classical Approaches to the Study of Religion*. The Hague: Mouton, 1973.

---. "Research on Meaning in Religion." *Religion, Culture and Methodology*. van Baaren and Drijvers 109-36.

Wach, Joachim. "Introduction: The Meaning and Task of the History of Religions (Religionswissenschaft)." Kitagawa 18.

Walt, Steven. "Rationality and Explanation." *Ethics* 94 (1983-84): 680-700.

Whorf, Benjamin Lee. *Language, Thought and Reality*. Cambridge: MIT P, 1956.

Wiebe, Donald. "The failure of nerve in the academic study of religion." *Studies in Religion/Sciences Religieuses* 13 (1984): 401-22.

Wilson, Bryan R., ed. *Rationality*. New York: Blackwell, 1970.

Winch, Peter. "Understanding a Primitive Society." Wilson 78-111.

INDEX

238

TORONTO STUDIES IN RELIGION

This series of monographs and books is designed as a contribution to the scholarly and academic understanding of religion. Such understanding is taken to involve both a descriptive and an explanatory task. The first task is conceived as one of 'surface description' involving the gathering of information about religions, and 'depth description' that provides, on the basis of the data gathered, a more finely nuanced description of a tradition's self-understanding. The second task concerns the search for explanation and the development of theory to account for religion and for particular historical traditions. The series will, furthermore, cover the phenomenon of religion in all its constituent dimensions and geographic diversity. Both established and younger scholars in the field will be included and will represent a wide range of viewpoints and positions, producing original work of a high order at the monograph and major study level.

Although predominantly empirically oriented the series will also encourage theoretical studies and even leave room for creative and empirically controlled philosophical and speculative approaches in the interpretation of religions and religion.

Toronto Studies in Religion will be of particular interest to those who study the subject at universities or colleges but will also be of value to the general educated reader.

Bruce T. Riley

THE PSYCHOLOGY
OF RELIGIOUS EXPERIENCE IN ITS PERSONAL
AND INSTITUTIONAL DIMENSION

American University Studies: Series VII (Theology and Religion). Vol. 49

ISBN 0-8204-0862-X   377 pages   hardcover US $ 47.70*

*Recommended price – alterations reserved

This book employs the basic concept of a religious problem as the necessary condition of religious experience. The connection between different kinds of religious problems and corresponding types of religious experience and behaviour is traced.

Religious experience as it occurs institutionally is considered at length. Relationships between experiences and institutions are examined in depth, as they pertain to the orign, expansion and decay of religious institutions. Of particular interest is the examination of present day cults as a symptom of religious decadence, including the analysis of why they arise, what their defining characteristics are, and the mechanisms which provide their dynamic. Although the study is undertaken from a naturalistic point of view, it is in no way inimical to religious beliefs already held.

PETER LANG PUBLISHING, INC.
62 West 45th Street
USA – New York, NY 10036

Anthony J. Blasi

EARLY CHRISTIANITY
AS A SOCIAL MOVEMENT

Toronto Studies in Religion. Vol. 5
ISBN 0-8204-0581-7   248 pages   hardcover US $ 34.50*

*Recommended price – alterations reserved

Early Christianity as a Social Movement is a social scientific study of the first half century of Christianity, from its development after the lifetime of Jesus of Nazareth into the 80's of the first century C.E. The literary evidence, separated into five separate stages of the movement's history by means of source analyses of the early writings, is subjected to content analysis to depict early Christianity as a new religious movement. This movement is found to be largely unlike most of the modern new religious movements.

« Blasi's book represents an innovative, challenging, multidisciplinary attempt to assees the character of the early Church as a social movement from the text it has left us. It should provoke discussion among both social scientists and students of the Bible. The book contains enough sophistication to satisfy specialists, but is also general enough to appeal to a wider body of readers. »
(William H. Swatos, Jr., Sociological Analysis)

PETER LANG PUBLISHING, INC.
62 West 45th Street
USA – New York, NY 10036